SEVENTEENTH CENTURY LIFE
IN THE COUNTRY PARISH

T0370928

SEVENTEENTH CENTURY LIFE
IN THE COUNTRY PARISH

WITH SPECIAL REFERENCE TO
LOCAL GOVERNMENT

BY

ELEANOR TROTTER, M.A.

Author of
Life in Olden Times in Babylon and Assyria.

CAMBRIDGE
AT THE UNIVERSITY PRESS
1919

CAMBRIDGE
UNIVERSITY PRESS

University Printing House, Cambridge CB2 8BS, United Kingdom

Published in the United States of America by Cambridge University Press, New York

Cambridge University Press is part of the University of Cambridge.

It furthers the University's mission by disseminating knowledge in the pursuit of education, learning and research at the highest international levels of excellence.

www.cambridge.org
Information on this title: www.cambridge.org/9781107688896

© Cambridge University Press 1919

This publication is in copyright. Subject to statutory exception and to the provisions of relevant collective licensing agreements, no reproduction of any part may take place without the written permission of Cambridge University Press.

First published 1919
First paperback edition 2014

A catalogue record for this publication is available from the British Library

ISBN 978-1-107-68889-6 Paperback

Cambridge University Press has no responsibility for the persistence or accuracy of URLs for external or third-party internet websites referred to in this publication, and does not guarantee that any content on such websites is, or will remain, accurate or appropriate.

This book is dedicated to the memory of my beloved Father, JOHN OUTHWAITE TROTTER, whose public work during a life of 82 years spent wholly in the North Riding was witness that Englishmen give time and energy in as great a degree as formerly to the affairs of their district and county; and of my dear friend MARY LOUISA STRETTON without whose encouragement and help it might never have been written.

PREFACE

In the following pages an attempt is made to show how the ordinary business of government—the maintenance of justice and the preservation of law and order—was carried on during that most troubled period in the life of our race—the Seventeenth Century.

This generation has seen the horrors of the Russian Revolution and has noted in how many points it resembled the French Revolution. We look back with wonder and a certain admiration at the English Revolution, which was achieved in a very different manner; there was indeed loss of life, for the Puritans struck at the highest in the land, but they put their king to death because—rightly or wrongly—they believed he was the cause of the Civil War; nevertheless, in the puritan revolution in the middle of the century and in the political one towards its close, there is a moderation and restraint—a regard for political considerations which is not found in the same degree in the revolutions of other races.

During those years of civil and religious warfare in the Seventeenth Century, though there might be intolerance and harsh administration of the law owing to partisanship, yet there was no indiscriminate plunder, no ruthless slaughter of men and women without trial, while peace and order were steadily maintained in the country districts.

The machinery for the administration of the laws and the maintenance of peace was so decentralised that the life of the average man flowed on undisturbed, though faction poured out its strong currents of feeling and caused an ebb and flow of everchanging opinion at Westminster.

A comparison of revolutions gives rise to the thought that when a nation is faced with a crisis in its history, it is not civilisation but character which is the dominant factor—not a specially formed and wrought out character but that which is inherent in the race, that which has been hammered out through generations of the national life.

The great majority of the men who took their share in the government of England in the Seventeenth Century had neither learning nor culture, some probably were not able to write their own names; nevertheless through being made responsible for the well-being and the good order of the little community to which they belonged they gained a considerable amount of political education. The work of local government, carried on voluntarily from father to son through untold generations, has produced certain characteristics—a moderation of outlook, a reasonableness and sanity of mind, an intensely critical faculty and a political insight—which are typical of our race. It is individuals who form the masses, and our history encourages us to expect that a people with such a record of governmental work has nothing to fear from further self-government. There is a fear lest the masses through ignorance of the work of their forefathers may demand a centralisation of governmental functions which is alien to the character of the English Constitution.

ELEANOR TROTTER.

6 Pierremont Crescent,
    Darlington,
        June, 1919.

CONTENTS

INTRODUCTION

I, North Riding, am for spaciousness renown'd,
Our mother Yorkshire's eld'st, who worthily is crown'd
The Queen of all the Shires.
        Speech of the North Riding.
                MICHAEL DRAYTON, *Polyolbion.*

IN the following chapters an attempt is made to show the
working of the Parish in the Seventeenth Century, the powers
and duties of its officials, their interaction and relation to
the supervisory jurisdiction of the Church and the local
Magistracy.

In this connection it is necessary to consider the manner
in which the Churchwardens became associated in civil duties
with the Constable, the Surveyor and the Overseers, and the
share taken by the Justices both individually and in Quarter
Sessions in the administration of Parish affairs. The most
important statutes affecting the Parish may be conveniently
examined in three divisions as they concern, first the Poor,
for whose benefit the Parish was specially adopted as a civil
unit; secondly the Labourers and Apprentices, who formed a
large proportion of the inhabitants of the Parish; and thirdly
the Rogues and Vagabonds, who were presumed to have no
right to be there.

Finally, since the Parish is a world in miniature, account
will be taken of those regulations (made either by Parliament or by the Justices) which affected the everyday life of
the individual often in the minutest detail. Though the
records from which this account of the Parish is derived
chiefly concern districts in the north of England, much

valuable information being gained from 'the various cases presented to the Justices of the North Riding and orders made by them in their Court of Quarter Sessions, yet in substance local government was very similar throughout the land, while so much divergence in detail is shown in the Riding itself that the conclusions arrived at may be typical of the "dull undated life of the country parish."

CHAPTER I

THE PARISH, THE UNIT OF LOCAL GOVERNMENT

DURING the Middle Ages the parish was the domain of the church. It was first recognised by the state as an integral part of the commonwealth in the sixteenth century. The social upheavals of that century caused by the destruction of the religious houses, the loss of common land to the working classes, and the general rise in prices, threw upon the government the necessity of making provision for the poor and destitute.

When the Elizabethan Parliament had to face this problem of pauperism, it found the solution in recognising the parish, hitherto the area of ecclesiastical jurisdiction, as a unit of local government, for the exercise of those functions which formerly the exclusive province of the church, were now first undertaken by the state. In medieval times the church alone cared for the relief of the impotent poor and enjoined on the faithful the giving of alms as a pious duty. During the Reformation period however, the ecclesiastical organisation being weak and disunited and poverty having increased in manifold degree, it became necessary for the state to enforce through legislation what had hitherto been accomplished promiscuously enough, it may be, through charitable use and custom.

With that feeling for continuity which is to some degree characteristic of English legislation, the Tudor Parliaments followed in the track laid down and gave statutory recognition to the existing organisation for poor relief—the parish— making it henceforth the civil area for such administration.

To the mind of the ordinary Englishman in the Middle Ages there was little distinction between church and state. At the parish meeting held in the church under the guidance of the priest, all matters affecting the well-being of the parishioners were considered. Thus, as regards its formation and province the parish meeting may be considered as in some measure the equivalent of the ancient folkmoot. The manorial courts insisted on the attendance of certain people, and the performance of certain obligations; over them the power of the feudal lord held sway. The church was free; in it the lord, though able at times to exercise considerable influence, was nevertheless one among many parishioners. Thus it came about that new matters, which cropped up from time to time, outside the sphere of the manorial courts but affecting the village community, were discussed in the parish meeting.

So well did the parish regulate its affairs, that, in the middle of the sixteenth century, when some definite area had to be made responsible for the repair of the highways, it was not the lay area of the manor, nor of the township, which was selected, but the ecclesiastical area of the parish.

Since the parish had always been the focus of the social life of the people it was natural that, when the strong central government of the Tudors attacked existing abuses and endeavoured to remove them by passing laws which regulated trade and labour, in accordance with the economic thought of the age, the administration of these statutes also should be delegated to it.

Reasons of state existed which may account in part for the selection of the parish as the unit of local government. The Tudor sovereigns were averse to any policy which would increase the feudal power of the lord of the manor; hence they preferred to make use of two strong organisations already in existence, each of which recognised the King's Majesty as the source of its coercive jurisdiction; the church and the local magistracy. By the Henrician legislation the church was definitely subjected to the control of the state, which in Tudor times was equivalent to the personal rule of the sovereign. Under this rule the power of the rector or vicar was confined to ecclesiastical matters, while the churchwardens, popularly elected, were employed as civil officers by the legislature. The Justices also received their commission from the King, and held it at his good pleasure. Moreover they were "specially under the eye of the Royal Council" and themselves subject to the jurisdiction of the courts of law if they transgressed in any particular their statutory powers[1].

Therefore the Elizabethan statesmen, following the principle already laid down by Henry VIII, took from the local organisations already existing in the country those elements which appeared most favourable for the administration of the new statutes, co-ordinated them, and gradually evolved that system of local government by which each parish regulated its own political affairs, executed the various and detailed statutes of the day, and maintained peace and order during times of great conflict and uncertainty.

It will be necessary to consider briefly the methods by which this end was achieved.

During the Middle Ages the churchwarden in the parish was the representative of the people for all those undertakings of which the church took cognisance; the constable in the township was the King's officer, responsible for good order. In the sixteenth and seventeenth centuries the churchwardens and constables of each parish were associated in the execution of the statutes which became law during that period, and were given for their assistance two new officials, the surveyor to take charge of the repair of the highways, and the overseer to help in the administration of poor relief. All these officers were elected yearly by the parishioners, were unpaid, and, unless they could plead privilege, were obliged to serve; the parish was for them "the unit of local obligation" and they were under the direct supervision of the Justices of the Peace.

The work of the surveyor will be noticed in connection with the statutory duty imposed on the parish of repairing

---

[1] F. W. Maitland, *Constitutional History*, p. 209.

the highways, but the spheres of activity of the constable, churchwarden and overseer intersected at so many points the life of the community that their functions and powers will be considered separately in later chapters. Considerable help was given to these officials by the Parish Priest and the Country Justice, whose legislative and administrative powers make up the tale of local government in the seventeenth century. But certain services necessary for the benefit and good order of the community were performed by individual parishioners, whose duties may be briefly considered here. Much of the work which is done at the present time by inspectors and other officials appointed by the Local District or the County Council, the Local Government Board or the Board of Trade, was carried out by amateurs who received payment from fees or a yearly salary.

The wellmaster had to see that the water supply was forthcoming and the well kept in repair. His work was under the supervision of the Court Leet. If, however, a leet was not held the inhabitants could always appeal to the Court of Quarter Sessions[1]. In 1688 the Justices held a session at New Malton and the court was informed "that the common well in the town of New Malton is in great decay for want of repairing and, by reason of the contest and difference between the Lords of the Manor of Malton, no Court leets of late hath been kept there, where the persons that neglected to contribute towards the repair thereof were usually punished"; whereupon the Magistrates ordered the inhabitants to contribute towards the repair of the well and pay the money to the wellmasters. The aleconner or ale-taster[2] tried to ensure that the community drank good beer,

---

[1] Presentments at the Quarter Sessions. *N.R.Q.S.R.* vol. I. p. 87. Helmsley, Oct. 6, 1607. "That one common well at Aymonderby doth ly open in the street there, which is very dangerous, etc." (Per homag. et per sacrm. Rog. Ringrose.)

[2] *Ibid.* vol. III. p. 269. Thirsk, Oct. 1628. "A Snainton man for refusing to sell his ale and beere to Tho. Clitheroe Clarke, N. Skelton, tailor and John Richardson, Aletaister there, having sufficient drinke in his house, and monie being tendered to his wife for the same, etc."

and ate wholesome bread of full weight and measure[1]. The alnager or searcher of broadcloth[2] examined all woollen material to make sure that it was woven the correct length, and stamped with the town seal[3]. In the small towns the clerk of the market attended fairs and markets from 10 o'clock until sunset; no buying or selling could take place before his bell[4] rang; he inspected weights and measures to prove that they were of the standard size[5], and he was authorised to take "due and lawful toll for every horse[6]" or other animal brought for sale.

The office of hogringer was a yearly one and the appointment was made at the Court Leet. The hogringer had to go to the commons and see that all the swine had rings in their noses to prevent them rooting up the turf. Any without rings he put in the village pound and charged 1d. for each one impounded and 6d. for putting a ring through its nose; doubtless also he superintended the work of the swineherd[7], who was hired to keep the pigs from straying off the common. The neatherd[8] minded the cattle and prevented them

---

[1] *N.R.Q.S.R.* vol. I. p. 150. Thirsk, Ap. 1609. "Eliz. Metcalfe and Margt Stevenson both of Bedall presented for breaking the assize of bread."

[2] *Ibid.* vol. V. p. 3. Thirsk, Oct. 1647. "Rich. Johnson Cloathworker to serve in the office of searcher of Broadcloth for Massam for one year."

[3] *Ibid.* vol. VI. p. 251. Thirsk, Ap. 1676. "A New Malton yeomn. for using a false and illegal seal under colour of the office of Alniger."

Ibid. vol. IV. p. 73. Thirsk, Ap. 1637. "A Northallerton weaver professing to be an Aulnager for extorting with a counterfeit warrant to seal woollen cloth, 17s. etc."

[4] *Ibid.* vol. I. p. 213. Thirsk, July, 1611. "John Sonley and Will Leafe of Ampleforth, for using the trade of a baker contrary etc. and buying of corne before the corne-bell ringe."

In some parishes, e.g. Knaresborough, a bell is still rung when the market begins.

[5] *Ibid.* vol. I. p. 122. Helmsley, July, 1608. "Chr. Carter of Great Ayton, blacksmith, for having and using a weight called vi pound weight, two ounces short as tried by the Clark of the Markett."

[6] 31 Eliz. cap. xii.

[7] *N.R.Q.S.R.* vol. I. p. 99. Malton, Jan. 12, 1608. "Will Splett of Nunnington, being the hired servant for keeping there towne-swyne, for departing forth of their service before the end of his tearme, etc."

[8] *Ibid.* vol. I. p. 30. Thirsk, Jan. 1605–6. "Whereas Chr. Pressick of Carleton for sundry misdemeanours proved against him before Sir

from straying on to the highways. The scavenger at the bidding of the surveyor removed out of the street the heaps of refuse which were thrown down anywhere outside the houses with no care for the public health.

Not the least important members of the community were the parish servants; the clerk, the beadle, and the sexton, who received a yearly salary out of the church funds augmented by fees and contributions in money or kind. At Houghton-le-Spring on March 25, 1611, the gentlemen and most of the "Four and Twenty" agreed "that the clerk shall have from henceforth of every plough within the said parish in lieu and full satisfaction of his boon at Christmas 2d. in money and for his eggs at Easter one penny." The appointment seems to have been made by the select vestry when one existed, in which doubtless the parish priest had considerable influence. In 1660 when a new clerk was appointed at Houghton, the entry runs: "It is agreed and concluded by the gentlemen and 24 that Jo Philpott is to be admitted clerke of the parish of Houghton-le-Spring, and also by the consent of Dr Barwick then Rector of Houghton aforesaid, and the churchwardens." Probably different customs held in different parishes, but it seems clear that when once appointed the parish servants could not be dismissed without cause shown.

The clerk rang the bell for service, set in order the Bible and Prayer-book for the clergyman and made the necessary provision for Christenings and Communions. He wore a surplice and was the leader of the congregation in the responses of the public prayers. The office was one of trust and public confidence, but the clerk did not always rise to the dignity of his position, for at times he was convicted of

Henry Jenkins...that he shall enter Recognisanzes of £40 for the good behaviour, and also other Recogns. of £100 for the bringing in of a boy which he did beat, being late neathird of Carlton mentioned in an Order made in the last Six Weekes Sessions holden at Gisborough: or else bring a true certificate of what is become of the boy....And if the boy be dead to bring a true certificate where and how and when he died. And that he appear at the next Sessions bringing said boy or said certificate, etc."

being drunk and disorderly[1], and even of assault[2]. In country villages the parish clerk also performed the duties of vestry clerk and at times his office was combined with that of the sexton. The sexton was entitled to certain dues at Christmas and Easter in addition to the fees he was allowed to charge for digging graves: in the vestry book at Houghton is the following entry:

It is concluded and agreed upon by the gentlemen and 24 that James Dobson of Houghton is to continue in his father's plaice as Sexton, and to haive the dues belonging to the plaice as it apeares by an order sett downe in this book: that is 2*d*. or bunns at Christmas, and eggs at Easter, for a grave in the churchyard 2*d*. in the church 4*d*. in the quire 6*d*. and for every cottage a ob[3].

The sexton was responsible for the cleaning of the church, the lighting of fires, the opening of pews, the digging of graves, and the general charge of the building. The beadle's chief work was of a punitive nature; he was expected to help the constable in apprehending and punishing rogues[4]; he wore a special dress and carried a whip or wand[5] in his hand with which he drove the dogs out of church[6]. When necessary the beadle filled the office of common driver; that is, he impounded stray cattle found on the roadside or

[1] *N.R.Q.S.R.* vol. I. p. 192. Helmsley, July, 1610. "Tho. Thompson, parish clerk of Kirkby Misperton for being drunk on the Sabboath daie, on divers occasions and is addicted to quarrellinge and disorder when he is so drunck."
[2] *Ibid.* vol. I. Richmond, Oct. 1607. One "Chas. Parishe of Midleham, Parish Clerke, for receiving divers persons into his dwelling house during the time of Divine Service, and permitting them to play at unlawfull games, viz: Shovell a board, etc., and also for an assault in the parish church of Midleham on one Brian Sweeting, etc."
[3] ob = obolus = small Greek coin used here for half-penny.
[4] *N.R.Q.S.R.* vol. I. p. 196. N. Allerton, July, 1610. "The inhabts of West Runckton for not keeping due watch and for want of a Bedle contrare to the Order of the Justices."
Ibid. vol. I. p. 163. Rich., July, 1609. "The Constable and inhabts of Bockby, of Brompton, of Holme and of Holgrave for not keeping a Bedell to apprehend and punish rogues and according to the Articles set down by the Justices."
[5] In 1887 at Wensley Church the wands were still to be seen. They were six in number, and were attached to the front of the churchwardens' high pews.
[6] Vestry Book, Pittington, *S.S.P.* vol. LXXXIV. p. 104. "Maie 3, 1646: John Lazing was appointed to be bedel for driving doggs out of the church in time of public worship, and other necessary dutys."

intruding on the common; also that of hayward—he inspected the hedges and fences round the open fields, to see
if they needed mending[1]. As his name implies[2] it was his
duty to bid people to the parish meetings; therefore in some
places the beadle was also the town crier[3].

Some of the expenses of government which are now met
by taxation or through private charity were borne by the
parish. Such were the upkeep of the prisons and hospitals,
and pensions for disabled soldiers.

Every parish had to contribute a sum not exceeding 6*d.*
or 8*d.* a week levied on Sundays for the maintenance of poor
prisoners in the county gaol. The whole sum paid by the
Riding in the early part of the century was 40*s.*, therefore
the amount from each parish was very small, yet if the payment was neglected the Justices received a demand for it
from the Council of the North[4]. This "Rogue money," as it
was generally called, was in some villages paid out of the
church expenses[5].

Not less than 20*s.* was to be sent out of the Riding every
year as a relief for the prisoners of the King's Bench and
Marshalsea, and in the early part of the century this sum
appears in the hospitals and bridges accounts of the Riding[6].

During the Civil War the payments seem to have lapsed;
in 1651 the treasurer of the hospitals for the east division
of the Riding asked the Bench for £13. 11*s.* 6*d.*, which he

---

[1] T. Smith, *The Parish*, p. 192.
[2] A.S. *beddan* = to bid, invite.
[3] S. and B. Webb, *The County and the Parish*, p. 127 n.
[4] *N.R.Q.S.R.* vol. I. p. 39. "The Justices in every severall wapentake
which have (not) paid their ratable proportion for the relief of the poore
prisoners in York Castle, according to the direction of the Rt. Ho. the Lo.
President his letters, shall presently cause to be levied and paied all such
sommes as are arrere to Mr Will. Wharton, Gaoler of the said Castle,
without delay. The whole rate for the N. Riding is xls. (side-note: At the
making of this order Sir Wm. Bamburgh for Bulmer and Mr Will Mau-
liverer for Laugburgh affirmed were paid)."
[5] It appears regularly in the vestry book of Pittington and was included
with the maimed soldier money and the assessment for the houses of correction. Vestry book of the parish of Pittington, *S.S.P.* vol. LXXXIV. pp.
19, 20, 22, etc. and p. 48. "Item payed to Mr Calverlay's clerke for Rogge
monie and Soger monie the v of June viij*s.* vij*d.*"
[6] *N.R.Q.S.R.* vol. II. p. 275.

had paid "to the Lord Chief Justice Roby as arrears due
from the North Riding for the poor prisoners in the Upper
Bench and Marshalsea with charges about paying in the
same[1]." The last entry previous to this was in the year
1637. The sum was raised to 28s. at some date after 1662[2],
one of the results of the Restoration being the increase of
money required from every county for the London prisons.
Certain sums were granted by the Justices in Quarter
Sessions to the county hospitals which were at Old Malton
and Scarborough. There was also one at New Malton which
was "utterly dissolved" by the Court of Quarter Sessions
in 1619, pensions being given to the old and impotent people
living in it[3].

In the October previously the Justices had been dubious
as to the "lawfulness" of the hospital at Old Malton, but
they continued its grant[4]. The sums given to the two county
hospitals were very small[5]; the method of helping the lame
and impotent by weekly relief was preferred in the seventeenth century.

PURVEYANCE

While all people had to pay certain rates for their parish
and county, other assessments reminded them that they
were part of a larger community. A sum of money was paid
yearly[6], instead of the oxen, which in olden times the North

---

[1] *N.R.Q.S.R.* vol. v. p. 73. Thirsk, Ap. 8, 1651.
[2] *Ibid.* vol. vi. p. 61. Thirsk, in 1662 the payment was 20s. for the
year. In Oct. 1665 "The Tr. to pay unto John Chapman Dep. Sheriff
56s. being the proportion for the N.R. for the prisoners of the King's Bench
and Marshalseas till Midsummer 1665." Evidently this was a payment
for two years. At Helmsley, July, 1673, the Bench orders "the Tr for
L.S. and Hospitals to pay 28s. which was due at Midsummer last for the
relief of prisoners in the King's Bench and Marshalsea."
[3] *Ibid.* vol. ii. p. 192. Helmsley, Jan. 1619.
[4] *Ibid.* vol. ii. p. 183. Malton, Oct. 1618.
[5] In 1608 Malton received £13. 6s. 8d.; Scarborough, £5. *N.R.Q.S.R.*
vol. ii. p. 257.
[6] In 1613 the sum was £152. 15s. 7d. (vol. ii. p. 6); in 1636 it had risen
to £235. 16s. *N.R.Q.S.R.* vol. iv. p. 55. Malton, July, 1636. "Whereas
the sume of £235. 16 to the Kinges Purveyor for his Maties Howsehold
Provision, whereof there was £208 borrowed of Mr Shallcrosse, citizen of
London for repayment whereof Mr Henry Bellassis Esq. with some other

Riding had to furnish for His Majesty's household provision. In 1613 the sum was £152. 15s. 7d. It was evidently rising, as in 1616 the Justices arrange to meet in York Minster to "compound for the rate of oxen to be sent forth of the North Riding for the provision of His Majesty's household[1]." In 1636 the amount had risen to £235. 16s. The money had to be collected by the high constables of the wapentakes, and it seems that the Justices made themselves responsible and even provided it when it was not paid up to time. For it was not given willingly. Many indications show that Parliament in denouncing purveyance was giving voice to a real grievance felt by the country. Constables neglected to levy the rate[2], or were assaulted when they went to claim it[3]. But though the Yorkshiremen disliked paying money, they were still more averse to giving up their horses, whether for conveying criminals to London or for other services demanded on behalf of the Crown. One John Egglefield of Topcliffe comes before the court

for making resistance against the Petty Constables there...they beinge taking of post-horses, and for that the said John in contempt of the said service rode awaie with his mayre.

Two men of Thirsk are presented because they resisted the constable "and would not suffer him to take their horses for the Kinges business."

However, there was no escape from assessments levied in an agricultural county like the North Riding; every householder possessed a certain amount of moveable stock, which was seized and driven away, if the owner refused to pay his

Justices did enter bond unto the said Mr Shallcrosse, and £27. 16 was disbursed by Mr Moor, Clark of the Peace, Ordered that the H.Cs of the N.R. shall at once pay £183. 6. 8 to Mr Moore and the Thr for the Hospls the further sum of £52. 9. 4 Mr Moore being authorised by the Court to pay Mr Shallcrosse the aforesaid sum of £208."

[1] N.R.Q.S.R. Vol. II. p. 125.

[2] Ibid. vol. II. p. 250. "Will Archer Constable of Norton Conyers for not executing a precept from the High Constables for money due for the provision of the King's Maties. Household, etc."

[3] Ibid. vol. II. p. 253. "Will Gilminge of Helmsley for offering to assalt Geo. Shepherde Constable there, when he went to demand his assistance for purvey-money."

rates[1]. These steadily increased during the century, and though purveyance ceased after the downfall of Charles I, hearth money and excise duties more than filled its place.

SOLDIERS AND SAILORS

Another obligation which rested on the community was the provision and equipment of soldiers and sailors for the army and navy. From every parish so many men were required to serve in the trained band of the Riding. If no one could be found willing to do this, men were pressed. Shakespeare has given for all time a vivid picture of the way in which recruits were enlisted in the England of his day. Though Falstaff and Shallow may exaggerate their type, yet it cannot be doubted that there were many Bardolphs who let off the "likeliest" men if they could give him "four Harry ten shillings in French crowns," and took instead the women's tailors, and "the little lean, old, chapped, bad shots," who had no money wherewith to bribe the corporal.

It is possible, however, that after pensions were granted by statute to soldiers and mariners who could prove that they were pressed[2], less unwillingness was shown to go to the wars. In the coast towns men were pressed for the navy, nor were there wanting in the seventeenth century agitators, who attained a certain amount of success, but could not escape the vengeance of the law. In 1667 a Sneaton man is summoned

for uttering these words against Fr Comyn, Rob. Bushell, Egidius Wigginer gentn and Tho. Skipton, Esq., who had received authority from our Sovereign Lord the King to press men for his Majesty's naviall service, viz: that they had no authority to impress any men for his Majesty's naviall service, and the persons needed not to obey their authority; and also did invite and encourage one man to pro-

---

[1] *N.R.Q.S.R.* vol. VI. p. 80. Richmond, July, 1664. "A marriske yeoman for rescuing a cow distreyned for taxes."

[2] *Ibid.* vol. I. p. 257. Thirsk, Ap. 1612. "That Geo. Watkins L.S.* shall have 13. 4 paid him for his relief until next Sessions, when he must prove where he was pressed, and where he was born, etc."

* L.S. = lame soldier.

cure a Goadland gentn to join with him in throwing the said four gentn. or any of them over the bridge at Whitby into the river, and he would justify them therein and be their warrant for so doing; likewise he did say that, if he were in the case of those persons that were pressed he would be hanged before he would serve the King and that those persons that were impressed needed not to be subject to obey their impression: which speeches did cause many of the persons so impressed to run away and abscond themselves[1].

Various statutes were passed to provide for soldiers and sailors in the reign of Elizabeth. A final one in 1601 designed "to provide reliefe and maintenance to souldiers and Mariners that have lost their limbes, and disabld their bodies in the defence and service of Her Majesty and the State," ordered that every parish should be charged with a weekly sum at the discretion of the Justices in Quarter Sessions so long as no parish paid more than 10d. nor less than 2d. weekly, as in the case of the gaol money. Some parishes only sent the exact minimum[2], for the rate was unpopular. In the first few years after the passing of the act, church-wardens were frequently presented for not paying their lame soldier money. Probably they had no lame soldiers living among them[3], and as feeling was extremely local they had no desire to contribute to the maintenance of people in other parishes. Since each village was expected to provide two, three, or four soldiers as the case might be for the trained bands, and these men were generally pressed into the service, it was eminently just that provision should be made by the community for them, and their wives and families. Only those men, however, who could prove that they were pressed were given pensions. Later in the century the grievance lay

---

[1] *N.R.Q.S.R.* vol. VI. pp. 122–3. Thirsk, April, 1667.

[2] In the Pittington parish accounts 8s. 8d. appears regularly every year for lame soldiers.

[3] *N.R.Q.S.R.* vol. I. p. 2. Thirsk, Ap. 1605. "Michael Meeke Church-warden of Kirby on the Urske was presented for not paying the sum due for Lame Soldiers and Hospitals." According to the statute his fine was 20s. In July of the same year the churchwardens of Deighton, Sigston and Wattset were also presented and in April, 1612, those of Marske, Melsonby, Barton Maryes, Cowton and Forsett, Coverham, Massam and West Runcton were all presented for not paying their lame soldier money. Vol. I. pp. 253–4. Thirsk, April, 1612.

in the fact that Royalists at heart had to pay the rate to
provide for men who had fought against them, and in like
manner Parliamentarians after the Restoration.

The churchwardens of Dighton, a small rural township in
the parish of Northallerton, were particularly obstinate, and
were presented no less than seven times in four years[1] for
refusing to pay their soldier money. In the case of such
refusal, the constable and churchwarden were empowered
by the statute to levy the sum by distress and sale of the
offenders' goods, therefore, since the parish officers had power
to distrain, they, ultimately, were to blame, and the constable
as well as the churchwarden was presented if the money was
not forthcoming[2]. The churchwardens were probably given
a year's grace, then they were summoned before the Court
of Quarter Sessions and presumably had to pay their 20s.
fine[3].

Unlike the Marshalsea money, which remained constant,
the lame soldier rate increased greatly, as might be expected
after the Civil War, and was a heavy burden on the Riding.

For just as the sums given to the Parliamentarians were
diminishing through the gradual decease of the holders, the
King was restored and further provision had to be made for

[1] *N.R.Q.S.R.* vol. I. The Churchwardens of Dighton for non-payment
of assts. in behalf of L.S. and H. were summoned at
               Thirsk, April, 1606
               Richmond, Oct. 1606
               Thirsk, Ap. 1607
               Richmond, Ap. 1607
               Malton, Jan. 1607
                 ,,   ,,   1608
               Richmond, July, 1609
               Helmsley, Jan. 1615

[2] *Ibid.* vol. I. "Will Lockwood, constable of Crake, Giles Parkes and
John Overan churchwardens for the year 1615 for refusing to pay their
money for lame soldiers and hospitals for the quarter ending Christmas
last, being 4s. 4d.; also Will Nicholson late constable there and Tho. Crake
and Richard Grayson, churchwardens for 1614, for the like as to the
quarter ended at Michaelmas last."
[3] *Ibid.* vol. III. p. 251. Richmond, Oct. 12, 1625. In 1625 the churchwardens of Masham, Coverham, Grinton, Aysgarth, East Bolton, Redmire
and Wensley for the years 1624 and 1625 were all presented. These
parishes are situated far up in the dales and they may have escaped the
high constable's notice for the pressing of soldiers.

the Royalist veterans. In many parishes all the assessments which the churchwardens had to collect were included in the church expenses, and either paid out of the parish income or levied as a single rate. The gaol, lame soldier, and hospital money was collected for the high constable of each wapentake, who paid it to the county treasurer appointed to distribute it according to the several purposes for which it was required.

The parishes in the North Riding are extensive in area, frequently comprising three, four or more townships. In the seventeenth century the population of the townships had become unequal; some villages were entirely rural, containing few inhabitants, others in which the church was situated or where the manor house had survived being fairly populous. It was obviously beneficial to the community that the parish rather than the township should be the area of local government, because all taxation was on land, and the larger area rendered more attainable the equalisation of assessments. Nevertheless, feeling was extremely local and there are many indications that the smaller method of division was favoured. As will be noticed later, churchwardens and overseers were chosen to represent each township, and finally they succeeded in establishing the principle with regard to poor relief, that each township should assume responsibility only for those poor within its area. After 1662 an order from the Bench was necessary to make a township contribute to the poor of the parish living outside its own boundaries[1].

As will be seen later this division of the unit of local government had disastrous consequences on the morale of the English people.

[1] *N.R.Q.S.R.* vol. VII. p. 26. Richmond, July 22, 1670. "Whereas it appears to this Court by the petitions of the inhabts of Ainderby Steeple that they are over-burthened and charged towards the maintenance of the poor within the said town and that the town of Warlaby within the said parish hath few or none within it: Ordered that the inhabrs of Warlaby do contribute towards the poor of Ainderby Steeple according to the statute of the 43rd of Elizabeth."

APPENDIX A

PENSIONS FOR LAME SOLDIERS

A lame soldier impressed in Yorkshire, sent by certificate from London back to Yorkshire to be pensioned by the county.

Whereas it appeareth by the Certificate of Sir Thomas Dowton, Knight, that the bearer of this John Huntley, Corporall of the... Company of Sir Tho. Dowton, is so hurt and maymed in the warres as he is not able to serve anye longer, forasmuch as by reason therof he is to be relieved by virtue of the Stattut established in the last Session of Parlyament for releiffe of hurt and maymed Souldiers. It is therefore not to be doubted but that you, the justices of the Peace, and others the treasorers for the County of Yorck, where he was impressed, will have a care to see him provided of such a yearly stipend for his releiffe and mayntenance as by the tenour of the said Stattut is ordained to a Servitour of his place and quallety.

From the Tower in London this vith of September 1606

W. Waad.

To the right wo(rshipful) the Justices of the Peace and otheres the Treasorers of the monie collected for the releiffe of hurt and maymed Souldieres in ye County of Yorck.

Mid'sex. Geven this berer to passe this countye, 11th September, 1606. 9*d*.   Wm Megges, Thresour.

Hertf(ordshire) the 14th of September to the bearer 12*d*.

(undecipherable)

Cantebr'. Given this bearer the 15 of September for his releife to passe this Countye, 12*d*.

William Pitcher, Treasorer.

Cambridg. Given to this bearer to passe this towne, 6*d*.

Richard Cr...Tresurer.

(fo. 52) Countie Hunt. Given this bearer the 19 of September 1606, to passe this Counte, 12*d*.

Mathewe Marshall, Tresurer.

I pray you give the bearer hereof halfe a crowne out of your mony. This shall be atte ye Sessions a discharge to you.

Ra Eure.

Geven this bearer to pass this Northrydding of the County of York for his releif, the 22 of Octr 1606., 2s. 6d.

Edmund Cloughe, Treasurer.

Mr Clugh, we pray you give this bearer 2s. 6d. for his releife unto the Sessions and this shall be your descharge at the Sessions.

Willm Mauleverer, Cha. Layton. John Constable

More payd to this bearer, 25th of November, 1606 for his releife till the next Sessions by the comandment abovesaid. 2s. 6d.

Edmunde Cloughe.

Ad general' Sess' pacis tent' apud Helmesley, xi° die Januar', 1624.

John Huntley came into the Courte and desired further pension, having one Petition, one Passe, two severall Certificates, and one Letter from the Lordes of his Maties most hon^ble Privie Counsell, which being showne unto the Courte, and compared with Sir Will. Waade's Certificate, and finding that he had received a gratuitie from the Countrie after the Justices had granted him £5, in regard he should never require anie further pension, he stole forth of the Courte and left his writinges for feare that he should have bene sent to the House of Correction.

Which see in the bundles amongst L. Soldiers passes and Certificates.

Se an Order in libro presentationum 1605, fo. 59. (For this, see Vol. I. p. 64, where Huntley "consents tò take 20s. in full satisfaction of all claim, and subscribes the Roll to that effect with his own mark.")   (fo. 55) Apud. Thirsk. 29 April, 1606.

N.R.Q.S.R. vol. II. p. 289.

CHAPTER II

THE CHURCHWARDENS

IN the thirteenth century, the English clergy succeeded in throwing upon their parishioners certain charges hitherto borne by themselves. Such were the repair of the nave of the church, and the provision of surplices, books, furniture, etc., used in the services. The people who were called upon to pay these charges were the landowners.

> The duty of repairing the parish church is analogous to the duty of repairing the County bridges; it is planted in the soil, and to the soil it has ceded. The Sheriff takes from every hide in the county toll for pontage and the Rector takes toll for Church repair.[1]

The writers of *The History of English Law* take the view that it is a moot point whether already in the thirteenth century the parishioners elected churchwardens; "they and their legal powers are to our thinking the outcome of two movements, one in the world of fact, the other in the world of legal thought."

Lawyers were beginning to hold that the parson was in some sort the owner or tenant of the churchyard and the glebe. It also became necessary to find an owner for what in the past had been chattels possessed by a saint[2].

From ancient times it had been the custom for the priest to meet his people in the church to consult with them about the parish business. At such meetings, when the need arose, the parishioners were accustomed to elect certain persons from among themselves to take charge of moneys bequeathed by will, to provide for the upkeep of the church and to buy books, communion cups or other furniture necessary for the services.

---

[1] Pollock and Maitland, *History of English Law*, Book II. ch. iii. p. 602.
[2] *Ibid.* Book II. ch. iii. p. 603.

The parish meeting, held at first in the church and later in the vestry, consisted in theory of all parishioners. Actually, however, in many places, a certain number of persons established the right to represent the rest of the inhabitants of the parish; these representatives were called "the vestry" from the place of their meeting; they held their office for life, and when a vacancy occurred it was filled by co-opting another parishioner.

The parishioners comprising these select vestries were generally (in the north of England) twelve or twenty-four in number[1]. In the seventeenth century they wielded considerable and extensive powers; they appointed the churchwardens and audited their accounts[2]; imposed the church rate, and authorised churchwardens to distrain for it by their warrant on the goods of any parishioner refusing to pay[3]; exercised a certain amount of supervision over the officers and servants of the parish, and took a large share in conducting its affairs.

The origin of select vestries is in many cases wrapped in obscurity. Sometimes they seem to have arisen because the parish business, which was the work of everybody, was done by nobody. In the sixteenth century the parishioners of Pittington in Durham chose twelve of their number to

---

[1] Twenty-four at Barnard Castle, Masham, Northallerton, Houghton-le-Spring, St Oswald's and St Nicholas, Durham; twelve at Pittington.

[2] Vestry Book of the Parish of Pittington, *S.S.P.* vol. LXXXIV. p. 23. "In primis receaved by us, the foresaid James Huntley and John Wheatlay, Churchwardens, in monie of the xij in the day and year aforesaid, xxij, *s.* vj. *d.*" (The money was the balance from the previous year's account, paid to the vestry by the outgoing churchwardens.)

[3] *Reports of the Resolutions of the Court of Common Pleas*, by Sir Ed. Lutwyche, 1718, vol. II. pp. 436–7. "Batt etc. late Churchwardens of Massam versus Watkinson. (2 W. & M.) Suggest: for a prohibition to the Consistory in York on a suit there to compel the Plaintiffs being Churchwardens, to give in their accounts there; because within the said Parish from the time whereof etc., there have been 24 Parishioners called the 24 that on the death of one the others have elected another, and that they have made Rates etc., and the Wardens have distrained by warrant of the 24, and that the Wardens have given their account to the 24 and thereby have been discharged etc. The Court, after several great debates, was of opinion the custom was good and reasonable, and a prohibition was granted absolutely."

represent them and to manage their concerns[1]. In the vestry books they are mentioned as "the twelve"; they transacted the main business appertaining to the parish, but on especially important occasions others of the most influential inhabitants were associated with them; for example, the "Gentlemen and twelve of the Parish" made a bye-law that no one was to entertain a tenant without acquainting the twelve[2]; they also made assessments for general purposes, such as the provision of the common armour[3]; and laid down rules for the better ordering of the parish[4].

Select vestries acted as an advisory committee to the churchwardens, who, when in doubt with regard to procedure guarded their action by obtaining the approval of some members of the twenty-four[5]. Since the churchwardens usually held office for one year only[6] the continued existence of the vestry gave stability to the parish government, though it tended to produce narrowness in policy.

The churchwardens, however, were, as their name implies, the legal guardians of property belonging to the parish and its church. When Lambard wrote, the custom which still prevails was already established, namely, that if a man took anything into the church it thereby became without word or writing the possession of the parish, and the churchwardens

[1] Vestry Book of the Parish of Pittington, *S.S.P.* vol. LXXXIV. p. 12. Anno 1584. "Then it is agreed by the consent of the whole parishe to electe and chuse out of the same xij men to order and to define all common causes pertaininge to the churche, as shall appertaine to the profit & commoditie of the same, without molestation or troublinge of the rest of the common people."

[2] 1624, Vestry Book of the Parish of Pittington, *S.S.P.* vol. XLVIII. p. 84. "Memorandum that it is agreed uppon by the Gentlemen and twelve of Pittington parish the day and yeere above written, that no inhabitant within the parish of Pittington shall receive harbour and entertaine any stranger to be his tenant or tenants into his house or houses before he acquaint the twelve with his entent, and shall himselfe and two sufficient men with him enter into bond with him to the overseers that neither his tenant, wife, or children, shall be chargeable to the parish for five years next following uppon paine and penalty to forfeit tenn shillings for every moneth."

[3] *Ibid.* p. 85.   [4] *Ibid.* pp. 310–11.

[5] See Barnard Castle churchwardens, *S.S.P.* vol. XXII. p. 141.

[6] 27 H. VIII, cap. XXV. sec. XXIII. No churchwarden to remain in office more than one year.

were bound to maintain an appeal of robbery against anyone (even the donor) who took it away[1]. Lambard held the view that for some purposes churchwardens might be considered a corporation "That is to say persons enabled by that name to take moveable goods or chattels, and to sue and be sued at the Law concerning such goods for the use and profit of their parish."

This, however, did not apply to immoveable property: "if the walls, windows or doors of the church be broken, or the trees in the churchyard cut down, or the grass thereof be eaten up, then the Parson or Vicar shall have the action for it[2]."

Probably a man once elected by the vestry could not refuse to serve, even in early times. If he did so without any adequate reason he was liable to be excommunicated. Certainly after becoming a civil officer he was presented at Quarter Sessions[3]. He might, however, be allowed to appoint a deputy[4]. The churchwardens were usually elected at the vestry meeting held on Easter Tuesday[5], and they were either sworn in church on the following Sunday by the rector, vicar, or curate in the presence of the parishioners, or they took the oath in the archdeacon's court at his visitation[6].

The oath administered for the diocese of Durham, which may be taken as fairly typical of that sworn in most dioceses, was as follows:

You that be chosen to be Churchwardens of this Churche or chappelle for this next yere doe swere by God and the holly Gospell before yow laide, that yow shall execute the said office effectuallie

---

[1] 2 H. IV, cap xii; 1 H. VII, cap. xii.

[2] Lambard, *The Duties of Churchwardens.*

[3] *N.R.Q.S.R.* vol. v. p. 193. Bedale, July, 1655. "John Colton of Burtreside to be Churchwarden for Askricke or, appear before the next J.P. and shew cause etc. within eight days, and if he refuse to be bound, etc."

[4] Vestry Book of the Parish of Pittington, *S.S.P.* vol. LXXXIV. p. 73. "April 12, 1618. The election of the new Churchwardons for this yere: William Shandfourth, and George Cooke *for* Mr Antho. Cockson."

[5] Toulmin Smith, *The Parish*, pp. 83 and 92, quoting Canon 90.

[6] Bishop Barnes appointed Ascension Day for the election throughout his diocese and ordered them to be sworn on the following Sunday. *S.S.P.* vol. XXII. p. 23.

and diligently, to the advancement of Godde's glorie and the commoditie of this Churche and parishe. The Quene's Iniunctions and
the Ordiniare's monicions ye shall observe, and in so far as in yow
liethe cause others to observe; and the violators of the same yow
shall duely and without all parcialitie present and detecte (to) the
Quene's Highnes Commissioners for causes Ecclesiasticall within the
Dioces or to the iuartes[1] and sworne men or to the Chauncelor. And
yow shall yeilde and give vp at the yere's ende a faithefull and true
accompte of all somes by yowe received and laide out for the use of
this Churche; and all suche somes of money Church implementes
furnitures and bookes as then shall remayne and delyver to your
successors. So God yow helpe by Jesu Christ[2].

When the oath had been sworn the minister read the
Queen's Injunctions and the Ordinary's Monitions.

By the Queen's Injunctions the churchwardens were to provide in every church "a comely and honest pulpit[3]" and a
strong chest with three keys for alms and oblations[4], "one
book of the whole Bible of the largest volumn in English,"
and Erasmus's Paraphrases on the Gospels[5]; they had also to
keep a book of register in which the dates of weddings,
christenings and burials were entered by the vicar[6]. In
addition the canons enjoined the provision of certain books
for use in the services; from time to time the bishop or the
archdeacon at his visitation ordered the churchwardens to
buy works relating to doctrine[7]. A memorandum in the
Vestry Book at Pittington runs

that it was agreed upon the xvii day of October, 1613, by *Mr Vicar*
and the most part of the xii men of this parishe, that a sesment of
ii*d* the pound should be presently leveyed by the Churchwa: within
this parishe of Pittington for the byinge of Mr Jewell's booke[8],
enjoyned unto us by my Lo. of Durham.

---

[1] jurates.
[2] Injunctions of Bishop Barnes, *S.S.P.* vol. XXII. pp. 26–27.
[3] Queen's Injunctions XXIV, 1559.
[4] Queen's Injunctions XXV, 1559.   [5] Queen's Injunctions VI.
[6] Queen's Injunctions X, Vestry Book of the Parish of Pittington,
S.S.P. vol. LXXXIV. pp. 74–75. Dec. 20, Anno 1618. "Item payed to Mr
Vicar for writinge the names of all Christnings Weddings and Buryalls in
our register booke, which we were commanded to bringe into the Court
before Mr Dcr. Colmore, Febru, 20 v. s."
[7] Vestry Book, Pittington, *S.S.P.* vol. LXXXIV. pp. 65, 66. 1613.
[8] Probably *The Apology of the Church of England.*

It seems that the cess was not paid; for the cost of the book
is entered in the yearly account. " Item payed for the booke
bying Jewell and Hardin workes so called xxs." So long as
the ecclesiastical courts were in existence, if the church lacked
any of the requisite service books the churchwardens were
promptly cited before them.

In 1579, Ralph Wright, the churchwarden of Stockton,
was haled before the judge and excommunicated because his
church lacked a communion book. He evidently obtained one
promptly as he is absolved in the same entry[1].

At Trimdon both wardens are in trouble "for their church
lacks the Postills, the Defence of the Apology, My Lord's
Monitions, and a pulpit[2]."

The bishop of the diocese issued monitions from time to
time reminding churchwardens of their duties with regard
to the cleansing and repair of the church, the care of its
property, the rendering of full and perfect accounts to their
successors, and the presentment without partiality at every
general chapter of all people who transgressed the Queen's
injunctions or the bishop's monitions.

Bishop Barnes also enjoins the churchwardens

to take order and diligently see that no fairs or markets be holden
or kept upon Sundays nor any pedler or other open or sell any wares
in any churches, church porches or churchyards at any time at all
or in any place in time of divine service, of sermons or ministrations
of Sacraments, nor that during such times any beggar be suffered to
sit, lie or stand begging abroad, nor that any taverns ale houses or
victualling houses during such time be kept open, or any victual
sold or any gaming used[3].

---

[1] *S.S.P.* vol. xxii. Injunctions of Bishop Barnes, p. 116. In 1578–9,
8 March, Stockton. "The Office of the Judge against Ralph Wright, Churchwarden. They lack the Communion Boke Excommunicated Absolved."
[2] *Ibid.* p. 119. 1579, Trimdon. "The office of the Judge against Robert
Jackson and Robert Taliour Wardens. They lacke the Postills, the Defence
of the Appologie, my Lord's Monicions, and a pulpit."
[3] *S.S.P.* vol. xxii. Injunctions of Bishop Barnes for year Oct. 1577,
p. 24. That the monition was not unnecessary is seen from the *Quarter
Sessions Records* (vol. ii. p. 103), July 14, 1615. "Richard Metcalf, Tho.
Rogers, Chr. Metcalfe and Edmund Coates, Churchwardens of Askrigg
presented for suffering a markett to be kept in the Churchyard there."

The oath, the injunctions, and the bishop's monitions relate solely to the ecclesiastical functions of the churchwardens, which may be summarised as follows:

1. The repair of the church, provision of surplices, books, furniture, and all other necessaries for the service and the care of the church property.

2. The account of all moneys received and paid out by them.

3. The presentment of all offences within the cognisance of the church courts.

The select vestry, moreover, in those parishes where it exercised general supervision over the churchwardens, was only concerned with those matters, ecclesiastical and lay, which were regulated by the church in the Middle Ages; it had no part in the statutory duties of the churchwarden; for the due performance of these, he alone was answerable to the state.

The province of the churchwarden therefore comprised both ecclesiastical functions and civil duties. In many cases, however, no clear line of division can be drawn between these two spheres of work. As will be seen later, the churchwardens were in large measure the servants of the ecclesiastical courts; nevertheless, as custodians of the parish property, they were considered by the judges to be temporal officers. Though they were sworn into their office by the archdeacon, yet the latter had no power to elect or control their election[1]; he could not refuse to swear a man into his office even though he might consider him unsuitable for the position. The churchwarden could only be displaced by the parishioners; moreover he could exercise the duties of his office before he was sworn[2].

As trustees of the parish the churchwardens collected, took charge of and paid out on its behalf all moneys, including

[1] T. Smith, *The Parish*, p. 90, quoting 1 Raymond's Reports, p. 138, Chief Justice Holt.
[2] *Ibid.* p. 91, quoting 1 Ventris' Reports, p. 267.

those which concerned the parishioners alone, as well as those pertaining to the church.

The main expenses, however, were connected with the upkeep and repair of the church, the maintenance of the services, the wages of the parish clerk and sexton, the fees for the visitations and the out-of-pocket expenses of the churchwardens.

The churchwardens provided out of the parish funds the church plate, robes for the clergy[1], a surplice for the parish clerk[2], and a dress for the beadle[3]. They bought; sometimes unwillingly, those books which were recommended by the bishop or the archdeacon[4], though, as we have seen, a special assessment might be levied for such books, or for service books[5], when they were too expensive to be bought out of the yearly income.

The quantity of wine used for communions was so great that in some places a special assessment for this also[6] was

---

[1] Vestry Book of the Parish of St Nicholas, Durham, 1674, *S.S.P.* vol. LXXXIV. p. 235. "For a new surplesse being 10 yards of fine cloth att 2*s.* 6*d.* per yard 1 L 5*s.* For makeing thereof 5*s.*"

[2] Vestry Book of the Parish of Pittington, 1620, *S.S.P.* vol. LXXXIV. p. 79. "Item for the clark's surples and for the making of it, xviij*d.* Item for our charges that day when we bought thes things ix*d.*"

[3] Vestry Book of the Parish of St Nicholas, Durham, 1676, *S.S.P.* vol. LXXXIV. p. 240. "To Thomas Binyon for the beagle's coate makeing 3*s.* 6*d.* For trimming to it 1*s.* 6*d.*"

[4] Vestry Book, St Oswald, Durham, *S.S.P.* p. 184, 1630–1631. "A Bible of the largest volume and latest edicion, as by the book binder's acquittance appeareth 21. 16*s.* 0*d.* To one that was purposely sent about itt 1*s.* For a service book for the Communion table of the best sort 9*s.* King David his psalmes translated by King James and commanded to be had in all churches 2*s.* 4*d.* To John Cowper for mending and binding the Paraphrases of Erasmus, and making a new cover to itt, 9*d.*"

[5] Vestry Book, Pittington, *S.S.P.* p. 94, 1632. "Item collected of a cessement of 6*d.* in the £ for the buying of a Church Bible 21£ 16*s.* 7*d.*"

N.R.Q.S.R. vol. V. p. 21. Helmsley, 1648–9. "The parishioners of Scawton to pay a man presenting a petition the sum charged upon them by way of asst. for a Church bible, and in case of refusal the next J.P. to bind the offenders, etc."

[6] Vestry Book, Houghton-le-Spring, *S.S.P.* vol. LXXXIV. p. 328, 1661–2. "For 7 gallons of wine against Whitsonday and towle 16*s.*" "For bringing the wine home 1*s.* 6*d.*" "For bread to the Communion 10*d.*" "For wine against Christmas 1£ 4*s.* 0*d.* For bringing it home 1*s.* 4*d.* For bread to the Comunion 1*s.*" "For 17 gallons and a pinte of wine against Easter 1£ 17*s.* 6*d.* For bringing it home 1*s.* 4*d.* For bread to the Communion

made. Charges for riding round the boundaries of the parish
on the Rogation days, called in the north "Gang Week[1],"
were fairly heavy, since all who accompanied the procession
received bread and drink afterwards at the parish expense.
The visitation was a great day for the parish in which it
was held; the bells were rung[2], a store of wine and sack was
laid in[3], and a "treat" was provided for the parson by the
churchwardens[4].

The parish clerk received a shilling per annum for keeping
the churchwardens' accounts[5]. But the vestry books were
not treated with the respect given to them to-day, for
at Houghton-le-Spring the churchwardens were so in the
habit of tearing sheets out of the account book that the
vestry, to prevent further destruction, authorised them
each

> to provide and buy himselfe a penyworth off cleane writing paper
> and put itt in their accounts, to the end they may all be provided
> and stored with paper upon all occasions and services belonging to
> their offices, and that hereafter the leaves of this booke be not torne
> or cutt outt by any on paine of vs. Signed by the gentlemen and
> fower and twentye: Thomas Delavall, etc.[6]

When a large item of church repair occurred special
benevolences were asked[7] or an extraordinary assessment

2s. 2d." p. 182. St Oswald's, 1628-9. "45 quarts of wine for the whole
year at 8d.; and more for a quart 8d."

[1] Vestry Book of the Parish of Houghton-le-Spring, 1667, *S.S.P.*
vol. XLVIII. pp. 335 *seq.* "Paid for charges at rideing the perambulation 7s."
In 1668 it was 2s., in 1669 9s. 6d., in 1670 5s. 3d., while in 1699 the
charges had risen to 17s. 2d."

[2] Easter, 1630-31, *S.S.P.* vol. XLVIII. p. 184. "Bells rung. At the Bishopps
going in his visitacion, we being formerly fined for not ringing, 2s. 6d."

[3] Vestry Book, Houghton-le-Spring, *S.S.P.* vol. LXXXIV. p. 337. "For
wine and sacke against the Archdeacons visitation, 13s."

[4] Vestry Book, St Nicholas, Durham, *S.S.P.* vol. LXXXIV, p. 251. "1683–
For the treat to the parson att the Visitacion day 12s. 6d."

[5] Vestry Book, Pittington, *S.S.P.* vol. LXXXIV. p. 63, 1611. "Item
payed to the clarke for writing xiid."

[6] Vestry Book, Houghton-le-Spring, *S.S.P.* vol. LXXXIV. p. 323.
"Ordered the 25th day of March 1658."

[7] Henry Best in 1616 paid to the C.W. of Baintry (Essex) "for my
benevolence towards the building of the gallery 16d." Rural Economy in
Yorkshire, *S.S.P.* vol. XXXIII. p. 149.

was levied[1]; sometimes even, the Court of Quarter Sessions was petitioned for a donation out of the county funds[2].

During the interregnum the repair of churches was somewhat neglected, since, after the abolition of the church courts and in the troubled period of the Civil War there was no central authority in the church to keep the vestry or churchwardens up to their work. Presently the Court of Quarter Sessions stepped into the breach and forced individuals or parishes to make the necessary repairs according to their liability[3].

In some cases the justices gave information to the court[4]; the churchwardens doubtless presented rectors who would

[1] Vestry Book, Parish of Pittington, *S.S.P.* vol. LXXXIV. p. 59. "May 20, 1609. Mem. that it is agreed by the consent of the xij men of this parishe of Pittington, that a sesment of ij*s.* the pounde shalbe leveyed presently through this parish towardes the repayringe of the steple, and other necessaryes about the church."

[2] *N.R.Q.S.R.* vol. II. p. 229. Richmond, 1619–20. "Leminge Chapel certified to be in great ruine: the inhabts. by reason of the great charge required and their great povertie, unable themselves to repaire yt: Therefore the Courte (for the furtherance of soe charitable a worke) Orders that 40*s.* be paid by Mr Rich. Bland, Thresr. for the Hospitalls, and if more be wanted, further consideration, etc."

[3] *Ibid.* vol. v. p. 39. Thirsk, Oct. 1649. "Dame Anne Hutton impropriatrix of the Rectory of Sutton on the Forest for not repairing the quire or chancell belonginge to the Church thereof."

Ibid. vol. v. p. 251. Thirsk, Oct. 1657. "The inhab. of Newsam and Breckonborough for not repairing the Churchyard of Kirby Wiske."

[4] *Ibid.* vol. v. p. 119. Thirsk, Oct. 1652. "Upon information of Luke Robinson Esq., J.P. that the quere or chancell of the Parish Church at Kirbymoorside is in great decay and like to fall by which means the inhabts. of that parish resorting to that Church may be in danger, and for that it is likewise informed that Mr Rob. Otterburne senr. and Tobias Thurscrosse senr. ought to uphold and repair the same, the Bailiffs of Ridall to carry them before the next J.P. to enter bond to repaire the same before the 1st Dec. next or appear etc." At Kirbymoorside, in the following January, Ordered "Whereas Tobias Thurscrosse and Rob. Otterburne gent. of Kirbymoorside impropriators of the Rectory of Kirbymoorside, have not repaired the chancell of the parish church there, as by law and custom they ought to have done, but have longe neglected the same to the great hazard and damage of the inhabts theis are to require you to demand £1 of good money of the said Toby Thurcrosse and Rob. Otterburne as a fyne the law appoints them to pay unto the poor of the parish to be distributed amongst them and in case they do not forthwith pay the same, to leavy it upon there goods and chattels by distresse and saile sending what remains and hereof yow are not to faile. To the Parish offrs of Kirbymoorside." Vol. v. p. 125.

not repair the chancel, while the vicar probably brought the law to bear on negligent churchwardens[1].

PARISH INCOME

The yearly accounts which the churchwardens were obliged to render of their receipts and expenditure show that the incidental expenses of the parish were lumped together with the statutory assessments for poor prisoners, house of correction, lame soldiers, and hospitals.

The income was mainly derived from rents of houses and lands bequeathed to the church, fees from lairstalls[2], and rents, or payments upon entry, for pews[3].

There were also various local methods of raising money: church ales were very popular in the south of England, and it may be that "the Feast" still held in the country villages is a reminiscence of them in the north.

In the parish of Pittington, in Durham, a flock of sheep was kept by the farmers in the proportion of one sheep for every £4 of rental[4]; and for forty years the parish flock paid all the parish expenses, a cessment being made only for exceptional expenditure.

If the income derived from trust property, fees and offerings was not sufficient to meet the expenses, then an assessment was ordered at the vestry meeting, sometimes by the select vestry alone, sometimes together with other parishioners[5].

[1] *N.R.Q.S.R.* vol. v. p. 212. Thirsk, April, 1656. In 1656 the churchwardens of Hovingham are presented for not repairing the church leads, walls and bell strings.

[2] Lairstalls were graves made within the Church. The usual charge was 3s. 4d. for an adult and 1s. 8d. for a child.

[3] Generally 4d. See Vestry Book of St Oswald, Durham, *S.S.P.* vol. LXXXIV. p. 168.

[4] Vestry Book of Pittington, *S.S.P.* vol. LXXXIV. p. 15. "Item yt is also agreed and set downe by the aforesaid xij men that everie iiij pounde rente within this parrishe as well as of hamlets as tounshipps shall gras winter and somer one shepe, for the behoufe of this churche."

[5] Vestry Book, Houghton-le-Spring, *S.S.P.* vol. LXXXIV. p. 286, 1606. "It is agreed by the gent. and xxiiii that a sesment of a grote of the pound shalbe collect and gathered by the Cunstables of everie towne and hamlet next adjoyninge unto them for the repairing of the Church, and to be

This was the church rate, the oldest form of local taxation in England; it was imposed by ancient custom and had no statutory authority[1]. Like other assessments it was levied on real property; every man who farmed land, whether rented or owned by him, was a parishioner[2] and had to pay a rate in proportion to the amount of land he held. Hence, since every house possessed a minimum of four acres of land, the rate was paid by all householders in the seventeenth century. Every man had to attend the church to which he paid his dues, but when a parish contained two churches, then dues were paid for the one situated in the township in which his land lay, and he was at liberty to attend either church[3].

After religious difficulties troubled the land it was the office of the churchwardens to see that every parishioner went to church on Sundays. If any person was absent without sufficient excuse, then (under the warrant of a justice) the fine of 12d. was levied according to law[4] for the use of

brought in before Lammas next to the hands of the churchwardens upon there perrells (perils) the day and yere above written."

[1] Except during the Commonwealth by an ordinance of the Long Parliament of 9 Feb. 1647. Scobell's *Acts and Ordinances*, 1658, Pt 1, p. 139, quoted by Toulmin Smith, p. 583.

[2] Cannan, *History of Local Rates in England*, quoting Coke, *Reports*, pt. v. pp. 67–8.

[3] *N.R.Q.S.R.* vol. III. p. 245. Malton, Oct. 1625. "A warrant etc. to attach Edw. Coley of Brompton and John Agar of Stockton gent. for refusing to paie all their arrearages imposed on them for repaire of the Chappell for the poore L.S. and Hosps. and other servies of his Matie. and to appear, etc."

Sleights is a farm in the township of Amonderby in the parish of Appleton-le-Street. In Jan. 1626 the matter was arranged at Helmsley Sessions as follows: "Edw. Caley of Brompton and John Agar of Stockton, gentn. to paie their rates and cessmts for the lands they hold in Sleights and West Inges, and all parochial duties to Amonderby Church and all arrears as the same have been anciently and accustomably paid: and to be discharged from paying any such duties to Appleton-le-Street Church, but notwithstanding to be at liberty to repaire to either of the said Churches, as they thinke fitt." *N.R.Q.S.R.* vol. III. p. 254.

[4] Houghton-le-Spring Vestry Book, *S.S.P.* vol. LXXXIV. p. 295. 1624. "In charges for going with our warrant about the parish for 12d. a Sunday being absent iis. iid.; for going to Durham with recusans iiiid."

N.R.Q.S.R. vol. II. p. 172. Helmsley, July, 1618. "A Thirske tanner for an assault on Tho. Watson and Tho. Williamson, Churchwardens of the said parish, being about to levie diverse summes of monie fo severall persons, being negligent commers to Church, by warrant of his Maties Justices of Peace."

the poor. In the first half of the century the chief offenders in this respect were Roman Catholics. These defaulters, if they continued to absent themselves from the services, were presented at the visitational court by the churchwarden, or a list of their names signed by him[1] was given to the constable to be presented at the Quarter Sessions. The statutes[2] were rigorously enforced by the justices in the North Riding. Long lists of recusants were given in to the court from time to time, and constables[3], ministers, and churchwardens[4] were fined when they did not make their returns. In the early part of the century the penalty of £20 on a master and £10 on his servant for every month's absence from church was exacted[5]. People who did not bring their children to be christened within a month of birth[6] were severely punished; in some cases recusants were confined within a radius of five miles from their homes[7]. When a recusant conformed he

---

[1] *N.R.Q.S.R.* vol. III. p. 234. Helmsley, J. 1625. "Tho. Trattle of Appleton le Street for refusing to deliver a warrant from the Justices for the maintenance of a poor widow woman and her children directed to him, being then one of the Churchwardens of that parish, and also refusing to sett his hand to the bill for the Recusants thereof."

[2] Laws relating to Recusants: 1 Elizabeth, cap. ii; 23 Eliz. cap. i; 29 Eliz. cap. vi; 35 Eliz. cap. ii; 3 and 4 Jac. I. cap. iv and v.

[3] *N.R.Q.S.R.* vol. II. p. 100. Richmond, July, 1615. Twenty-six constables fined 20s. each because "being summoned to appear etc. and make presentments of such Popish Recusants and all housekeepers as remaine with in, etc." they made default. Two ministers (of Hipswell and Hutton Longvillers) fined 20s. each because they did not make presentment of their Recusants.

[4] *Ibid.* vol. III. p. 334. Malton, July, 1632. "The Churchwardens of Brotton-cum-Kilton to appear at next Sessns. and bring in a Bill of Recusants within their parish, or otherwise a warrant, etc., those of Easington, Great and Little Aiton, Thornaby, Carlton and Biland the like. The like as to all the Churchwardens of Hovingham parish."

[5] *Ibid.* vol. I. p. 95. Richmond, Oct. 8, 1607. "Rich. Mennell of Dalton Gent.... also for having kept Anne Dunn, a Recusant, in his service by the space of eight monethes contrary etc. fyned upon the orig: presentr. for the said 8 moneths LXXX£, etc."

"Chr. Smith of Ravensworth for keeping Geo. Syre, a Recusant, at dyet in his house by the space of XII moneths: fined ut supra cxx li."

[6] *Ibid.* vol. III. p. 246. Richmond, 1625. "Will Greene of Lanmouth gentn. Recusant, for not having a male child of his duly baptized within a month of its birth at his parish church of Leake, or in any other church (Penalty £100)."

[7] *Ibid.* vol. I. p. 128. Richmond, 1608. "Brian Smithson thelder and Brian Smythson the younger of Cowton Graunge, being obstinate Recusantes and by the law confyned within 5 miles of their said dwellinges,

must produce in court a certificate, signed by the minister and the churchwardens, that he had attended his parish church and received the sacrament according to the rites of the Church of England. In 1616, at the Helmsley Sessions[1],

It was CERTIFIED by Patrick Robinson, Minister of Seamer in Pickeringlieth, and by Will. Dixon, John Candler, Tho. Harnett and John Milles, Churchwardens of the same, that Alice wife of John Ripley of East Aiton, Popish Recusant, convicted, conformed and went to her parish church (that of Seamer) in time of Divine Service and there received the Sacrament, etc.

Perhaps, with the ascendency of Cromwell and his Independents, the feeling against "obstinate convicted Popish Recusants," gradually died down. After the Restoration the Quakers and Nonconformists were added to the list of people who had to pay a fine for not repairing to their parish church[2], but the first hint of toleration appears when in 1660 the fine of 1s. only is levied for negligence, not obstinacy[3]. In 1684, the fact that "desenters and absentees" are informed that there will be no process against them if

and on the sworne information of James Hawkesworth, Vicar of Middleton Tyas, it appears that the said Smythsons have insolently behaved themselves, and that thelder Bryan hath travelled long journeyes from the place where he was so confyned...a Warrant be made to apprehend and bring both the said Smithsons before etc., and be bound etc., to appeare at the next Quarter Sessions to be holden within Richmondshire to take the oath of Supremacy and in the meantyme...."

[1] *N.R.Q.S.R.* vol. II. p. 153. Helmsley, Oct. 1616.

[2] *Ibid.* vol. VI. p. 79. Helmsley, July, 1664. "John Dickeson of Burniston,—neglecting to go to the parish church or any place of Common prayer upon Sundays and festivals bet. 1st May and 1st June." Side note to Minute:

QUAKERS.

23 men whose names are given "for assembly at the house of John Dickenson under pretext of religious worship contrary to the statute, etc."

[3] *Ibid.* vol. VI. p. 31. Helmsley, Jan. 1660. "The Court being informed upon oath that Henry Pownall of Hawnby Gent. and Johanna his wife were not at their parish church nor any other church upon the several Sundays hereafter following, to witt Nov. 11th, 18th, and 25th; Dec. 2nd, 9th, 16th, 23rd, 30th, doth order that the Churchwardens of Hawnby levy of the goods and chattels of the said Henry Pownall 16s. for his and his now wife's neglect of coming to the Parish Church." Henry Pownall was fined again in 1661.

they pay their fine[1], shows probably that the toleration which the Whigs desire for Nonconformists will inevitably have a favourable effect on the position of Roman Catholics.

The churchwardens, as representatives of the parish, were expected by both church and state to exercise supervision over the conduct of the parishioners, even sometimes over the parson himself[2].

Twice a year the archdeacon held his court in some central church, the summoner having given notice previously of the time and place of the visitation to all the churchwardens and sidesmen of the parishes in the archdeaconry[3]. These were expected to attend the court and present all offences against the Canons, the Queen's Injunctions or the Bishop's Monitions, the Act of Uniformity, and the statutes against recusants, and any other cases which came within the cognisance of the Church's jurisdiction. The most serious offence was immorality, of which a person was liable to be accused on the mere suspicion of his neighbours[4]. People who stayed away from church without a sufficient excuse, or who talked and otherwise misbehaved themselves during the service, schoolmasters who taught without a licence, parishioners who refused to pay the Church Rate, were summoned before the ecclesiastical courts. One Rouland

[1] *N.R.Q.S.R.* vol. VII. pp. 69-70. Stoxley, July, 1684. "Ordered by the Court and agreed on by the Jury that desenters and absentees from the Church presented by the Petty Constables be only indicted for absenting from the church for three Sundays last past; Ordered that process of re. fa. be made and issued out against all desenters and others that are indicted or presented at these Sessions, and the usual and legal process against all other persons heretofore indicted or informed against, and that the respective Baliffes of each weapentake and their Deputies do make particular returns in writing of what they shall severally do in pursuance of such process; Ordered that if any person presented at these Sessions for excusancy shall within a month before the next Quarter Sessions or at any time betwixt now and then pay 3s. due upon the said presentment, or bring a certificate of writing under the hands of the Parish Offrs. of the respective places where they live that they have paid the same to the use of the poor there, and pay all due fees to the Clerk of the Peace, that then no further process shall be issued out against them."

[2] T. Smith in *The Parish*, p. 94, quotes from the articles of Montagu, Bishop of Norwich in 1638, questions issued to the churchwardens regarding the deportment, behaviour and dress of their minister or curate.

[3] Ware, *The Elizabethan Parish*.   [4] See below, pp. 34, 35.

Bell was cited because "He will not suffer his doge to be whipped out of churche in tyme of devine service but kepithe him uppe in his armes and gevithe frowarde words." Rouand Bell appeared, gave froward words to the court, and was therefore ordered to pay 2s. to the poor[1].

At St Oswald's, Durham, the vicar, churchwardens and vestry drew up certain rules regarding seats, with penalties for default, and had them confirmed by the bishop, so that if any were broken the offending parties could be presented at the visitational courts[2]. Some of the regulations are very quaint, showing the good order in which the youth of the parish were kept. No young man, journeyman, or apprentice was to presume to sit in the choir unless he could read and help to say the service; in that case he was to have a convenient place assigned to him by the churchwardens. Nor were the journeymen to sit upon the sides of the women's stalls. No young women or maid servants were to presume to sit in any wives' stalls above the cross alley. The fine was 2d. for every default. A self-denying ordinance was also made, by which a vestryman was to forfeit 12d. to the poor if he absented himself from any meeting for the good of the church, "warninge beinge gevine in the churche and he beinge in the towne and havinge no lawfull lett."

While the incumbent was expected to present the negligent churchwarden, he himself was liable to be presented by that same warden if he gave occasion for blame.

A curious series of complaints was made in 1587 against the priest of Barnard Castle, Thomas Clark[3]. The churchwardens were a husbandman, Thomas Vinte, and a labouring man, Richard Sanderson, neither of whom could write, for they attest their signature to their depositions by their mark. They accused the priest of not signing the children upon the forehead with the cross, of two suspicious marriages

---

[1] 1579, 16 May, Branspethe, *S.S.P.* vol. XXII. p. 122.
[2] Vestry Book, St Oswald, Durham, *S.S.P.* vol. LXXXIV, pp. 213-5.
[3] *S.S.P.* vol. XXII. pp. 139-141.

of refusing at the last Rogation Days to walk the perambulation of the parish according to the Queen's Injunctions, of refusing to christen a child on a working day unless its father swore that the child was going to die, "though he had christened wealthy men's children," of refusing to administer the communion to a sick man although he had obtained the required number of people to receive with him, and of not being at home to bury two corpses. Then the churchwardens related that they met the bailiff, Thomas Rowlandson, together with three other parishioners, and as all the company were of the "twenty-four" of the parish, they thought it good to shut the church doors and not allow the curate to say the service until some improvement took place in his conduct. Whereupon two Justices of the Peace, Sir George Bowes and Mr Middleton, put the three churchwardens into the Tollbooth and finally the matter came up at the visitation.

The democratic character of the vestrymen is remarkable, as is also the supervision exercised by the churchwardens over their vicar.

On the other hand, if, at the half-yearly inspection of the archdeacon, the requisite number of books was not provided, or the necessary repairs not made[1], if offences of the parishioners were not duly presented[2], or the orders of the Bishop carefully performed[3], then the churchwardens were sum-

---

[1] *S.S.P.* vol. XXII. p. 118. Visitational Courts of the Diocese of Durham, 1578–1587. "1579 28 March Seham. The office of the Judge against Henry Liddel and George Parkins, Churchwardens. They do not demaund the fyne of 12*d.* upon those that doothe absent themselves from devine service. They have not a decent pulpitt. Ther Churche's dore ys broken, so that swyne or other beasts maye come into the Churche; they want the appologie. Suspended."

p. 123. The Churchwardens of Hantwesell are admonished because "their Churchyerd unfensed a pece of a wyndow not repaired, Church unwhited."

[2] *Ibid.* vol. XXII. p. 117, 1578–9, "13 March. Long Newtone, The office of the Judge against William Newham, Churchwarden. He refused to sett his hand to the presentment of faltes with his fellowe Churchwardone."

[3] Vestry Book, St Oswald, Durham, *S.S.P.* p. 184, 1630–1631. "To Thomas Atkinson for drawing a note or roll in parchment for two years burialls, christenings and weddings according to the canon, we being com-

moned in their turn and were liable to be suspended or
excommunicated; nor did they receive absolution until
they produced evidence that the matter about which they
were cited had been rectified. The penalty imposed by the
visitational courts was usually the greater or lesser excommunication. The church had no power to fine or imprison,
but heavy court fees were exacted before an excommunicated
person received absolution. If, however, an offender remained obstinate he was summoned before the Court of
High Commission.

In the seventeenth century also the dignitaries of the
church were generally made Justices of the Peace[1], and
their advice was frequently asked by the Sovereign when
commissioning new Justices[2], thus the influence of the
bishops among the magistrates was considerable, and doubtless therefore the church used the civil arm if need arose,
to enforce its decrees.

The procedure of the ecclesiastical courts was informal.
There was no jury and the old method of compurgation was
still in use. If the accused person could find four or five
men to say on oath that they believed him, he was acquitted;
but men seldom knew when they had been charged, and
even if the suspected person were proved innocent, he had
to pay the cost of the court fees[3]. Such a system produced
spies and no one was free from the libellous statements of
malicious people, who seem to have gone scatheless, even
when their indictments were refuted. It is not difficult to
appreciate the unpopularity of the church courts in the
seventeenth century. The case of John Johnson of Shincliffe
gives an example worth relating. Johnson was presented by

manded by the Bishopp and his officers to exhibite the same into the
Consistory Court, 2s. 4d."
    [1] Vestry Book, Houghton-le-Spring, S.S.P. vol. LXXXIV, p. 278. "For
going to Durham about her Maties business when we were commanded by
Mr Deane and the Justices xijd." The Dean seems to have been Chairman
of the Court of Quarter Sessions.
    Also, Ware, The Elizabethan Parish, quotes Bancroft's letter 1605,
"We that are Bishops being all of us as is supposed J.Ps."
    [2] Ware, The Elizabethan Parish, quoting Mary Bateson, Camden Mis-
cellany, IX. 1895.   [3] S.S.P. vol. LXXXIV. p. 362.

the Churchwardens on suspicion of incontinency with another man's wife. He was cited, and threatened with excommunication if he did not appear; at length he presented himself and denied the charge. The apparitor promoted the office of the judge against him. His accusers were required to adduce proof, and they produced nine inhabitants of Shincliffe who swore to the general belief in his guilt. Johnson being called upon to reply again denied the charge on his oath *ex officio*. He was then required to produce four honest neighbours as his oath helpers, *i.e.* to swear that they believed him to have sworn truly. He did so and was acquitted. The suit was nine times before the Court and was protracted from June 1600 to May 1601. Johnson was compelled under pain of excommunication to pay the whole cost of the suit amounting to £1. 3s. 4d. in spite of the fact that he had been unjustly accused.

The fees of the ecclesiastical courts and the expenses incurred in attending them swallowed up a considerable share of the parish income. Fees were paid when the churchwardens were sworn[1]; regularly, every half year when they attended the visitation[2]; generally, also, whenever they were summoned to appear at the monthly court of the archdeacon[3].

[1] *S.S.P.* vol. LXXXIV. p. 217. Vestry Book of the Parish of St Nicholas, Durham. "Disbursements 1665. 19th May '65 paid for swearing the Churchwardens and Sidemen att the Bishop's Visetation, 5s. 6d."

[2] Vestry Book of the Parish of Pittington, *S.S.P.* vol. LXXXIV. p. 48. 1600. "Item given to the sumner the first day of October, when we wer before Mr Huton xvjd. Item given for our expences the same day xijd."
    "Item given to the sumner the xxj of Aprill, when we wer before Mr Huton, and for our expenses the same day xviijd."

[3] The Vestry Book of the Parish of Pittington, *S.S.P.* vol. LXXXIV. pp. 54, 55. 1605. "Item given to the sumner the vij of June when we wer before Mr Huton xvjd. And for writinge our presentment, 4d. Item for our charges the same day viijd."
    "Item given to Thomas Kinge the xxvj day of July when we wer before Mr Huton iiijd. And for our expences the same day with our syde men xxijd."
    "Item given to the sumner the xvij day of October, when we wer before Mr Huton xvjd. And for our dinners the same day xijd."
    "Item given to the sumner the xxix of Aprill when we wer before Mr Huton with our syde men, xvjd. And for our expences the same day, xvjd."

For this reason possibly, when difficulties arose regarding the church rate in which the whole parish was concerned, the churchwardens had recourse to the court of Quarter Sessions, which was less expensive and had a much stronger executive power.

After the abolition of the ecclesiastical courts that portion of the churchwarden's work which had hitherto been supervised by the archdeacon was placed under the jurisdiction of the Justices of the Peace by an ordinance of Parliament in 1647. Henceforth the churchwardens were to be chosen in Easter week and within a month were to be allowed under the hands and seals of two Justices of the Peace. They were authorised with the consent of two Justices of the Peace to raise assessments, and for the only time in English history the Church Rate was levied by Parliamentary decree.

In the Middle Ages, just as the constable was the executive officer of the township, the civil unit, so the churchwardens were the administrative and judicial officers of the ecclesiastical unit, the parish. This is shown by their election in the vestry and their oath in the parish church. Moreover, being elected by the parishioners the churchwardens stood out in a special measure as the representatives of the parish; therefore, when the Tudor legislators determined to make each parish responsible to the state for conformity in religion and for the good order of its inhabitants and the relief of its poor, they found in the chief parochial officers suitable persons for carrying out this work.

Thus it came about that the churchwardens were associated with the constable in the administration of the social statutes connected with ale-houses, vagrancy, profane swearing, the keeping of the Sabbath day, and with the surveyor in the repair of highways and bridges, while they were *ex officio* overseers of the poor.

The churchwarden's manifold duties in connection with the statutes for the relief of the poor will be considered in connection with the functions of the overseer, and his association with the surveyor will be noticed in the account of the highways and bridges. It only remains now to consider his general relations with the parish.

Where a parish consisted of several townships the churchwardens, like the overseers, were frequently elected so as to represent each township, but the jurisdiction of a churchwarden extended over the whole parish, being in this respect unlike that of the constable, whose authority was bounded by the limit of his township.

The churchwarden was associated with the petty constable in the enforcement of the numerous statutes by which the early Stuart Parliaments endeavoured to repress drunkenness.

The fines for offences against these statutes were to be devoted to the use of the poor, and if not paid within six days the parish officers could obtain a warrant from a justice to levy the sum by distress and sale of the offender's goods. In 1664 the Bench at Thirsk ordered the constables and churchwardens of New Malton

to levy 20s. of the goods of John Story for the use and behoof of the poor, for keeping an alehouse without license, and if he have not sufficient goods whereby the said sum may be levied, or shall not pay the same within six days then the said Constables are to whip him openly for the said offence[1].

Anyone convicted of drunkenness had to pay a fine of 5s. within a week to the churchwarden, while the ale-house keeper paid a heavy penalty if he allowed a man to sit drinking in his house, if he sold his ale without a licence, or demanded more than the fixed rate for it[2]. One full alequart of the best beer or ale cost 1d., while two full alequarts of small beer could be bought for the same sum, but 1d. represented half the wages of an unskilled workman for a day, so the price was more than is paid at the present

---

[1] N.R.Q.S.R. vol. VI. p. 78. Thirsk, 1664.
[2] 21 Jac. I, cap. vii and xxviii; I Car. I, cap. iv. The fine for every offence was 20s. Alehouse-keepers were frequently presented in N. Riding, e.g. N.R.Q.S.R. vol. III. p. 358. Richmond, July, 1633.

time. The fine for every offence against the statutes was 20s. yet innkeepers were frequently summoned. In July, 1633,

A Swinton Alehouse-keeper is to be suppressed from brewing for three years and to pay a fine of twenty shillings to the Churchwardens for the use of the poor, for selling ale at more than 4d. a gallon.

If the constable and churchwardens neglected to carry out their part of the statutes relating to ale-houses, they forfeited forty shillings for every default; this also went for the use of the poor. Any other indifferent person in the parish could accuse these officers of neglect and by a warrant from a justice could levy the distress; if the fine was not paid within six days, or if there was not sufficient distress then the unfortunate parish officers were to be committed to the common gaol. So runs the Act. Doubtless it was seldom carried out in all its severity.

As an offshoot from their duties respecting the relief of the poor, the churchwardens had to collect those moneys mentioned above, authorised by statute, and assessed on each parish by the Justices in Quarter Sessions.

These were:

1. For the relief of the poor prisoners in the county gaol[1].

2. For the relief of the poor prisoners in the King's Bench and Marshalsea, and for the county hospitals and almshouses[2].

3. For the relief of maimed soldiers[3].

Other duties devolving on the churchwardens, as the representatives of the parish, were the repair of the schoolhouse[4], the supervision of hawkers and pedlars, who were

---

[1] 14 Eliz. cap. v, sec. xxxviii.
[2] 39 and 40 Eliz. cap. iii, sec. xiii.   [3] 43 Eliz. cap. iii.
[4] *N.R.Q.S.R.* vol. v. pp. 81–82. Richmond, 1651. "Three gentn of Northallerton to examine the receipts and disbursements of the late Churchwardens and if any moneys appeare to be in their hands due to the town, they are to pay john Rymer for repair of a schoolhouse and other worke he did by appointment and if there be not enough for his satisfaction, then the present Churchwardens to pay him out of the rate they have made or shall make."

not allowed to trade without a licence, the extinction of vermin, the arrangement for the burial of unknown corpses[1], the care of the armour, provision of muskets, powder and match, and equipment and payment of the soldiers who served for the parish in the trained bands[2].

The churchwardens and six other parishioners could tax anyone who possessed land or tithes in the parish, in order to raise money when necessary for the extinction of vermin[3]. The Act was designed to preserve corn and the thatch of houses, barns and ricks; rewards, however, were given not only for the eggs and heads of crows, choughs, rooks and other birds, but also for the heads of badgers and foxes[4]. Usually no special tax was raised, the foxes' heads, together with other expenditure directly concerning the parish, being included in the churchwardens' accounts.

Curious items appear in those accounts. At one time the churchwardens give 10s. "to a preacher which maid us a sermon wanting a place he desyring our benevolence[5]." A sermon was a not too common luxury in the seventeenth century, since only those clergymen who were licensed by

[1] Toulmin Smith, *The Parish*, p. 154.
[2] Vestry Book, Houghton-le-Spring, *S.S.P.* vol. LXXXIV. p. 293. 1618. "Item it is agreed by the gentlemen and the twenty-foure that the sesment of xij*d.* of the pound shalbe leved through the parishe for the byeinge of comon musk and the use of the church betwixt now and the fourth day of Aprell next 1619, and payed over to the churchwardens." p. 295. A.D. 1624. "For powder and match to the souldiers, vis.; for dressing of the common armor, 1s. July 4th. For mending the capp of the armor of East. Renton viii*d.*; for dressing the armor of West Herrington ...for mending the muskat of John Welsh vi*d.*; for a scourde and a worm to the muskat of Robt. Guy vii*d.*; for a pyke to West Herrington iiis. viii*d.* Given to the souldiers in number 15 xs. (twice); for fyve pykes to the souldgers vis. ix*d.*; for dressing a swhord and new scabart 1s. vi*d.*"
[3] 8 Eliz. cap. xv.
[4] Vestry Book of the Parish of Pittington, *S.S.P.* vol. XLVIII. p. 60. 1609. "Item given for tow foxes' heads iis."
Ibid. p. 91. April 20th, 1628. "It was agreed uppon by the gentlemen and twelve of this parish, that whosoever shall take any fox, or pate, or badger, in this parish, and bringe the heade to the church, shall have twelve pence paid by the Churchwardens."
Vestry Book, Houghton-le-Spring, p. 287. 1606. "To the fox-catcher for two fox heades 11s." p. 294. A.D. 1623. "For two graisheads (*i.e.* badgers' heads) to John Robinson 8*d.*"
[5] *Ibid.* 1624, *S.S.P.* vol. LXXXIV. p. 295.

the bishop were allowed to preach to their flocks. In some parishes there was a preaching fund under the control of the churchwardens[1], to pay for a licensed preacher. Donations also were given by the parish officers to distressed travellers and people who had lost their money through fire or misfortune. Foreign clergy occasionally visited England, seemingly to beg for funds; in 1611 Pittington gave 3s. 7d. "to the bishope of Gerese[2]." No small amount of the parish revenue went to provide drink for the ringers or for the plumber, the mason, or the carpenter[3], and even for the officers themselves when superintending repairs.

The churchwardens, as was only just, were allowed the cost of their dinners and other expenses when they attended the Assizes[4], the Quarter Sessions[5], the Visitation, or the Court of High Commission[6].

[1] Vestry Book, St Nicholas, Durham, vol. VI. p. 259. A.D. April, 1696. "Memd. Whereas one bond of ten pounds dated the one and thirtieth day of January (89) and another bond of twenty pounds dated the third of February (89) being the gift and moneys of Mrs Mary Fenwick late diceased of St Nicholas in the city of Durham towards the fund for a preaching minister for the said parish, the said two bonds are now delivered up into the hand of John Gordon Esqre now present, Major, and John Hall Alderman and Trustee for the said moneys by Mrs Margaret Trotter, relicte of Mr Ralph Trotter, the then churchwarden. Test. Joseph Dun, Ralph Gelson, Willm. Midleton."

[2] Vestry Book of Pittington, S.S.P. vol. LXXXIV. p. 63.

[3] Ibid. p. 25. "Item given to Thomas Bird's wife for bread and drinke which the ringers toke on the coronation day vjd." p. 27. "Item given for drinke to the ringers the xix of November vjd." Ibid. p. 208. St Oswald's, Durham. 1688–9. "For the ringers for ringing the young prince 3s. 6d.; at Ral. Robinson's drunk for joy of the young prince 7s. 6d.; to the ringers for joy etc. 8s.; to the ringers in drink for the young prince 1s."; p. 36 Pittington: "Item payed for drink to the wrights and masons vijd." p. 330; Houghton-le-Spring, "In drink when the great bell was cast 5s. 6d." p. 341 "To the wrights in drink when they began the Vestery and helping up with the tymber 4s."

[4] Vestry Book, Houghton-le-Spring, S.S.P. vol. LXXXIV. p. 295. A.D. 1624. "For charges 3 dayes waiting for giving in our presentment at the Syezes, is."
Vestry Book of the Parish of Pittington, S.S.P. vol. XLVIII. p. 82. "Item for my dinner when I gave in the presentment att the Assizes, vid."

[5] Ibid. vol. LXXXIV. p. 63. 1611. "Item payed for our dinners at Michelmas at the Quarter Sessiones iijs. vjd."
Ibid. vol. LXXXIV. p. 55. 1605. "Item given for our dinners the seventh of November when we wer before the Justices conceninge the recusantes, xijd."

[6] Ibid. vol. LXXXIV. p. 55. 1605. "Item given for our expences the xvj day of Januarie when we wer before the great Comission concernynge the recusants, vjd."

Finally, there was included in the parish expenses the charge for those convivial meetings without which Englishmen do not conduct public affairs, and which have their use in promoting good-fellowship. The Pittington churchwardens began and ended their year of office by eating a dinner in company with Mr Vicar, the cost of which is regularly entered in the parish accounts[1].

APPENDIX B

COST OF RE-CASTING THE GREAT BELL AT HOUGHTON-LE-SPRING

April 25, 1671. Order that the great bell be new cast and the bell frames repaired at the charge of the parish.

1676–7. Orders for assessment of 20s. in the pound, only for new casting of great bell and making new bell frames (May 28 and Aug. 27).

When we agreed with the bell founder about the bells, 5s.; in earnest 1£; going to Lumley Park about wood 1s.; three tun and halfe a foote of timber, 6£. 5s. 6d.; charges when we bought it 2s. 6d.; getting the wood over the water, 5s. 6d.; porters for helping to load it, 2s. 6d.; boards for the bell wheales, 18s. 8d.; to the bell-founder for casting the great bell, 40£; for writeing the bell-founder's bond, 2s. 6d.; our charges when we paid him his money, 4s. 6d.; for 13 foote and some more of timber for the steple 15s. 2d.; for 40 dales at 10d. a piece, 1£. 13s. 4d.; in drink when the great bell was cast, 5s. 6d.; when the great bell was taken downe our charges was, 2s. 6d.; for ashe wood for rowlers, 4s.; for soape for the rowlers, 6d.; for leather for the bells, 1s. 10d.; when all the bells was hung, 2s. 6d.; charges at the first rinning and exercizeing the two new bells, 3s.; for carrying a letter to Farr Weermouth, 6d.; to John Langshaw (plumber) for rinning the brasses for all the bells, 2£. 1s. Disb. 122£. 18s. 0½d. Rec. 116£. 11s. 1d.

Vestry Book of the Parish of Houghton-le-Spring, *Surtees Soc. Pub.* vol. LXXXIV.

[1] Vestry Book of the Parish of Pittington, *S.S.P.* vol. LXXXIV. p. 63. 1610. "Item for our dinners, the old Churchwardens and the newe, with Mr Vicar iijs."

CHAPTER III

THE ANGLICAN PRIEST AND THE CHURCH

In the seventeenth century the Anglican priest played a smaller part in the general life of the parish, through the growth of puritanism and the increasing influence of the Scottish presbyteries; in some cases the clergy were not men of much standing[1], nor did they behave in a manner fitted to entitle respect for their office. There are cases of extortion[2], drunkenness, and assault. Some of them kept alehouses, which, though possibly intended as an augmentation of income, was hardly a dignified calling for the parson[3]. In many cases it seems clear that their income was a mere pittance, since what had sufficed in the Middle Ages for a celibate was totally insufficient for a married priest with a wife and family to support, in times when the cost of living had increased.

The parson was associated with the churchwardens and constables in the execution of the statutes. He signed the certificate allowing a labourer to leave the parish; he was expected to be present when rogues were whipped, to register the punishment and to sign the testimonial with which the

---

[1] *N.R.Q.S.R.* vol. VI. p. 77. Thirsk, Ap. 1664. "Tho. Parker of Thormandby Clerk for neglecting to hang three gates, the same for uttering approbrious words; the same for assault; and again for being a common drunkard."

[2] *Ibid.* vol. VI. p. 140. New Malton, Jan. 1670. "A Lestingham Clerk for extortion of 23s. 6d. for proving a man's will."

Ibid. vol. II. p. 171. Helmsley, July, 1618. "Henry Jeffrey of Alne, Clerk, being Commissary of the Peculiar Jurisdiction of the late Treasury of the Cathedral Church of S. Peter at York for extortion in obtaining under colour of his office 4s. as his fee for writing of proof of the will of Mary Hall, widow lately deceased, all whose goods rights and credits at the time of her death were under the value of £5. etc."

[3] *Ibid.* vol. II. p. 16. Thirsk, Ap. 1613. "Rob Tose of Skelton, Curate there, for keeping an alehouse there contrarie, etc."

Ibid. vol. III. p. 359. Thirsk, Oct. 1633. 198 alehouse keepers suppressed, among them one is "clericus."

rogue was sent back to his native place[1]. He could license sick people to eat flesh on statutory fish days, and he was allowed to charge 4d. for registering this in the church books[2]. If the churchwardens failed to prosecute recusants for absenting themselves from church, the vicar did so[3]; he required a convicted recusant to make public confession and submission during the service. He also conducted the penance imposed on offenders either by Quarter Sessions or by the ecclesiastical courts[4].

The fierce strife which raged in London was reflected in the country parish. Little respect was shown to religion; the congregation was locked out of church[5], tumults arose during the service[6], the vicar was assaulted[7] and interrupted[8], sometimes even the preacher was expelled[9] from the sacred edifice.

[1] The fine for default was 5s.

[2] *The Exact Constable*, by E.W., Ed. 1682, pp. 115–119, gives the duties of Church-Ministers.

[3] *N.R.Q.S.R.* vol. IV. p. 74. Thirsk, April, 1637. "Complaint made by Mr Edw Thursby, Parson of the parish of Kilvington, that diverse of his parishioners have absented themselves from Church for three Sundays past—therefore a warrant etc., to the Constable of the said place to take all such delinquents before the nearest Justice etc."

[4] *Ibid.* vol. I. p. 44. "Geo Nelles of Danby for his slanderous speeches against the Justices (he said that he could not have right and that the Bench did him wrong, vol. I. p. 30) be fined xxs. and on Sunday next in his parish church openly in the time of Service after the Gospell make confession that he hath highlie offended, etc."

Ecclesiastical Proceedings of Bishop Barnes, *S.S.P.* vol. cxix. 1579, 11 May, Darnetone. "The office of the Judge against Brian Todie Robert Croften and Thomas Heughe 'They dyd not receyve at Easter the pennance in their parish church in their usual dress having etc., above the same'; to receive and to certify."

[5] *N.R.Q.S.R.* vol. v. p. 236. "North Allerton, Ap. 1657. A Cowsby man for locking the Church door and keeping out the minister and people."

[6] *Ibid.* vol. v. p. 116. Thirsk, Oct. 1652. "A draper of Easingwold for assault and affray upon a woman in the parish church upon the Lord's Day (pleads the Act of Oblivion)."

[7] *Ibid.* vol. VI. p. 248. Rich., Jan. 1676. "Two Northallerton labr for assault on the Rector of Birkby in the parish church in the time of divine service."

[8] *Ibid.* vol. VI. p. 7. New Malton, July, 1658. "A husbn for uttering malitious and seditious words to the great disturbance of the Minister of Coxwold and the whole congregation there."

Ibid. vol. v. p. 151. Northallerton, Jan. 1654. "A Crake spinster for maliciously and unlawfully interrupting the Minister of Craike when he was preaching the Word of God to the congregation (Comitt to the gaole for three moneths); a labr of the same place for the like (like sentence)."

[9] *Ibid.* vol. VI. p. 183. Thirsk, Ap. 1673. "Three Malton yeomen for

Curious scenes must have been witnessed in many of the villages during the Interregnum; vacancies which occurred in livings whose patrons were Royalists[1] were filled up by the Parliament; Anglican priests were displaced, and Puritans nominated to their cures. In some cases when the nominee of Parliament arrived, possession was withheld[2]; and doubtless much of the disorder which occurred during the middle years of the seventeenth century arose from dislike of the compulsory changes in religion. After the abolition of the church courts, clergy who offended in ecclesiastical matters against the ordinances of Parliament were presented at Quarter Sessions[3], and were required to find sureties for their good behaviour in future. The chief difference imposed by Parliament was the new requirement regarding marriage[4] of the appointment of a Parish Register,

forcible and riotous entry on the parish church on a Sunday and for expelling the preacher."

[1] *The Church under the Commonwealth*, by W. A. Shaw, vol. II. p. 188, quoting L.S. VII. 24. 14th Oct. 1644. "Forasmuch as the parsonage of Kirklington in the North Riding of Yorkshire is lately become void by the death of Mr Doggett, late minister and that the advowson doth belong to Sir Edward Osborne who hath been in arms against the Parliament as guardian to George Wandesford, his Majesty's ward, therefore the Lords and Commons nominate Wm. Clarkson to the living."

[2] *N.R.Q.S.R.* vol. VI. p. 227. Thirsk, Oct. 1656. "Leon Conyers of Lastingham Clerke for disturbing of Wm. Locke Clerke (entered traverse) vol. v. p. 253, on traverse declared by jury not guilty." Vol. v. p. 236. "N. Allerton, Ap. 1657. Leon Conyers of Lastingham for assault upon Phil. Peckett, Clerke (to be traversed). The same for the like (to be traversed); the same for withholding possession of the Vicarage house from Ph. Peckett Clerke (to be traversed) the same ag. for forfeiture of a recognisance (to be traversed)."

[3] *Ibid.* vol. v. p. 97. Malton, Jan. 1651. "A warrant against Edw. Manwaring of Sowerby clarke to be bound etc. to answer for marrying people privately and using the Comon prayer book; a warrant against 3 men to present evidence against Wm. Headlam for keeping Crucifixes and other...in his howse, not acquaintinge some Justice of Peace herewith." *Ibid.* vol. v. p. 179. Richmond, Jan. 1655. "A warrant for good behaviour of Ch. Beaverley Clerke of East Witton for marrying Rich. Hambleson and Eliz. Pratt contrary to law."

[4] *Ibid.* vol. v. p. 205. Kirbymoorside, Jan. 1656. "Upon a petition of Lawr. Jackson and Ellen Younge of Kirkeleadtham, whereby they set forth they have been published three times at the Markett Cross of Stoaxley, and that the Parish Register of Stoaxley certifies the same, and that they desire to proceed to marriage, Ordered that they may proceed to marriage accordingly."

who does not seem to have been a satisfactory official, since various Parish Registers were summoned before the court for betraying their trust[1] in the short time during which the position was held.

It was an age of little culture and there were few schools. Yorkshire, however, was better off in this respect than many counties[2], money having been bequeathed to various parishes for the maintenance of a school[3]. In some places it is probable that the parson in addition to his spiritual duties also taught the village school, as he was accustomed to do in the sixteenth century[4]. Schoolmasters still required a licence from the bishop of the diocese[5]. Fugitive priests frequently became the tutors of the children of Roman Catholics, and recusants who were forbidden by law to teach were often in trouble for continuing their profession[6].

---

[1] *N.R.Q.S.R.* vol. v. p. 162. Malton, July, 1654. "Mr Hugh Lenge, Clerke, Parish Register of Huttons Ambo having confessed in Court that he in Dec. last did marry 2 persons together contrary to law and thereby betrayed his trust, to be discharged of his said employment and the parishioners to elect and chuse a fit person to be their Parish Register and present the same to the next J.P. to take the oath etc."

[2] In 1546–7 there were schools at Topcliffe, Thirsk (G), Richmond (G), Rumbolde (G), Bedall (G), Well (G), Malton (G), Northallerton, Pickering (G); Leach, *English Schools at the Reformation*, pp. 284–9 (G = Grammar School). There is mention also in the Records of schools at Kirkby Hill, Topcliffe, Formanby, and Hutton Rudby.

[3] Leach, p. 286. "The Wapentake of Gyllingwest. 3. A Grammar Skole. Rumbolde. Memorandum: That there is in the sayde paryshe (Rumbolde) one gramer scole for the better brynging up and instructyng of the inhabatauntes children there dwellyng. The master of the sayde scole is Michell Horner, having yerely for his stipend or wages £3. 6. 8 paid out of a stocke which remayneth in the handes of the paryshoners of the same parishe £3. 6. 8."

[4] *Ibid.* "The Wapentake of Hangaest. 89 A Stipendare or Service. Bedall. Memorandum: That there is in the sayd paryshe (Bedall) one stipendarye preste called John Grege, doing dyvine service in the sayde churche and teching a grammar scole in the sayde town for the which there was certen landes and tenements geven to the yerely value of £7. 11s. 4d."

[5] *N.R.Q.S.R.* vol. vi. p. 147. Richmond, July, 1670. "Oliver Nicholson of Hutton Rudby scholemaster for presuming to teach boys without any license from the Bishop of the Diocese."

[6] *Ibid.* vol. v. p. 86. Thirsk, Oct. 1651. "2 women for that they are Roman Catholiques to find sureties not to teach any children till next Easter Sessn. and then to appear and not to depart the Court without license."

Vol. vi. p. 8. New Malton, July, 1658. "A warrant against Rob Roger-

The church was still the chief meeting place[1]: there the High Constables rendered accounts to the Justices of the Peace; the overseers received and lent out the parish stock to those needing it[2]; the fathers of bastard children paid the money for their weekly maintenance[3] to the mother. Chapels of ease were at times used as lodging houses[4], while in some places the village school was held in the church[5].

The fabric of the church required almost yearly expenditure. In the early seventeenth century some churches were still unflagged[6], the bare earth of the floor being covered with rushes or straw[7].

It was the desire of many people to bury their dead within the church. The consent of the churchwarden was

son of Farmanby to appear before the next J.P. to answer wherefore he continueth to teach a school there being a convict Recusant."

N.R Q.S.R.. vol. III. p. 250. Richmond, Oct. 1625. "Jas. Page Schoolmaster of East Witton presented as a Recusant."

Depositions from York Castle, No. xl. p. 47. John Thopson a Roman Catholic priest. "Hee is by profession a schoolmaster."

[1] *N.R.Q.S.R.* vol. I. p. 266. Northallerton, July, 1612. "That Tho Jackson one of the High Constables of Hang East, shall repair to the Church of Pattrick Brompton on Monday next, to render account to Sir Comers Darcy and Sir Arthur Dakins of all moneys received by him for bridges or other matters."

[2] Vestry Book of the Parish of Pittington, *S.S.P.* vol. XLVIII. p. 91. "Money given to the stocke of the poore of the parish of Pittington and delivered to the Overseers of the same parish and lent to the parties whose names are here underwritten, Aprill the 22nd, 1627. The money was paid in Pittington Chancell; the Overseers stand bound to the parish to pay it the next yeere."

[3] *N.R.Q.S.R.* vol. III. p. 238. Richmond, July, 1625. "The father of a bastard child to pay the mother thereof 4*d.* a week until the child be 7 years old, the payment to be made week by week in Catterick Church on the Sondaie, before noone."

[4] *Ibid.* vol. I. p. 137. "Geo Firbanck of Sutton for keeping of inmates in the Chappell at Sutton and in his house at the townes end."

[5] Ware, *The Elizabethan Parish.*

[6] Vestry Book of the Parish of Houghton-le-Spring, *S.S.P.* vol. LXXXIV. pp. 280–282. 1604. "Mem. That the xth of June, 1604, it was agreed and sett downe by the newe churchwardens and xxiiij of that parish that were then present that, whereas Mr Docter Hutton the parson there is contented in his devotion to beare the charge of the floringe of the church, that a cesse iij*d.* the pound shalbe levied for the winninge of flaggs for that purpose and for the bryngynge of bords for loftinge of the lower lofte of the belhouse so sone as may be."

[7] Vestry Book of the Parish of Pittington, *S.S.P.* vol. LXXXIV. p. 55. 1605. "Item given for twoe thrave of strawe for the stalls in the church vi*d.*"

always necessary for this, a fee being charged for the lairstall[1]. From the amount of money received from fees for lairstalls in some parish accounts it would appear that the church floor was being disturbed continually. So much was this the case at Houghton-le-Spring, that in 1657 an order was made that any harm done either to the pavement or seats of the church by making a grave was to be repaired within fourteen days, "and the rubbish remayning to be cleane carried forth of the Church[1]"; the sexton also was ordered to take up the pavement stones carefully without breaking them and to make every grave within the church 1½ yards deep at least[2].

The number of intramural burials must have been extremely unhealthy and undoubtedly produced a very disagreeable odour. To counteract this, juniper, benzoin, and frankincense were burnt in the church on festivals and great occasions, such as the Bishop's Visitation[3].

Fresh rushes were always laid down for Whitsunday[4] and the branches of birch which had been carried in the perambulation of the parish boundaries on the Rogation days previously were set up in the church[5].

Other items of expenditure were lime for whitening the walls according to the desire of the Puritans[6], lead for the roof, glass for the windows, cushions, stool, etc., for the

---

[1] Vestry Book of the Parish of Houghton-le-Spring, *S.S.P.* vol. LXXXIV. pp. 310, 311.

[2] *Ibid.* vol. LXXXIV. p. 311.

[3] Vestry Book, St Nicholas, Durham, *S.S.P.* vol. LXXXIV. p. 247. "Anno 1680; For frankincense, benjanin and juniper att the Bpp's preaching 2s. 6d. Item for birkes and to Robert Cogdon for putting them up 3s. 6d." Vestry Book of the Parish of Pittington, *S.S.P.* vol. LXXXIV. p. 28. A.D. 1589. "Item given to Bettres Dobson and her daughter for bringinge of twoe burthen of jenepers to the churche iijd."

[4] Vestry Book of the Parish of St Nicholas, Durham, 1670, *S.S.P.* vol. LXXXIV. p. 228. "For Birkes for the Church at Whitsontide, 1s. 8d." p. 238, 1676. "For birkes and rushes, being 4 of birch and 6 of rushes 4s. 6d. For the church and pewes clensing and the birkes putting up and the rushes stroweing therein, 2s. 6d."

[5] *S.S.P.* vol. LXXXIV. p. 228 note.

[6] Vestry Book, St Nicholas, Durham, *S.S.P.* vol. LXXXIV. p. 253. 1684-5. "For whitening the Church 3£. For plaistering and whitening the Vestrey 1s. For lime and the Porch whetening 10s. 8d. Item for drink 4s."

furnishing of the interior[1], and numberless articles, collars, cods, houpes, imps, bawdricks, gudgeons, etc., connected with the machinery of the bells.

For the bells played a loud and important part in the parish life of seventeenth-century England. They rang out on all occasions of rejoicing, on every anniversary[2], and to celebrate any important event[3]; they filled the place of the newspaper of the present day[4]; and they cost the parish a considerable sum of money every year in the wages of their ringers, and in payments for repairs[5]. While some remote country parishes in the north of England were dependent for the music of the service on the local band of violins far into the reign of Queen Victoria[6], others already in the seventeenth century were using an organ[7], which seems however in some parishes to have been frequently out of repair.

[1] Vestry Book, St Oswald, Durham, *S.S.P.* vol. LXXXIV. p. 186. 1631–2. "For two frames for two formes to stand at the Communion table for the churchwardens and others to knele at the Communion 6s. 8d. For kersey to cover them 5s. To Stephen Arundell for fringe and other necessaries, and for making them upp as appeares by his acquittane 10s."
Vestry Book, Houghton-le-Spring, *S.S.P.* vol. LXXXIV. p. 296. A.D. 1625. "For a rope for the great plume of the clock, 2s. 6d. for V quarters of fustian for boddoming the pulpit qushine 1s. 2d."

[2] Vestry Book, Houghton-le-Spring, *S.S.P.* vol. LXXXIV. p. 287. 1606. "To the ringers the V of Novermber ijs. vjd." "To the ringers upon the Kinge day vis." 1607. "For ringers of the belles of St James day xijd." "For ringing of the belles the fifte of Aug. ijs. vjd." (The day of the King's escape from the Cowrie conspiracy.) "Payed to the ringeres the fower and twenty of March, vis. iiiid."

[3] Vestry Book, St Oswald, Durham, *S.S.P.* vol. LXXXIV. p. 187. 1634–5. "To the ringers when the Bishop came first to Durham 1s. 8d." "To the ringers at the Bishopp's visitation 3s. 10d. Do. on the 5th of November 3s. 4d. Do. on the 27th of March 3s. 4d."
Vestry Book, St Oswald, *S.S.P.* vol. LXXXIV. p. 208. A.D. 1685. "To the bell-ringers for ringing the 6th day of July 1685, when Monmouth was taken 7s." "For ringing the 26th day of July 1685 being a day of Thanksgiving 7s." "To the bell-ringers upon the King's birthday 7s." "To the bell-ringers the 6th of February 7s." "To the bell-ringers on the King's Coronation Day 7s." "To the bell-ringers the 6th of October 1686, 7s."

[4] Vestry Book, Houghton-le-Spring, *S.S.P.* vol. LXXXIV. p. 342. "1688–9. To the ringers for ringing for the young Prince, 3s. 6d. at Ral. Robinsons' drunk for joy of the young Prince 7s. 6d.; to the ringers for joy etc. 8s.; to the ringers in drink for the young prince 1s....for coales to a bone fire rejoyceing for the young Prince 10d."

[5] See Appendix B for cost of the Great Bell at Houghton-le-Spring.

[6] *e.g.* at Fingall in Wensleydale.

[7] Vestry Book, Houghton-le-Spring, *S.S.P.* vol. LXXXIV. p. 296. "For

By the common law naves of churches were free to all parishioners, who had equal rights to accommodation therein, subject to the power of the churchwardens or of the vestry[1] to grant them their places. The tenure of a certain house or farm carried with it the right to a pew in the parish church, and the occupants of pews were expected to repair them[2]. The names of the seatholders were written inside the pews, and a man was not expected to sit elsewhere in the church[3]. In an age when attendance at church was compulsory, it was necessary that churchwardens should know exactly where each parishioner sat. When further seating was necessary those requiring it asked permission of the vestry to be allowed to provide[4] it. Though the vestry made arrangements in 1584 for the stalls of all the husbands in Pittington, it was not until 1625 that the women of the

a loft for the Clark to stand to play in the organs." Vestry Book, Houghton-le-Spring, *S.S.P.* vol. LXXXIV. p. 296. A.D. 1626. "For mending of the organes the 19th March 1£ to the organnes 27th March 5s."

[1] Pittington Vestry Book, *S.S.P.* vol. LXXXIV. pp. 13–15. The select vestry of Pittington made the following arrangement regarding pews in 1584. "Item it is agreed by us the aforesaid xij men for the better hearinge of divine servis that everie householder, as well gentlemen as also husband-men and cote men shall taike suche place as is appointed for them, hear-after followinge, payinge for the same, for so many roumes as everie man shall have iiij*d*. a roume att everie first entrye. In primis the aforesaid xij men have appointed for Ludworthe the first stall on the southe side of the quere door of twoe roumes. Item for the maner of Pittington the first stall on the north side of the quere door, of fower roumes, which said stall Maister Anderson haithe builded at his owne proper charges."

[2] *Ibid.* p. 14. "Item for Cunan Bras, Richarde Dobson, Thomas Dobson and Christofor Whitfelde, the third shorte stall on the south side of the quere doore." Added later: "(which stall was repaired by these 5, 1625)": ..."John Whitfeild, William Nicholson, Mich. Pattison, William Hall, one for Sr Hen. Anderson's cottage 1625."

[3] *Ibid.* p. 14. "Item for the rest of the cotigers in Shearborne, the last shorte stall on the south side of the quere doore: (This stall was repaired the same yeare, and those whose names are underwritten must sitt in it.)"

[4] Vestry Book, Houghton-le-Spring, 1658, *S.S.P.* vol. LXXXIV. p. 324. "And lastly, upon the request and desire of sundry of the parishioners that are farmers, tradesmen youemen and others that either want seates in the church or are inconveniently placed, Wee do give consent that they shall have liberty at their own proper costs and charges, to erect and build a gallery over the cross North angle twixt the East end of the first pillar and over the doore goes up to the steeple, provided the same be strongly made of oake wood, and handsomely wrought as other pew work in the Church, and noe nusance of hurt to any whose pewes shall happen to be underneath the said gallery."

T.   4

parish had seats in church allotted to them. Thus it is clear that long after the Reformation men and women still sat apart in church[1]. Many heart burnings arose regarding stalls; everyone wanted the first room[2], and disputes sometimes had to be settled in the ecclesiastical courts or (after their dissolution) in the Quarter Sessions of the Justices[3]. There is little to be found in the records of either parish or county regarding the work of the county parson: being probably the only man of learning in many villages he doubtless gave both advice and help to the unlettered parish officials in the various duties imposed on them by the central government.

[1] Vestry Book of Pittington, *S.S.P.* vol. LXXXIV. pp. 86–87. "An. Dom. 1625. Martii XXV. It is agreed uppon by the xij of the parish of Pittington the day and yeare above written that the women of the same parish shall have theire seats in the church in manner following.

"In primis John Swalwell's wife of Ludworth, Simon Lackenby of Shadforth, two roomes or seats; for two farmes in Pittington belonging to Sir Henry Anderson, two seats; William Hall's wife of Shadforth and Raiphe Huntley's wife of the same, have first stall appointed for them..."

[2] "Whereas some of the women were not content with any roomes in the stalls but the first, contending for the first places, to avoid suits in law and to restraine the pride of such, it was agreed uppon by the twelve of the parish of Pittington that everyone should take their place as they came, such as came first to the church should have the first place in the stall appointed for them."

[3] *N.R.Q.S.R.* New Malton, July, 1657. "The Churchwardens and Overseers together with the Minister of Whitby to examine the truth of the petition annexed and to make an agreement betwixt them of the pew in the church if possible, otherwise to certify the two next Justices what they conceive fit to be done therein that the public peace may be kept."

CHAPTER IV

THE OVERSEERS OF THE POOR

Be it enacted that the churchwardens of every parish and four substantial householders there, being subsidy men, or (for want of subsidy men) four other substantial householders of the said parish, who shall be nominated yearly in Easter week under the hand and seal of two or more justices of the peace in the same county, whereof one to be of the quorum, dwelling in or near the said parish shall be called overseers of the poor of the same parish[1].

Thus came into existence the statutory office of overseer of the poor.

Rarely, however, did English legislation create new offices: in this case, for instance, Parliament merely recognised and made permanent an office foreshadowed even so early as the reign of Edward III.

The overseer is the descendant of those collectors of parish alms, who are mentioned in the year books[2], and who were authorised by later statutes[3].

It has been noticed that the Tudor statesmen in considering the question of poor relief took as a basis the existing parochial organisation and made the churchwardens responsible for the execution of the Acts. They recognised, however, the onerous nature of the duties involved by this legislation; therefore in 1563, the first poor law of Queen Elizabeth enacts that "two able persons or more shall be appointed gatherers and collectors of the charitable alms of all the residue of the people inhabiting in the parish whereof they be chosen collectors for the relief of the poor[4]."

These collectors, "the Sunday next after their election, or

---

[1] 30 and 40 Eliz. cap. iii. section i.
[2] Toulmin Smith, *The Parish*, p. 178, ed. 1857, quotes 44 Ed. III, fo. 18 and 19.
[3] 27 Henry VIII, cap. xxv.; 5 and 6 Ed. VI, cap. ii.
[4] 5 Eliz. cap. iii. sec. ii.

the Sunday following, if need require, when the people are at the church at divine service, shall gently ask and demand of every man and woman that they of their charity will be contented to give weekly towards the relief of the poor[1]."

If any person refused his charitable alms, the parson and churchwardens were to exhort him gently, and if he refused to be so persuaded, "the Bishop of the Diocese or the Ordinary shall send for him, to induce him by charitable means to extend charity to the poor"; if he still remained obdurate then the bishop or the ordinary could bind him to appear before the Justices of the Peace, and if he would not be bound could commit him to prison[2].

The collectors were to distribute weekly the parish alms to poor and impotent people and to enter in a register kept for the purpose all sums of money received and distributed by them.

Possibly it had not been easy to procure men willing to undertake the collection and distribution of poor relief, for in 1572 the Justices of the Peace were ordered to see that collectors for one whole year were appointed, and to appoint in addition "overseers of the said poor people by their discretions, to continue also for one whole year; and if they do refuse to be overseers, then every of them so refusing to forfeit 10s. for every such default[3]."

The overseers were to justify their name; rogues and vagabonds, born within the county or settled there for three years, were "to be holden to work by the oversight of the said overseers[4]"; able-bodied aged people also were to be set to work, and if they refused were to be whipped or put in the stocks[5].

From the Queen's Injunctions[6] it is clear that the overseers were expected to help the churchwardens in their ecclesiastical duties. In every parish the ordinary was to

---

[1] 5 Eliz. cap. iii. sec. ii.   [2] *Ibid.* sec. vii.
[3] 14 Eliz. cap. v. sec. xvi.   [4] *Ibid.* sec. xxiii.
[5] *Ibid.* sec. xxii.   [6] Queen's Injunctions, xlvi.

appoint three or four discreet men who were diligently to see "that all the parishioners duly resort to their Church upon all Sundays and holy days there to continue the whole time of the godly service"; and "to admonish and denounce to the Ordinary all such as were found slack or negligent therein." That this injunction was obeyed is shown by the commission directed to Gateshead in 1572 by Bishop Barnes, authorised to appoint four parishioners of Gateshead as overseers, to swear them into their office openly in the parish church and to admonish them "to be diligent, and the parishioners to be obedient to them, not diminishing the authority of the Churchwardens, but adding theise (theirs) unto them in aid and assistance[1]."

In the Act of 1598 the office of collector was combined with that of overseer and a definite sphere of action was allotted to these parish officers, namely, the administration of the Act for the relief of the poor. The area of administration was the parish, the churchwardens were *ex-officio* overseers, and the remaining three or four substantial inhabitants who held the office were nominated at the vestry meeting. But the overseers no longer helped the churchwardens with their ecclesiastical duties; their office was henceforth purely civil, and after nomination at the vestry meeting they were appointed "under the hand and seal of two or more Justices of the Peace." In this way the parish—the new unit of civil government—was associated with the supreme local authority. Before the overseers put into force any important provision in the Act they had to obtain the assent of two Justices.

Before considering the working of the poor law in the parish government, it is necessary to take some account of the attitude of legislators towards the poor at the end of the sixteenth century. The statutes passed in the reigns of Henry VIII and Edward VI[2] had looked upon poverty

---

[1] Proceedings of Bishop Barnes, *S.S.P.* vol. xxii.
[2] 22 Henry VIII, cap. xii.; 3 and 4 Ed. VI, cap. xvi.

almost as a crime, and had enforced severe punishment of
"valiant beggars."

The Elizabethan statesmen endeavoured to repress voluntary paupers by re-enacting Henry VIII's and Edward VI's
laws, and taking measures for the punishment of rogues
and vagabonds; but they recognised also that poverty may
be involuntary, and they attempted to strike at its root by
providing work for vagrants and for destitute persons, and
by regulating trade and labour. Moreover, in the first poor
law of the reign, they made provision that the "impotent
feeble and lame which are the poor in very deed" should be
helped[1], thus recognising that the state was responsible for
the care of such people. Various experiments, beginning
with the attempt to enforce voluntary charity, were made
during Elizabeth's reign, and her Parliaments showed an
earnest desire to improve the social and economic conditions
of the lower classes. Finally, they combined the most
practical of these experiments with useful customs already
in operation in many parishes, and embodied them in the
great Poor Law of 1598. The administration of this law was
the particular function of the overseer of the poor.

The interpretation of the term "poor relief" was wide,
and the duties of the overseers were extensive. They may
be summarised as follows:

1. To give weekly relief, usually in money, to the poor,
lame, blind, old and impotent.

2. To keep a stock of raw material to provide work for
those who could not obtain it, and to set to work all people
who had no daily trade by which to earn their living.

3. To build houses on the common land for the destitute.

4. To take charge of and educate the children of the poor
and to bind them as apprentices.

5. To take charge of and administer money or lands left
for the use of the poor.

---

[1] 5 Eliz. cap. iii. sec. i.

It may be useful to examine the overseers' work and its supervision by the Justices from these five points of view.

I. POOR RELIEF

In the early part of the seventeenth century comparatively few orders for relief were made by the Court of Quarter Sessions, from which it may be inferred that the Act was efficiently administered, possibly also that the poor and destitute were not very numerous in the North Riding. The orders given for maintenance vary considerably in amount, presumably in accordance with the circumstances of the case. The Justices insisted that good provision should be made for the wives of men pressed to serve as soldiers: in 1608[1] the Bench ordered

that upon a petition and upon credible information of the poore estate of Elizabeth wieff of Arth. Valentyne, who was lately pressed for and from the towne of Topcliffe to serve as a souldier in Ireland ...her means of subsistance thus taken from her and herself great with child etc....inasmuch as her husband was pressed from Topcliff the said Elizabeth be relieved there, and have 12*d.* weekly from the assessment for the poor up to the time of her delivery and ability to travel to her husband[2]; and she shall have also allowed her for her better relieff in her childbed 5*s.* paid unto her by the Thres*r.* for the Hospitalls for this Division, and a warrant to be made to the Constable, Overseers and Churchwardens of Topcliff accordingly.

But it is only the wives of soldiers who receive the good round sum of 12*d.* a week; usually the amount varies from 4*d.* to 10*d.*[3] The overseers of Helmsley are to pay "a very poor infirm woman 4*d.* weekly," those of Rievaulx are to give the same sum "to a very poor aged and impotent man towards the maintenance of himself and family[4]," while "the Parish offrs. of Newbiggen are ordered to pay a poor woman with six small children 10*d.* weekly."

Some of the entries respecting relief give a pitiful descrip-

---

[1] *N.R.Q.S.R.* vol. I. p. 115. Thirsk, April 5, 1608.
[2] In July, 1609, the Bench gave her 13*s.* 4*d.* so that she might go to join her husband in Ireland. *Ibid.* vol. I. p. 160.
[3] *N.R.Q.S.R.* vol. VI. p. 158. Helmsley, July 11, 1671.
[4] *Ibid.* vol. VI. p. 258. Richmond, July, 1676. "The Overseers of Ravensworth to pay a poor impotent aged lame man 6*d.* weekly."

tion of the state of society: "a woman with seven children is to have 12*d*. weekly until her husband come out of gaol[1]." Two girls "forsaken by their father and mother, now in York gaol, and not able to maintain themselves by reason of their minority" are allowed 8*d*. weekly[2].

It was an age when many people were sent to prison not merely for criminal offences, but often for conscience sake, or perhaps for inability to pay a fine incurred through some negligence of office. Both the above cases seem so palpably necessitous that some reasons might be expected why the overseers refused to grant the relief and allowed the cases to be presented before the court. Possibly they desired to make some relative of the distressed parties provide for them, or it may be they disputed the liability to give the relief.

The records show that, as early as the seventeenth century, there is the fear of a tendency to throw on the rates the responsibility which should be borne by the family. A curiously careful order is made at the Helmsley Quarter Sessions in 1627 for "two children left orphans at Helmsley to be taken, the one of them by her grandfather on the mother's side, and the other by his grandmother on the father's side, and to be educated and maintained with meate and drink, clothinge and lodginge and all other thinges need-full for their education[3]." If such relatives refused, the overseers appealed to Quarter Sessions for authority to levy the sum by distress. Another instance occurs where a man from Crayke was ordered to pay 8*d*. weekly to his grand-children[4], and if he refused the parish officers were author-ised "to levy the same sum and the arrears thereof from time to time upon his goods and chattels." Bearing in mind that "goods" in the seventeenth century generally meant living creatures, it seems that the parish officers were

---

[1] *N.R.Q.S.R.* vol. VI. p. 137. Richmond, July 20, 1669.
[2] *Ibid.* vol. VI. p. 146. Stoxley, July 12, 1670.
[3] *Ibid.* vol. III. p. 284. Richmond, Jan. 16, 1627.
[4] *Ibid.* vol. VI. Thirsk, Oct. 1660. See also the case of Ruth Barton, vol. V. p. 188 and p. 205.

intended to lead away a sheep or a cow, sell it, and use the proceeds for the maintenance of the children; when more money was required more goods and chattels were requisitioned, it may be that the grandfather at Crayke acquiesced, since many people prefer to lose their possessions rather than to pay out money, but it is evident that he had a sufficient income to maintain his grandchildren, although he was content to allow the parish to provide for them.

But if one of the great evils of the Elizabethan poor law system—the loss of self-respect consequent on the rejection of responsibilities—was as yet a mere germ, the other greater abuse connected with settlement, by which a man was tied down to his own parish, became a vigorous growth in the latter half of the seventeenth and during the eighteenth centuries. After the passing of the last Act of Settlement in 1662, which enacted that 40 days should constitute a settlement, it was the object of every overseer to prevent labourers from coming to live in the parish, lest they might at some future time become chargeable to it.

The following order made at Helmsley on July 11th, 1671, constitutes in itself a criticism of the whole system:

Complaint being made by the Overseers of Thirske that a Thirske lab[r]. hath contemptuously disobeyed the orders made at Thirske May 2nd, 1671 whereby he was ordered to repair to Seazey, there to be settled according to law: Ordered that the aforesaid Order stand ratified and confirmed, and that the Constables of Thirske immediately after the receipt hereof, do apprehend the said man and his wife, and carry them to Seazey, and deliver them to the Overseers there, to be provided for: and in case he shall refuse to obey the said settlement, or shall return with or without his wife to Thirske, then the said Constables shall apprehend them and carry them to the Ho. of Corr[n]. at Thirske, there to be dealt withall as stubborn, contemptuous disobeyers of the authority of this Court, there to be detained until they shall give security to a J.P. that they shall and will, within two days of such security, repair to Seazey, and there remain and settle themselves, according to the said recited Order, and be no further troublesome to the inhab[ts]. of Thirske[1].

[1] *N.R.Q.S.R.* vol. vi. pp. 156–7. Helmsley, July, 1671.

Thus a man's village became as surely his prison as the House of Correction itself. Such a system went on for a century and a half after this date, until year by year there gradually settled down over the minds of the strong and vigorous British workmen a feeling of helpless immobility and despair. As a consequence of the Act regulating settlement, arbitration in the incessant disputes between parishes, regarding their liability to give poor relief, constitutes a large part of the work of the Court of Quarter Sessions from the latter half of the seventeenth century.

Each parish tried to throw off its responsibility, and in so doing took no heed whatever of family ties. A baby, the infant son of Thomas Ord of Northallerton, is sent to Thirsk to be nursed; the overseers of Thirsk complain, and the court orders that the infant "be sent to Northallerton to his father being his legal settlement, there to be provided for[1]." The overseers gave no consideration to any private arrangement, which may have been made for the nursing of the baby; their chief fear was that when he grew up they might have to pay for his apprenticeship. It would be interesting to know in orders like these how the infants were conveyed; supposing the nurse refused to walk from Thirsk to Northallerton, presumably the petty constables would pass on the baby from one township to the next until he reached his legal settlement.

One infant has to be "safely conveyed" from Stokesley to Burton-upon-Ure, a long distance across country; he would change hands a good many times if he were sent from constable to constable[2].

The intricate disputes regarding settlement and poor relief were frequently delegated for arbitration to two or more Justices, who, living in the neighbourhood, could more easily get at the true facts of the case[3]. In 1676 the court sitting at

---

[1] *N.R.Q.S.R.* vol. VI. p. 66. Stokesley, July, 1663.
[2] *Ibid.* vol. VI. p. 162. Thirsk, Oct. 3, 1671.
[3] *Ibid.* vol. VI. p. 255. Helmsley, July 11, 1676.

Helmsley ordered "a man and his wife to remain and be settled at Newton unless it appear to Sir Jas. Pennyman and Edw. Trotter, Esq., that he did remain in service at Tocketts above forty days: and if, upon examination of the witnesses upon both parts, it be found that he hath been legally settled at Tocketts aforesaid, then the overseers there to provide him and his wife a convenient habitation, if it be so adjudged by the said two Justices, who are hereby desired to end and determine the same."

If the overseers neglected to give relief and the needy person petitioned the Court of Quarter Sessions, the matter was frequently referred to the nearest Justice[1]. Sometimes the order was given with great precision. In 1654 the parish officers of Bolton-on-Swale were to "provide a competent habitation for a poor man and his family and to pay him 6d. weekly, unless they show cause, etc., to Geo. Smithson, Esq., J.P., upon or before Saturday next, Jan. 20th[2]." As the Sessions were held on January 17th the overseers had not much time in which to formulate their excuses.

The court, moreover, enforced and upheld if necessary the order of an individual Justice[3].

But not only had the parish officers to provide relief for the poor and destitute; they were also expected to look after those people who were afflicted with insanity[4], or with some disease. An order, remarkable for its orthography, runs:

---

[1] *N.R.Q.S.R.* vol. v. "In 1654 the Parish officers of Sowerby having disobeyed an Order made last Sessions at Thirske, Oct. 4, 1653, and a former Order touching the weekely maintenance of a poore ould man not able to maintaine himself, the said Parish Offrs. to pay unto the petitioner all the arrears of his weekly maintenance, formerly Ordered him, and 8d. weekly from this time forward, and in case they refuse, the Constables of Sowerby to carry them before the next J.P. to enter recogce. to answer their contempt or shew cause, etc."

[2] *Ibid.* vol. v. p. 149. Kirbymoorside, Jan. 1654.

[3] "Whereas there was an order made by Sir Salomon Swale that the Overseers of Kirby Hill should pay 6d. weekly to a very poor woman, or otherwise relieve her, and they not observing the same, it is ordered that they appear before Sir Rich. Grahm with sufficient sureties to be bound etc., and that he proceed further therein as he shall think most convenient." *N.R.Q.S.R.* vol. VI. p. 143. Thirsk, Ap. 1670.

[4] *Ibid.* vol. VI. p. 127. Richmond, 11 July, 1668. "The Parish Officers of

the inhabitants of Hudswell to receive and take care of a man by reason he is distracted, and not to suffer him to wander about the country, by which he may do either himself or others harm, and also to repair to some able phisition for the recovery of his health.

And a few years later the parish officers of Ainderby Steeple are enjoined to pay 4*d*. weekly to a poor sickly creature, who, like Julius Caesar, hath the falling sickness[1]. When they were remiss in this respect it seems probable that a petition on behalf of the sufferer was made to the Justices, who gave the order for relief.

Occasionally the parishioners themselves required that poor relief should be given. In 1680 the overseers of Middleton Tyas are ordered "to pay a very old blind man 2*s*. per week, it being the request and desire of the inhab^ts. of Middleton aforesaid."

II. PARISH STOCK

A determined effort was made by the Elizabethan legis-lators to prevent people being out of work.

In 1576 they ordered a stock of raw material to be kept in cities and corporate towns, and in market towns "so that every poor and needy person able to do any work shall not for want of work go abroad either begging or committing pilferings[2]." The same statute provided for the building of Houses of Correction, where also a stock was to be kept for "setting on work Rogues and such as be inhabiting in no parish," and also those persons who spoilt or embezzled the county stock. In 1598 this principle was extended to the parish.

The overseers were empowered to raise "A convenient stock of flax, hemp, wool, thread, iron and other stuff to set the poor on work[3]."

Barton to provide for a poor woman according to her condition, by reason she is distracted and not to suffer her to wander about the country."

[1] *N.R.Q.S.R.* vol. VII. p. 33. Thirsk, Ap. 1680. The parish officers of Ainderby Steeple are "to pay 4*d*. weekly to a poor sickly creature who is troubled with the falling sickness." Compare *Julius Caesar*, Act I. Scene 2. "He hath the falling sickness."

[2] 18 Eliz. cap. iii. sec. iv.

[3] 39 and 40 Eliz. cap. iii. sec. i.

There can be no doubt that this provision took its origin in some known need of the time. In the seventeenth century it was possible for the great class of workers in country districts to provide a competency for themselves and their families; owing, however, to the conditions of trade and labour they could rarely lay aside even a small sum of money for emergencies; therefore, when any misfortune occurred, such as fire, bad harvest, disease among sheep or cows, they were immediately reduced to beggary. For individual cases of pauperism such as these, in which an industrious man required capital only (either money or specie) to enable him to recover his position, the parish stock completely justified its existence.

In some parishes the custom was already established. Money left by will or obtained by church-ales and donations formed the parish stock and was let out at interest to those needing it, such interest being used to help the poor and sick of the parish[1]. Parliament, therefore, made the useful example of the well-cared-for parish into a law incumbent on all overseers and benefiting every poor person. Any person might apply for the stock, and if the overseers refused to give it then such person might appeal to the Court of Quarter Sessions[2]. In the poor law, however, stock generally means raw material, not money, though sometimes instead of weekly relief being granted a man was given a lump sum of money in order that he might buy his own stock. At Thirsk in April, 1677, the parish officers of Tollerton are ordered "to pay a man 6d. weekly for his relief and maintenance, or 20s. at one time payment, for enabling him to buy skins to follow his trade of parchment maker[3]."

[1] See Vestry Minutes of Steeple Ashton 1603–1625 given in *The Parish* by T. Smith; also Vestry Book of the Parish of Pittington, *Surtees Soc. Pub.* vol. LXXXIV. pp. 626–644.

[2] *N.R.Q.S.R.* vol. VII. p. 24. Northallerton, July, 1679. In 1679 Sir Richard Grahm ordered "that the town of Romanby should not for the future pay any weekly allowance unto a certain widow there, or be further chargeable with her than the providing her a stocke." Presumably the widow was expected to earn her own living by spinning or weaving.

[3] *Ibid.* vol. VI. p. 271. Thirsk, April, 1677.

The difficulty about working this section of the Act seems to have been that, if adequately carried out, it would have taken up a large amount of the overseer's time. The raw material was given out to each worker; when the work was brought back if properly done it was paid for, if spoilt, then the worker was publicly whipped or sent to the House of Correction. It seems probable, therefore, that, except in rare instances, where the overseer was interested, or a man of leisure, this part of his work was never completely carried out: nevertheless it is evident from various references in the records that "setting the poor on work" by means of the parish stock was considered an important part of the overseer's duties.

Ralph Dunning, an enthusiastic admirer of the Elizabethan Poor Law, wrote in 1686 his *Plain and Easy method of showing how the office of Overseer of the Poor may be managed*. From his pamphlet it appears that more might have been accomplished in the way of employing the destitute, and he lays his finger on the reason for this neglect when he says: "There is scarce a great parish wherein there is not a person who for 40s. or 50s. per annum will undertake the setting up and continual management of giving poor work[1]." But the overseer was unpaid, and he had not time to organise the industry and to see that the people thus provided with work performed it satisfactorily[2].

Even if the industry of the poor could have been adjusted by the overseers, as a general preventive of destitution the principle broke down. This is clearly pointed out by Defoe in his tract published in 1704, *Giving Alms no Charity*, in which he shows that this method was "enriching one poor man to starve another, putting a vagabond into an honest man's employment[3]."

[1] R. Dunning, *Plain and Easy Method*, etc., p. 15.
[2] Cp. Statutes passed regulating this work. 7 Jac. I. cap. vii. "If poor do not spin properly, spoil or embezzle goods they are to be publicly whipt in their own town."
[3] Defoe, *Giving Alms no Charity*, p. 17.

III. THE PROVISION OF HOUSES FOR THE DESTITUTE

One of the most useful measures passed in the Tudor period was the law which provided that every cottage must have four acres of land laid to it[1]. The yield of corn from such land was expected to provide sustenance for one family. Hence the same law forbade people who inhabited cottages with this minimum of land to "entertain inmates," that is, to provide board and lodging for any person not a member of the family. Nor might a house be divided into two separate tenements unless four acres of land were laid to each[2].

This Act seems to have been rigorously enforced in the North Riding; men are frequently summoned for erecting cottages contrary to the statute[3] or for "harbouring under-settlers"—the name for additional inmates in Yorkshire. In October, 1607, at Richmond Quarter Sessions eleven people were summoned for having cottages without the four acres of land, and were all fined 40s., one of them,

Thos. Pybus for contynueing of a cottage erected etc. (contrary to the statute) occupied by James Gill of a second by John Greathead, and of a third by Chr. Sadler: fined 40s. in each case.

A case tried at Richmond in the year 1608 shows the reason why the parishes had a full appreciation of the value of the Act; it runs:

Whereas John Browne of East Whitton has erected a cottage in Burrell and not laid 4 acres etc....he is fyned 10s., and that he be bound etc. that neither Fr Marshall whom he hath placed tenant in the same, his wieff or his children shall become chargeable to the Parish[4].

It seems clear as one result of this law that the supply of cottages in the villages was never sufficient to meet the

---

[1] 31 Eliz. cap. vii.
[2] *N.R.Q.S.R.* vol. IV. p. 222. Thirsk, April, 1642. "A man for dividing a cottage into two separate tenements and letting them out, etc."
[3] At the same Sessions "Leon Marshall of Ravensworth for keeping of an undersettle (*i.e.* inmate) for the space of a moneth contrary, etc. fined 10s."
[4] *N.R.Q.S.R.* vol. I. p. 139. Richmond, Oct. 1608.

demand, since, owing to the increased value of land, yeomen and farmers were unwilling to build fresh cottages, because they did not want to lose the four acres of land which must also be provided.

Therefore the parish officers could (and must, if need be) build houses for the poor on the common or waste ground of the parish, provided they gained the consent of the lord of the manor[1]. Such houses might be erected without the provision of the four acres of land, but they were ever afterwards to be kept solely for the use of the poor[1].

There are indications that the building of these houses was not always popular in the neighbourhood, either with the lord of the manor or with the inhabitants. In 1620 a certain Ralph Huton, who is designated gentleman, and others pulled down a frame erected for a house to be built on a waste piece of ground "to harbour & relieve Will Dason his wife & children." This high-handed action is duly presented before the Justices, who order the house to be built up again by the parishioners of Long Cowton, and kept "for ever here after for the use of the poor[2]."

Sometimes certain Justices were directed to choose out a position for the house[3], and in no case could the overseers do anything without the consent of the lord of the manor; should such consent be withheld they might petition the Bench who at times put pressure on the unwilling party.

"lett Mr Alderud Brooke see this petition," runs an order in 1650, "and either give libertie for the Overseers of the poore for Lastingham to build houses upon the waist, for the poor people mentioned in the petition, or else show cause for his refusal att the next Sessions[4]."

The houses were made of wood, and thatched with

---

[1] 43 and 44 Eliz. cap. ii. sec. iv.

[2] *N.R.Q.S.R.* vol. II. pp. 250 and 253. Richmond, Oct. 10, 1620.

[3] "The Parish officers of Nawton to build a house on the waste of the said township as a dwelling for a poor man, the said house to be built in a place approved of by Sir Rich. Darley and Sir John Gibson." *N.R.Q.S.R.* vol. IV. p. 64, Thirsk, Oct. 5, 1636.

[4] *Ibid.* vol. V. p. 62. Thirsk, Oct. 1, 1650.

straw; the cost of building varied, but was probably about
£3. In 1654 the Bench made an order for "a poor woman of
Thorneton in the Street, who hath relief from the parish,
being in great want of harbour to have 20s. from the parish,
the better to inable her to build herself a howse"; from the
wording of the order this probably did not cover the whole
cost[1]. In some cases the churchwarden or overseer found
the money and reimbursed himself by a general assessment
on the parish. If the latter refused to pay then he got an
order from the Quarter Sessions. In 1622 an order is made
for

a general asst. to be presentlie made by the Churchwardens and
Overseers of Catterick for the sum of 58s. 6d. disbursed by Will.
Barker Churchwarden there for erecting of a house for a poor man[2].

In many cases when the house was provided by the parish
the occupier was expected to pay rent for it. In 1656
the parish officers of Wigginton are ordered "to provide
harbour for a poor ould man, who is to pay such rent as he
is able out of his labour[3]"; the rent being about 6d. a week[4].
Workhouses were not yet known, but there is mention in
1649 of a "House for the poor" at Brompton[5], which seems
to indicate that it was built for more than one family.
Usually, however, the house was built for the particular person needing relief, who was generally specified by name, as
in the following case:

The Churchwardens and Overseers of the towne of Boltby shall
provide a habitation and relieff for Ellen Killington according to
lawe, for that she hath dwelt there xxty yeares last; and that they
likewise put her children prentizes according to law[6].

[1] N.R.Q.S.R. vol. v. p. 165. Richmond, July 27, 1654.
[2] Ibid. vol. iii. p. 154. Richmond, Oct. 8, 1622.
[3] Ibid. vol. v. p. 220. Malton, July 15, 1656. Also vol. vi. p. 241.
Richmond, July, 1675. "The P.O. of Exilby Leeming and Newton to
provide a convenient habitation for a poor woman, she paying rent for
the same."
[4] Ibid. vol. ii. p. 27. "The Overseers of Masham to provide house
for a man and his family and give him 12d. weekly but until the house
is found he is to have 18d. weekly."
[5] Ibid. vol. v. p. 21. Helmsley, Jan. 9, 1649.
[6] Ibid. vol. i. p. 38. Thirsk, April 29, 1606.

T.							5

IV. THE EDUCATION OF POOR CHILDREN

Of all the overseers' duties the one most beneficial to the community was that by which the coming generation were ensured a fair chance in life. Parish officers had power to educate the children of paupers by apprenticing them to domestic service, or other occupations[1]. Such children were apprenticed as early as seven years of age, thus growing up away from the atmosphere of destitution, in homes where they were given board and lodging. The overseers could demand of any householder that he should receive one of these poor children as his apprentice; if he refused, they appealed to the nearest Justices[2], or in the last resort to the Court of Quarter Sessions[3].

Girls seem to have been frequently apprenticed to domestic service; and the whole of their labour was given to their employer without payment during the years of apprenticeship. While in many cases no doubt these orphans obtained comfortable homes, there are indications that the treatment of such poor children was not always of the best[4].

During the strife of parties in the middle of the seventeenth century the Justices ordered that the minister should be consulted as to which of his parishioners were suitable persons to receive apprentices[5]. Thus the authorities exercised care

---

[1] 39 and 40 Eliz. cap. iii. sec. iv.

[2] *N.R.Q.S.R.* vol. I. p. 87. Helmsley, October, 1607. "Tho. Nesse of the Sleightes for not keeping Rog Elmer his apprentice, being appointed unto him by the Justices." And vol. v. p. 121. Thirsk, Oct. 1652. "A boy of Crake having been presented to the J.Ps. within Bulmer Division, to be putt forth as an apprentice, and the Parish Offrs of Crake having nominated one Marm Mortimer to take him, but the said Mortimer having refused to take the said apprentice, three J.Ps to call all parties concerned before them, and to see right and justice done therein."

[3] *Ibid.* vol. III. p. 310. Gisborough, March, 1630. "Mark Liell of Cliffe gent, being a substantiall inhabitt. within the Parish of Kirkleathome for refusing to take an apprentice being lawfullie tendred unto him by the officers of the said parish to the hindrance of the execution of the Statute."

[4] *Ibid.* vol. II. p. 93.

[5] *Ibid.* vol. v. p. 41. Thirsk, Oct. 1649. The parish officers for Easingwold shall, with the approbation of the minister of the parish, nominate and certify the two next J.P.s "whoe is a fitt maister to take

and forethought in providing that children should be satisfactorily settled and grow up in an atmosphere favourable
to the political opinion of the day. Indeed the overseer
might be considered the trustee of the parish[1], being the
guardian of orphans[2] and of those poor little waifs who
were deserted by their parents[3]. Where special cases of
neglect occurred on the part of the overseers the Justices
empowered certain of their number to see that the orders of
the court were performed. Crayke was a village in which
were many factions; during the Civil War and Commonwealth frequent riots and disorders occurred. In 1651 the
Bench ordered that

forasmuch as complaint is made that the number of poore people
increaseth dayly, more and more in the parish of Crake, and that noe
care is taken by the Parish Offrs for the putting out of poore children
apprentices, these are to require the present Parish Offrs to certifye
the next two J.P.s whereof one to be of the Quorum, what children
are fitt to be put forward apprentices, as also the persons fitt to
receive them and the J.Ps to see the children placed according to
law[4].

Elizth. Baxter's grandchild, an apprentice, and the parties concerned
therein to repair before the two next J.Ps as aforesaid that indentures may
be entered according to law."
   [1] *N.R.Q.S.R.* vol. VII. p. 29. Helmsley, Jan. 1680. "Whereas a Cawton
woman late deceased, hath left a son about eleven years of age, and the
Overseers have not only taken care to pay her funeral charges but also
to provide for the said child since her death, and to put him to a trade,
and there being some household goods left by her: Ordered that the
Overseer be hereby impowered to enter upon all household goods left as
aforesaid and to sell or otherwise to dispose thereof as he shall think most
expedient, for reimbursing him the moneys laid out."
   [2] *Ibid.* vol. V. p. 180. Richmond, Jan. 1655. "The goods and chattells
given by will unto Wm Marg Harker by Eliz. Harker late of Staireton
being apprised to the value of £6. 6s. to be safely preserved and kept by
the parish officers for the maintenance of the children."
   [3] *Ibid.* vol. VI. p. 226. Thirsk, Oct. 1674. "The Overseers and inhabts.
of Swainby Holine and Ainderby Whearnhowe to contribute respectively
out of every of the said towns 3d. weekly towards the maintenance of the
young child which was lately found in the highway in the Constablery of
Scinderby and to continue the payment thereof unto the Overseers of
Scinderby until this Court shall otherwise Order."
   [4] *Ibid.* vol. V. p. 72. Thirsk, April, 1651.

V. THE ADMINISTRATION OF LANDS OR MONEY
LEFT BY WILL FOR THE USE OF THE POOR

The overseers shared in that function appertaining solely to the churchwardens in the Middle Ages, of administering the property left to the parish for the benefit of the poor. In this also they received help from the Justices[1], who in the Court of Quarter Sessions made dilatory executors deliver up their trust[2]. At times it seems clear that the Anglican priest was associated with the parish officials in this administration[3].

When the overseers of Easingwold complain that divers inhabitants in the town who hold lands which have been left for the use of the poor neglect to pay the rent of the lands, the court authorises them "to distreyne for the arreare of said annuities[4]."

SOURCES OF INCOME TO MEET THE EXPENSES
OF POOR RELIEF

To meet the considerable expenses necessary in order to perform their duties satisfactorily the overseers could draw upon three sources of income:

1. Lands or money left by charitable people for the use of the poor.

---

[1] *N.R.Q.S.R.* vol. v. p. 105. Thirsk, April, 1652. The parish officers of Kilburn are ordered "to pay the poore people of Ouldstead and Wasse the moneys arreare unto them by Mr Keye's will or give acct. before the next J.P. how the same is distributed."

[2] *Ibid.* vol. v. p. 189. Malton, July, 1655. In 1655 "the overseers of Kirkdaile are ordered to appear at the next Sessions and prove the coppie of Tho. Ellerton's will and Mr Tho. Savill or his assignes, to appear and shew cause wherefore they doe not pay 20s. yearly, given to the poor as is alleadged by the said Overseers."

[3] *Ibid.* vol. iv. p. 237. With reference to an annuity of £5 for a certain piece of land called Carleton Close payable to the poor of Thormanby it is "Ordered that the said Will Stanely who undertook the yearly paiment, doe forthwith upon sight here of pay the said annuity with all the arreares unto Rob. Oxley, Clarke, Parson of the said Parish, Tho. Thomlinson gentn. and to the Overseers and Churchwardens of the same, to be bestowed by them for the poore people's best advantage."

[4] *Ibid.* vol. iv. p. 249. Easingwold, Jan. 1646. 39 and 40 Eliz. cap. iii. sec. i.

2. Fines for the breaking of certain laws, assigned definitely by the statutes, to be given for the relief of the poor[1].

3. The poor rate, which the overseers with the consent of two or more Justices of the Peace were authorised to levy on all the inhabitants of the parish[2].

Some parishes received considerable sums of money for the use of the poor from the fines inflicted by the court either for negligence of office or for offences against the statutes. In October, 1607, at the Richmond Quarter Sessions the poor of Scruton by the iniquities of the rich seem to have benefited to the extent of £7. 13s. 4d.[3] All fines for breaking the severe game laws passed in the reign of James I went to the use of the poor. People were frequently presented and

---

[1] 1 Jac. I, cap. xxvii ⎫
7 Jac. I, cap. xi ⎬ : for infraction of the game Laws.
21 Jac. I, cap. xxviii ⎭

1 Jac. I. Fines alehouse keepers 20s. for allowing people to sit tippling in their houses or for selling for 1d. less than 1 qt of best beer and 2 qts of small.

4 Jac. I, cap. v: 5s. fine for drunkenness.

21 Jac. I, cap. vii: 3s. 4d. fine for sitting drinking in an alehouse in the offenders' parish.

3 Jac. I, cap. iv: fine of 1s. for absence from church.

21 Jac. I, cap. xx: fine of 1s. for profane swearing.

21 Jac. I, cap. xviii: for breaking regulations for cloth-making.

1 Car. I, cap. i: fine for meeting for games outside the parish on Sunday.

1 Car. I, cap. i: fine for meeting for unlawful games in the parish on Sunday.

3 Car. I, cap. ii: fine of 20s. for carriers driving on Sunday.

3 Car. I, cap. ii: fine of 6s. 8d. for butchers killing meat on Sunday.

All penalties for default in carrying out the provisions of the Act for Poor Relief. 39 and 40 Eliz. cap. iii. sec. xi.

£5 on J.P. failing to nominate overseers. 43 and 44 Eliz. cap. ii. sec. ix.

£3 at least on persons refusing to be treasurers. Do. sec. xiv.

20s. on churchwardens and overseers. 39 and 40 Eliz. cap. iii. sec. i.

The fine of 12d. for not attending service in church was levied by the churchwardens for the use of the poor.

[2] 43 and 44 Eliz. cap. ii. sec. i.

[3] N.R.Q.S.R. vol. I. p. 94. Richmond, Oct. 8, 1607. "Tho. Hutchinson of Scruton one of the Overseers of the poore there for not keeping his monethly meeting according to the Statute etc. fined 20s.; also Ralph Gaill, Chr Hawe and Tho. Orton, others of the Overseers for the like, and with like fines. John Richardson of Scruton, bruester, for breaking the assize of ale etc., fined 20s. John Stevenson and Arth. Pearson labr. both of the same and bruesters, for breaking etc., fined 20s. each. Tho. Hutchinson of the same, freholder, and Geo. Davison the younger, for playing at unlawfull games, as bowling and such like contrary to etc., fined 6s. 8d. each."

fined for "tracing hares in the snow[1]," or "for shooting in a gunne at hayres and pigeons[2]." But much more frequently are they fined "for sitting drinking and tipling in alehouses," or for playing unlawful games when they should have been attending the service in the parish church. When the Puritans reigned supreme many fines were estreated for profane swearing[3], and for not keeping the Lord's Day.

As we have seen, alehouse keepers were fined 20s. if they allowed people to sit drinking in their houses, or if they sold them less than one quart of best beer or two quarts of small for one penny, or if they brewed unwholesome ale. Perhaps a man got some satisfaction when paying his fine from the reflection that it would help to keep down his poor rate.

The overseers themselves occasionally had to lay down money for the use of the poor in the way of a fine. In 1655 the overseers of Smeaton are

fined 20s. apiece for neglect of executing their office, the Churchwardens and the Constable to leavy the same within fourteen days, and distribute it to the poor, and to certify the names of the poor who receive it to the next J.P.[4]

Evidently in this instance the churchwardens have succeeded in exculpating themselves; but more often they are included in the guilt.

In 1655 Lord Fairfax was fined 5s. to the poor; the entry recording it throws a vivid sidelight on Cromwell's government. The order runs:

the Constables and Overseers of Gillinge to leavy 5s. on the goods of Lord Fairfax to be distributed to the poor according to Ordinance of Parliament, for that it hath been proved that he was present when Tho. Carlton, Anth Chapman and others acted a comedy or stage play at Gillinge at Christmas last;

the like order is made "to the Constable, and Overseers of

---

[1] *N.R.Q.S.R.* vol. I. p. 111. "Two men of Sowerby for tracing and killing hares in the snow."

[2] *Ibid.* vol. I. p. 71. Thirsk, Ap. 14, 1607.

[3] *Ibid.* vol. v. Malton, July, 1652. "A man convict of swearing profanely to be fined 3s. 4d. which is to be distributed to the poor of Ayton."

[4] *Ibid.* vol. v. p. 193. Beadall, July 17, 1655.

Oulton against Lord Castleton; the like order to the Constable and Overseers of Bransby against Mr Cholmeley[1]."

The entry illustrates the nature of local government in England in the seventeenth century; whatever miscarriages of justice there might be, if arbitrary orders were given, they were given as much against the rich as against the poor; the liberty of the Parliamentarian was restricted in the same degree as that of the Cavalier.

Every inhabitant and every occupier of lands in the parish had to pay the poor rate; this was to be assessed by the parishioners themselves, or in their default by the churchwardens and constables. If, however, parishioners, churchwardens and constables could not agree, then the nearest Justices ordered the rate. After the assessment had been made by the parish it could only be altered by the same authority. The churchwarden of Bainbridge was summoned because he altered an assessment without the authority and consent of the neighbours[2].

Occasionally the overseers had to obtain an order from the court before they could induce people to render an account of their incomes[3].

If a man refused to pay the assessment, then the parish officers, by a warrant from any two Justices of the Peace, could levy the rate by distress and sale of the objector's goods[4], a proceeding which was never submitted to with equanimity and was the occasion of frequent assaults.

William Noble, a yeoman, overseer of Whitby, seized a certain pewter dish belonging to James Willie, alias Grenebancke, in lieu of poor rate, but James Willie made an

---

[1] *N.R.Q.S.R.* vol. V. p. 190. Malton, July 10, 1655.
[2] *Ibid.* vol. VI. p. 58. Richmond, July, 1662.
[3] *Ibid.* vol. IV. p. 65. Thirsk, Oct. 1636. "The inhabitants and freeholders of Thirsk at the request of the Parish officers of the same" are ordered "to make a particular of all their lands and tenements which they or their tenants shall yearly have that the said officers may know how to make their assts legally and the said officers to furnish to the said inhabts. etc., a particular of their several assts."
[4] 39 and 40 Eliz. cap. iii. sec. iii.

assault on the overseer and got back his dish "in the way of rescusse[1]."

Since the overseers were of the "substantial" inhabitants of the parish, they had to pay a considerable proportion of the rate which they levied. The Justices also, who sanctioned the rate, were concerned that it should not be too heavy. This circumstance acted as a deterrent against extravagant expenditure: indeed the overseers seem generally to have erred on the side of economy; frequent petitions for poor and other relief are presented to the Court of Quarter Sessions, as well as complaints against parish officers who have been negligent in the discharge of their duties or who have refused to give relief. In 1647 the Bench issued the following order:

> On general complaint that the Parish Officers of divers parishes in the N.R. have large sums of money in their hands which ought to be employed for the use of the poor, and that the poor complain for want thereof, Ordered that the said Parish Officers shall forthwith make acct[2].

Considerable sums of money passed through the overseer's hands and he was required to give an account of them to his successor. If he failed to do so his own goods were seized. In 1653 a warrant was issued "against the Overseer of Pickering to levy 50s. of his goods, for money due to the poor, still in his hands, and also 20s. more for neglecting the execution of his office as Overseer[3]."

Very full powers were given to the Justices of the Peace with regard to the assessment of the taxation for the poor law, and a considerable part of their time in Quarter Sessions was spent in hearing petitions from individuals or from parishes aggrieved at their assessment[4]. The Justices could

---

[1] *N.R.Q.S.R.* vol. II. p. 120. Hulton Bushell, April 5, 1616.
[2] *Ibid.* vol. IV. p. 273. New Malton, July 13, 1647.
[3] *Ibid.* vol. V. p. 145. Thirsk, Oct. 1653. The overseers of Thirsk are presented for not accounting for their receipts and disbursements and not handing over their balance in hand to the new overseers.
[4] 39 and 40 Eliz. cap. iii. sec. vi. "If any persons shall find themselves grieved with any cess or tax or other act done by the said Churchwardens

also at their discretion[1] in Quarter Sessions order one parish to help another "overburdened with poor people." This they frequently did at the request of the poorer parish, generally after having obtained from the Justice living in the neighbourhood some enquiry into the facts of the case: *e.g.* in 1632 the Bench ordered

the controversy between the Overseers of Barningham and those of Kirkby Ravensworth to be heard by Math. Hutton Esq., who is to certify at next Sessns what he thinks the Overseers of the latter ought to allow to those of the former, in regard this towne is thought to be greatlie charged with their poore, etc.[2]

Barningham and Kirkby Ravensworth are separate parishes but each contains part of the township of Newsham. Again in 1665 the Justices order

the inhabitants of Ainderby Myers-cum-Houltby to pay 6*d.* weekly to the Overseers of Hornby by reason Hornby is much charged with poor and impotent people and Ainderby Myers-cum-Houltby have none[3].

Ainderby Myers with Holtby is in the parish of Hornby and the entry is interesting as showing that the inhabitants of each township dissociated themselves from the entire parish, a custom which had obtained the sanction of Parliament three years previously[4].

STATUS OF THE OFFICE OF OVERSEER

The custom seems to have held in the North Riding that the overseers of a parish consisting of two or more townships or hamlets should be chosen to represent each township or each hamlet as the case might be. In 1608 Richard May of Catterick, John Calvert of Hipswell and Henry Tompson of Tunstall are overseers for the poor of Catterick, Tunstall

and other person or by the said Justices of peace, then it shall be lawful for the said Justices of peace at their general quarter sessions to take such order therein as to them shall be thought convenient."
[1] 39 and 40 Eliz. cap. iii. sec. ii.
[2] *N.R.Q.S.R.* vol. III. p. 336. Richmond, July 13, 1632.
[3] *Ibid.* vol. VI. p. 85. Thirsk, Ap. 4, 1665.
[4] 14 Car. II, cap. xii. sec. xxi.

and Hipswell being townships of Catterick[1]. In 1611 the overseers for West Tanfield, a parish which has no dependent townships but contains three hamlets, Nosterfield, Thornbargh and Brinsoe, "were Chr. Bourne of West Tanfield, Arth. Petty of Nosterfield, Will Ingleton of Thornbargh, Will Bradweth of Binsley[2]" (? Brinsoe).

The office of overseer seems to have been considered an honourable one. "The poor income I gleaned," says Tapwell, "hath made me in my parish, thought worthy to be scavenger, and in time may rise to be overseer of the poor[3]." The Act of 1598 specially enjoined that the overseers should be of the rank of subsidy men.

In 1607 the overseers of Scruton were Ralph Gaill, Thomas Hutchinson, Christopher Hawe and Thomas Orton[4]. Of these, the three latter were yeomen and freeholders. They all served at various times on the grand jury, therefore they must have had lands or tenements to the value of £20 a year or £500 personalty[5]. Ralph Gaill was probably a member of the Gaill family who bought the manor of Scruton in 1688, and who are known to have lived previously to that date in the parish. Thus, while the petty constable might sometimes be a labourer, it seems that, in the first half of the seventeenth century at any rate, the overseer was generally a yeoman. Indeed, only a man with a certain income could afford to pay the fine of 20s. levied for any default of office, a sum of money equivalent in those days to the value of six sheep[6].

In 1614 George Metcalf of Firby, gent. is nominated as overseer, and being of the rank of gentleman perhaps he felt

---

[1] *N.R.Q.S.R.* vol. I. p. 111. Also p. 231. Overseers of Kirklington are John Scurton, Math Wilkinson of Kirklington, Will Warcop of East Tanfield, John Pickering of Sutton Howgrave, the 2 townships of Kirklington.

[2] *Ibid.* vol. I. p. 231. Richmond, July, 1611.

[3] Massinger, *A New Way to pay Old Debts*, Act I. Sc. I.

[4] *N.R.Q.S.R.* vol. I. p. 94, see full entry note 3, p. 69.

[5] *Ibid.* vol. VI. p. 90. Richmond, Aug. 8, 1665. Two men are excused from serving as grand jurymen because they have not this amount of income or personalty.

[6] *Ibid.* vol. I. p. 8. Stokesley, July 9, 1605. "A labr. presented for stealing six white sheep at Alne, of the value of 20s."

it was beneath his dignity, for "he did contemne and scorn that office, saying he would not stirre to the doore about it," therefore a warrant was issued to attach him "for refusing to execute the office of overseer of the poor, being duly nominated[1]." Two years later the same man was treasurer for the hospitals for Richmondshire, a position of great trust and importance[2], to which only Justices of the Peace or people rated for subsidy at £5 land or £10 goods could be appointed[3]. The fact that the Justices nominated a man in his position to be an overseer shows that the office ranked considerably above that of a petty constable.

There is no indication that the outgoing overseers were expected to find substitutes to fill their places. As has been mentioned, the parish officers for the year were most probably arranged at the vestry meeting. The names of the overseers being generally given in the parish books after those of the churchwardens: the only difference is that the churchwardens are mentioned as "elected" while the overseers are merely named, since their election was not valid until sealed by the Justices.

ADMINISTRATION OF THE POOR LAW

The records of the Court of Quarter Sessions seem to prove that in the North Riding the Justices on their own initiative made a steady effort to administer the poor law, and to keep the overseers up to their work[4]. The overseers were presented by the chief constable[5], and also by the petty constable under the warrant of a Justice[6], but it is possible that petitions were sent direct to the Quarter Sessions, for at Richmond in October, 1605, the Justices order

---

[1] *N.R.Q.S.R.* vol. II. p. 50. Richmond, July 12, 1614.
[2] *Ibid.* vol. II. p. 155. Helmsley, Oct. 1, 1616.
[3] 43 and 44 Eliz. cap. ii. sec. xii.
[4] *N.R.Q.S.R.* vol. I. p. 1. Thirsk, Ap. 11, 1605.
[5] *Ibid.* vol. I. p. 36. Thirsk, Ap. 1606. "John Sakeld and Rynyan Wilson of Aynderby with Steeple Overseers of the Poor there for negligence in the execution of their office. (Per Tho. Warde et Geo. Robinson, Cap Const.)"
[6] *Ibid.* vol. III. p. 115. A petty constable refuses to apprehend the overseers on the Justice's warrant and is presented.

that a warrant per Curiam be made to commaund the Churchwardens of the townes of Screwton and Aynderby to be more diligent in relieving their poore that the Court be not troubled with any further claymours therein[1].

Neither Ainderby nor Scruton were fortunate in the choice of their overseers for in the following April the overseers of Ainderby were before the Bench for negligence, and in October, 1607, all the four overseers of Scruton were fined 20s. each for not keeping their monthly meeting[2]. In nothing is the Justice's power over the parish officers more apparent than in the fines he is able to inflict.

By the poor law the overseer was to be fined 20s. for every default, but in 1622 the Bench threatened a penalty of £5[3], and in 1651 when the Justices were freed from all central control they imposed a fine of £20 on the overseers "for contemning an Order and not paying moneys due[4]." The court evidently conceived that it had the right to fine recalcitrant officers according to the gravity of the offence and the circumstances of the case.

The law enacted that the churchwardens and overseers should meet together at least once every month on a Sunday in the church after divine service in the afternoon[5]. What they were expected to do on these occasions is shown in the presentment of "Tho. Solperwick als. Gillam, of Healey in Massam, Overseer," who is before the court

for that he and his fellowes have beene very negligent in their places, and have not mett monthly, nor sett anie poore on worke that lacked worke, neither have releived the impotent as they ought to have done, nor have put children to be apprentices[6].

---

[1] *N.R.Q.S.R.* vol. I. p. 22. Richmond, Oct. 4, 1605.

[2] *Ibid.* vol. I. p. 94. Richmond, Oct. 1607.
    Vol. I. pp. 111, 128, 136. The overseers of Middleton Tyas and Moulton, Ellerton and Scorton, Catterick Croft and Bolton upon Swale are summoned for not meeting monthly and providing for the poor.

[3] *Ibid.* vol. III. p. 154. Richmond, Oct. 1622. The overseers of Northallerton are ordered "to receive and provide for Jane Dawson als. Aselbie, and if they refuse, the lawful penalty shall be estrated against them, viz: in £5 a peece for everie Overseer that shall refuse."

[4] *Ibid.* vol. v. p. 81. Richmond, July, 1651.

[5] 43 and 44 Eliz. cap. ii. sec. i.

[6] *N.R.Q.S.R.* vol. II. p. 88. Thirsk, April 18 and 19, 1615.

It was necessary to enforce this provision if the Act was not to become a dead letter, since the effective working of the poor law lay in its prompt and detailed administration by the overseers. The Justices recognised this and insisted that monthly meetings should be kept, and that overseers should perform their statutory duties[1]. Nor might any one of them shirk his work. At Thirsk, in April, 1606, Richard Nicholson, junr., of Topcliff, was presented "for taking on himself the office of Overseer of the poor, but declining to fulfil the duties thereof in conjunction with his fellow Overseers[2]." In 1620 Edm. Hay of Newton is presented "for that being appointed Overseer of Pickeringe he refuseth to meet monthlie with the rest of the Overseers of the parish att his parish Church fr the reliefe of the poore etc.[3]"

From the records it might be supposed that the Justice was the advocate of the poor against the overseers who were continually striving to avoid giving relief; but behind the Justice was the Central Government which by orders and proclamations continually kept him up to his work.

As fluctuations in trade occurred, and as bad harvests caused scarcity, so the Privy Council issued letters of advice to the Justices.

A Royal Commission for the Poor was appointed in 1630, Wentworth being one of the Commissioners responsible for Yorkshire, and in January, 1631, a book of orders and

---

[1] In the early years of the seventeenth century overseers are more frequently presented for not keeping their monthly meeting, e.g. N.R.Q.S.R. vol. I. p. 99 } 1608 Overseers of Catterick, Well, Middleton Tyas,
p. 111 { Moulton, Bolton on Swale, Ellerton, Scorton
p. 128 { and Croft
p. 136 } 1610 Overseers of Topcliffe (for not relieving the poor).
Vol. I. p. 188
1611 Overseers of Wath, Burneston, Topcliffe, West Tanfield, Condall, Kirklington (for not relieving their poor). Vol. I. p. 231.
At the latter end of the century overseers are most frequently summoned for neglecting or refusing to execute the warrant of a Justice.
[2] N.R.Q.S.R. vol. I. p. 31.
[3] Ibid. vol. II. p. 231.

directions was issued to the Justices, to ensure the better administration of the Poor Law.

The Justices were to report their doings every three months to the sheriff, who gave these reports to the Justices of Assize, to be sent on to the Lords Commissioners. The Justices of Assize were specially enjoined to enquire if the Justices of the Peace were negligent, and if so, to report them to the King[1].

In Yorkshire the Justices divided out the Riding amongst themselves, and arranged to hold monthly meetings of the churchwardens, overseers and constables in each division. During the Commonwealth this custom fell into disuse. In 1661 it was re-established by an order of the court which declared

that by former experience it hath been found that the diligent observance of the monthly meetings of the Justices in their several divisions have prevented many disorders[2].

After 1662, however, the Justices seem to have had increasing difficulty in getting their orders performed. Frequently cases of relief which have been ordered by three or four Justices out of Sessions come before the court as not having been paid by the overseers.

It may be that occasionally, when the Justices were petitioned for relief, they gave it too readily[3]. In 1675 there are two cases at the Richmond Sessions where the parish officers show that the grant of relief should be reduced, one of which runs:

Complaint being made unto this Court by and on behalf of the inhabitants of Danby Wiske that a man, who now receives 12d. weekly towards his maintenance as a poor man, is not so indigent as to deserve so great a contribution: Ordered that the Parish Offrs of Danby Wiske shall only pay him 6d. weekly till further Order[4].

[1] See E. M. Leonard, *The Early History of English Poor Relief*, chapters viii and ix.
[2] *N.R.Q.S.R.* vol. iv. p. 31. Helmsley, Jan. 1661.
[3] *Ibid.* vol. vii. p. 51. Richmond, July 19, 1681. "A warrant against the Parson of Ainderby Steeple to find sureties etc. for reflecting on the Court for easy granting Orders for the relief of the poor of Ainderby Steeple aforesaid."   [4] *Ibid.* vol. vi. p. 241. Richmond, July 20, 1675.

As the century proceeds the records show clearly enough that the Poor Law had failed in its object and the question arises as to whether it had not helped to create that poverty which it was designed to abolish.

It is evident that there was an abundance of destitute people in the last quarter of the century.

In 1679 the inhabitants of West Tanfield (quite a small village) petition the court

that there is above twenty lame and blind persons in the parish that are more necessitous than a certain woman, and have no allowance but the alms of the parishioners, and if they had it, would utterly undoe the inhabts. to pay it.

In some cases the parishioners had ceased to give alms[1], since they had to pay the poor rate as well. No doubt the regular system of relief was better than indiscriminate charity, but from many orders and complaints it is a question, whether the really deserving poor always received the relief, or whether it was not given to the eager and importunate. In 1686 Ralph Dunning, himself an overseer of a parish in Devon, admits that the aspersion has been cast on the statute 43 Elizabeth for the relief of the poor, that the law had made multitudes idle and careless because they, having relief, had not taken care to provide for themselves, "the parish is, as they say, bound to find[2] them": but while he declares that the cause of the numbers of idlers and felons lay in the lax administration of the statutes regarding alehouses, rogues and vagabonds, labourers and apprentices, etc., he gives a trenchant criticism of the Act in these words:

The charge of the poor...is nearly double what it was thirty years since, and not occasioned by dearth or scarcity of necessaries because there was never a greater plenty, but by idleness, profuse expenditure, ill-bringing up of children.

[1] *N.R.Q.S.R.* vol. v. p. 156. Thirsk, April 4, 1654. "In regard the parishioners of Osmotherley withdraw their charitie, which formerly they gave at their doores to Alex Swailes, a poor man, it is therefore Ordered that the Parish Offrs there shall, for the future, pay the said poor man 12*d*. weekly." See also a note by Canon Atkinson showing that the custom of giving regular alms—in food—still held in Cleveland in the nineteenth century.
[2] *find* = provide for.

The real cause of the idleness of which the Devonshire overseer complains lay in the conditions created by the Poor
Law; the evils of the law of settlement, and the too indiscriminate giving of relief through the method of administration.

Of this also Dunning gives a useful illustration:

"Loose idle persons clamour for relief when they need none," he
says, "and if their demands be not satisfied complain to the J.Ps
who never do, nor can do less than order the Overseers to come
before them to answer and shew cause etc., and such Overseers as
live far from the J.P. will often give the clamourers relief merely to
save themselves a journey especially when they have the wit to
complain in a busy time[1]."

The overseer was unpaid, and he had to earn his own
living; in most of the townships of the North Riding he was
probably a small farmer. When a pauper threatened to
appeal to a Justice some distance away, in the sowing or
the reaping season, that was sufficient to gain the overseer's
consent to his importunity.

It is evident that the duties of the overseer, if they were
to be transacted with any degree of efficiency, were altogether
too extensive for the ordinary layman. They needed the
detailed, careful attention of a permanent official; they
could not be performed by the hard-working farmer or
tradesman in his scanty intervals of leisure.

[1] R. Dunning, *Plain and Easy method of showing how the office of Overseer of the Poor may be managed*, 1686 Ed. p. 13.

APPENDIX C

COPY OF AN INDENTURE OF AN APPRENTICE

North Riding of the County of York.

This INDENTURE made the seventh day of August in the year of Our Lord 1804, Between Michael Glenton and Robert Ward being the Major part of the Churchwardens & Overseers of the Poor of the Township of Wensley in the said Riding and Margaret Spensley a poor child of the said Township on the one part, and Robert Sweten of Barnard Castle in the County of Durham Weaver, on the other part, WITNESSETH, that the said Churchwardens & Overseers of the Poor have, by & with the Consent Allowance & Approbation of two of his Majesty's Justices of the Peace for the said North Riding put, placed, & bound the said Margaret Spensley as an apprentice to, & with the said Robert Sweten with him to dwell & remain from the Day of the Date hereof until the said Apprentice shall attain the age of Twenty one years, or Marriage according to the form of the statute made in that case & provided. During all which said Term her said Master well & truly shall serve, his Secrets shall keep his Commands (being lawful & honest) at all Times willingly shall perform; and in all Things as a good & faithful servant shall demean herself towards her said Master & all his Family And the said Robert Sweten, for himself, his Executors, Administrators & assigns, doth Covenant Promise and Agree to & with the said Churchwardens, Overseers, & his said Apprentice, that he will educate & bring her up in some honest & lawful calling, & in the fear of God. And the said Robert Sweten for himself his Executors & Administrators doth further Covenant Promise & Agree to & with the said Churchwardens, Overseers & this said apprentice that he will find, provide for & allow unto his said Apprentice sufficient wholesome & competent Meat, Drink, Washing, Lodging, Apparel and all other Necessaries meet for such an Apprentice during all the said Term. Provided always that the said last mentioned Covenant on the part of the said Robert Sweten, his Executors & Administrators to be done & performed shall continue & be in force for no longer than for three Calendar Months next after the death of the said Robert Sweten in case he the said Robert Sweten shall happen to die during the continuance of such apprenticeship according to the provisions of an Act passed in the 32nd year of the reign of King George the Third intitled, An act for the further regulation of Parish Apprentices.

In witness thereoff the said parties to these Presents have hereunto interchargeably set their Hands & Seals the Day & Year first above written

(*signed*)   MICHAEL GLENTON, Churchwarden.
ROBERT WARD, Overseer of the Poor.
ROBERT SWETEN, Master.

Sealed & delivered in the presence of
WM RIDLEY,
PAUL GREATHEAD.   (*signed*)

Allowed by us, two of his Majesty's Justices of the Peace for the said North Riding.
WM CHAYTOR,
WM CHAYTOR, Junr.

CHAPTER V

THE PETTY CONSTABLE

Shall not a man in authority be obeyed?
FORD, *Perkin Warbeck*, Act v. Sc. 3.

No account of the parish in the seventeenth century would be complete without a full and even detailed description of the office of the petty constable.

The parish might have existed without its surveyor, its overseers, or even its churchwardens, but assuredly not without its constable, since on him depended the continuance of order and stability in those restless and uncertain times. While estimating therefore the constable's position in the village cosmos, it will be necessary to discuss the origin of his powers and functions, and the sphere of his activity.

"By the ancient custom of the realm," says Lambard, "there is a great officer called the Constable of England who by means of the high authority which he had, was a principal stay unto the King's government[1]. The lower Constableship is a very finger of the hand of the Constable of England."

During the thirteenth century when legislation with regard to the maintenance of peace throughout the country (which had been initiated by Henry II's Assize of Arms and was finally summed up in the Statute of Winchester) was being gradually evolved, two officers called constables were ordered to view the arms in each hundred twice a year, and to enforce the ancient duties of watch and ward, hue and cry.

From very early times it was the custom for each township to elect in its local court certain tithingmen[2] to administer

---

[1] Lambard, *The Duties of Constables*, etc., Ed. 1631, p. 5.
[2] Blackstone, I. 356, 9th Ed. by Burn, 1783. "The Constable may do whatever the tythingman may but not e converse, the tithing man not having an equal power with the Constable."

its affairs. These men received the various titles of Reeve, Borsholder, Tythingman, Headborough, according to their various localities. It seems probable that for the aid and assistance of the constable of the hundred, one of these officials (the chief pledge or tithingman) was given the title of constable and held responsible by the Central Government[1] for the maintenance of peace within the township.

The tithingmen still continued to be elected, but the constable in virtue of the additional powers conferred on him by the state[2] took the chief place among them; witness for example, the importance with which Dogberry assumed the chief command, and the comparative insignificance of Verges. Lambard, who wrote in the seventeenth century an illuminating pamphlet on the duties of constables, declares that "where there be many tithingmen in one parish, there, only one of them is a constable for the king and the rest do serve but as the ancient tythingmen did[3]."

After he became a government official the constable received from time to time certain administrative powers, limited and defined by statute, for exceeding the authority of which or on the other hand for non-fulfilment he was liable to be punished; these later functions, however, were inferior to his ancient and customary rights and privileges[4].

For the constable held his office by no statute. His power was original and primitive, derived from ancient custom and recognised by the Common Law[5].

---

[1] At some period in the reign of Edward III. Blackstone, I. 356.

[2] 2 Ed. III, cap. iii. Petty constable in rural districts like mayors and bailiffs in urban districts to keep the peace.

4 Ed. III, cap. x. Constables designated as representatives of townships.

23 Ed. III, cap. i and 25 Ed. III, cap. i. Conferred powers on constables. H. B. Simpson, The Office of Constable, *E.H.R.* 1895.

[3] Lambard, *Duties of Constables*, Ed. 1631, p. 9.

[4] Coke, *Institutes*, Bk. IV. cap. liv. "Divers and many acts of Parliament have given Chief Constables and Petty Constables more authority and power than originally they had, but no officer constituted by Act of Parliament hath more authority than the Act which creates him or some subsequent Act of Parliament doth give him, for he cannot prescribe as the officer by the Common Law may."

[5] *Ibid.* Bk. IV. cap. liv. p. 265. Blackstone, I. 355, 9th Ed. by Burn, 1783.

He was elected and sworn in the Court Leet, a fact which in itself showed the antiquity of the office since the Leet "can be traced...to the earliest era of the English occupation[1]."

Sir Edward Coke declares

The Constable or Petty Constables are chosen by the Common Law at the Leet or Tourn and are by the Common Law Conservators of the Peace and may take surety of the peace by obligation and are as ancient as tourns or leets be.

Both Coke and Blackstone emphasise the fact that the petty constable had very considerable powers because he was an officer by the Common Law

"of the extent of which powers," says Blackstone, "considering what manner of men are for the most part put into these offices, it is perhaps very well that they are generally kept in ignorance."

The oath administered to the constable in the North Riding of Yorkshire was as follows:

You shall duly exercise your office of Constable of the township of A....and well and truly present all manner of bloodsheds assaults and affrays and outcrys there done and committed against the King's Majesty's peace: All manner of writs warrants and precepts to you lawfully directed you shall truly execute: the King's Majesty's peace in your own person you shall conserve and keep as much as in you lyeth: And in all other things that appertain to your office you shall well and truly behave yourself. So help you God and the contents of this book[2].

It will be noticed that no mention is made of recusants in this oath, as in that given by Dalton in *The Country Justice*. It is possible, therefore, that this may be the original oath taken when the petty constable first became the King's officer, at a time when there were no recusants, and his chief duties were the maintenance of the King's peace, and the execution of writs, warrants and precepts.

In the seventeenth century, if the constable could not be sworn in the Leet, he took the oath in the Court of Quarter

---

[1] Hearnshaw, *Court Leet, Introduction to Southampton Records*, vol. I. pt. i. p. ix.
[2] *N.R.Q.S.R.* vol. I. p. 183.

Sessions or, after the year 1662[1], in the presence of two Justices; since he was an officer at the common law he had to be sworn before he could legally perform his duties[2].

While possessing large and complete powers over the township by statute and by common law the constable was himself under the jurisdiction and command of the following officers:

1. The sheriff (as the King's representative in the shire) and his officers in the Court Leet.

2. The coroner, on whom he must attend "for the abjuring and conveying such persons as shall take the churchyard as a sanctuary for safeguard of their lives by occasion of any felony by them done[3]," and on whose warrant he must summon people competent to sit on a jury for a discovery of murder[4].

3. The bailiff of the liberty, or (4) the high constable of the wapentake, in which his township was situated. The latter exercised a general control over his actions and received in petty sessions the presentments he had to make, and the assessments it was his duty to collect.

But in their commission as conservators of the peace, the Justices were given a general supervision over all sheriffs, bailiffs, constables, etc., who had been careless or negligent in the execution of their duties and of the statutes[5]. As the influence of the sheriff declined before the growing power of the Justices, the high and petty constables came more and more under the supervision of these magistrates, whose sphere of action was local and direct, in contradistinction to the indirect and far removed control of the high sheriff of the county.

The Chief Constables presented to the Justices in Quarter

---

[1] 14 Car. II, cap. xii.

[2] *N.R.Q.S.R.* vol. v. p. 71. Thirsk Quarter Sessions, Ap. 1651. Information was laid by a sworn informer against Ralph Powthwaite "for arresting a man not being sworn beforehand."

[3] Lambard, *Duties of Constables*, etc., p. 26.

[4] See *The Compleat Constable*, J. Paul, 1785, p. 21.

[5] Commission for the Justices of the Peace, Clause ii. Prothero, *Select Statutes*, 3rd Ed., p. 45.

Sessions the offences of the petty constables in their several wapentakes; out of sessions also individual Justices exercised a very potent jurisdiction over the constables of the townships in their immediate neighbourhood.

Though the constable is mentioned with the churchwarden as a parish officer and in the administration of many Acts of Parliament was associated with the surveyor, the overseers, and the churchwardens, yet with the parish as a unit of government he was not concerned, for his jurisdiction extended only over his own township. Some parishes, therefore, had two, three or more constables according to the number of their townships. The parish of Burneston in the North Riding consists of the townships of Burneston, Carthorpe, Exelby Leeming and Newton, Gatenby and Theakstone. In 1615 the following men held the office of constable: Christopher Gatenby for Burneston, Christopher Raper for Carthorpe, Edward Atkinson for Gatenby, John Fall for Theakstone, Christopher Tennant for Exelby Leeming and Newton[1]. In such a case the remaining officers had to deal with each constable according to the particular locality in the parish over which his jurisdiction extended.

The arrangement, though unforeseen, was of advantage in the North Riding, where the parishes are extensive in area, for the duties of the constable so far exceeded in number and variety those of any other local official that it would have been impossible in a large parish for one man to perform them, and at the same time pursue his own occupation. As a general rule the area of a constabulary contained only one village or hamlet and the surrounding land which belonged to the original vill. In a case where a township consisted of two or more hamlets the constable was allowed to appoint deputies: in 1678, for example, the constable of the above-mentioned township of Exelby Leeming and Newton obtained power from the Court of Quarter Sessions to appoint two deputies, one for Leeming and another for Newton.

[1] *N.R.Q.S.R.* vol. ii. p. 104. Richmond, July, 1615.

THE DUTIES OF THE CONSTABLE

The work of the constable in the parish government, whether considered from the point of view of his duties at the common law or with regard to his statutory obligations, has for its main characteristic that of a police officer, a conservator of the peace.

If a quarrel broke out in his presence he must not let it go too far: when words ran high he must warn the disputants before they came to blows. He must discriminate as to what exactly was the distinction between a lawful and an unlawful assembly of people, and in the latter case he must command it to disperse. He must listen to all complaints, and decide whether a suspected person were guilty enough to justify a warrant of arrest, and, having arrested a man, he must keep him in safe custody until the day of trial. It was also his duty to see that the various statutes passed for the good ordering of mankind were not violated in his township; there must be no cursing and swearing, no unlawful games, no sitting tippling in alehouses, no eating of flesh on fast days, no profaning of the Sabbath Day, either by absence from church or by unlawful work; but every man must provide himself with suitable arms; the fathers must teach their sons the use of the bow; parents must bind their children apprentice; masters and servants must be content to give and receive neither more nor less than the wage laid down by the Justices of the Peace. Rogues and vagabonds must be summarily sent to their native places; minstrels and wandering players of interludes must not be allowed to corrupt the King's liege people; wherever a market was held, the various trade regulations affecting corn, butter, malt, weights and measures, etc., must be enforced. In short, the constable must apprehend, take charge of and present for trial all persons who broke the laws, written or unwritten, against the King's peace or against the statutes of the realm, and, when judgment was delivered, in many cases he had to inflict the punishment or levy the fine.

All rogues and vagabonds found begging, hedge-breakers, robbers of orchards and gardens, cutters of corn and wood, apprentices who had misbehaved themselves, were to be summarily whipped by the constable at the bidding of a Justice of the Peace, and should this unfortunate amateur policeman refuse to execute this part of his work, he could be sent to prison "there to be kept without bail or main-prise until he submitted."

The constable had moreover to carry out sentences inflicted on offenders by the Justices of the Peace, acting separately, together, or in Quarter Sessions, or by the Leet in places where the Courts Leet were still held. He must also execute the commands of the Justices of Gaol Delivery, of Oyer and Terminer, and of the Coroners. If a fire broke out in the parish, the constable had to be present to prevent any goods being stolen. If any particular bit of work had to be done for the good of the whole village, the constable commanded the various householders to come and give their labour. Henry Best of Elmswell notes down in his diary for Nov. 19, 1642: "I made the sheepe dike in the towne becke by How-samlane ende, and William Whitehead would not sende any helpe to make it, but gave the Constable Richard Parrat, ill wordes, and called him slave when he wished him to come to helpe; so that he is not to wash any sheepe there[1]."

In some cases he was the rate collector for the township, and was empowered to seize the goods of any person refusing to pay an assessment, sell them, and take the money for the rate, giving back to the owner the overplus. He was associated with the churchwardens in the administration of the Poor Law, and of the Statute of Labourers and Apprentices. He was also the executive officer of the surveyor, in that he must order people to come to their common days' work on the roads and present them if they refused[2]. Every year in Easter week, it was the duty of the constable and the church-

---

[1] Rural Economy in Yorkshire, *S.S.P.* vol. XXXIII. p. 163.
[2] See *N.R.Q.S.R.* vol. I. pp. 201, 212, 231.

wardens to call a meeting at which the surveyor was appointed and the time of the common days' works arranged.

Many were the meetings which the constable was expected to attend. Every month he had to meet with the other parish officers to consider the administration of the various statutes for which they were responsible. Four times a year it was his duty to attend upon the Justices in the Court of Quarter Sessions, on pain of a fine of 20s. for non-appearance.

Four times also in between the Quarter Sessions he had to attend the Statute or Petty Sessions of the High Constable.

Twice a year he was bound to appear before the Justices to give an account of the rogues and vagabonds found in his constabulary.

Such then being the chief duties imposed on the constable, it remains to be seen in what way and how far they were performed by him in the rural townships which make up a large part of the North Riding. The minutes and orders of the Court of Quarter Sessions held in the seventeenth century show that the Justices kept a steady control over both high and petty constables. From time to time as they awakened to the fact that certain evils were prevalent, they issued charges to the high constables, to be sent later to the petty constables in the several wapentakes.

If an affray took place in the presence of the constable, he had immediately to make proclamation "that the affrayers shall keep the King's Peace." When the affair seemed likely to become dangerous he had to part the fighters, and might even imprison them for a short time in the stocks "until their heat be over or until they should find sureties for the peace," but a quarrel was not to be considered an affray unless weapons were drawn, nor might the constable arrest the affrayors without a Justice's warrant, unless he had reason to think that someone was in some peril of death[1]. The constable in his role of peacemaker had

---

[1] Dalton, *The Country Justice*, chap. viii. p. 34.

not an easy task nor did he always come out of it scatheless.

John Stubbs of Wath was presented before the Court at Richmond for making an assault and affray (on Christmas last in John Tanfield's house) on one John Stapleton in Wath and also for abusing Jas Harrison Constable of Wath, reviling him and pulling away a great part of his beard, when commanding the said Christopher to keep the peace when he made the affray aforesaid[1].

Sometimes the injury was quite serious. A Crayke yeoman presented "for wounding and stabbing the Constable" of his village, on submission was fined £5[2]; from the heavy fine it may be inferred that the constable was severely hurt.

But taking into account the number of constables in the North Riding and the fact that the seventeenth century was an age when political and religious passions were deeply stirred, the presentments for abuse seem remarkably few. Probably even in his anger a man realised the constable was merely an instrument of the law, which he in his turn would have to execute. The constable, moreover, had the protection of the law beyond other men; even if, in his effort to keep order, he wounded or slew a man, yet he was held guiltless; moreover, if an assault were made on a Justice or a constable, the offenders could be summarily taken and put in the stocks and detained until they had found sureties that they would keep the peace.

The constable also could maintain the dignity of his office through his power of presenting offenders at the Quarter Sessions. At Thirsk in 1661[3]

A Glaisdale man was presented for speaking publishing and uttering divers false scandalous and approbrious words of the Constable of Glaisdale viz. "that he is a rogue and deserves a withy and to have

---

[1] *N.R.Q.S.R.* vol. I. p. 210. Richmond, Jan. 1611.

Vol. I. p. 241. Richmond, Oct. 1611. Thomas Walworth and his wife presented "for assault on the Constable of Birkby, also George Walworth of Birkby for beating the Constable and hurling stones at him."

Vol. III. p. 160. Richmond, Jan. 1623. Two yeomen and their wives and a third yeoman all of Gale are presented "for a riotous assault on Jenkin Rowthe, Constable there."

[2] *Ibid.* vol. v. p. 173. Kirbymoorside, Jan. 1654.

[3] *Ibid.* vol. vi. p. 34. Thirsk, April, 1661.

his ears nailed to the pillory," to the great damage and discredit of the said Constable in the execution of his said office.

"O that I had been writ down an ass![1]" said Dogberry, knowing that such an insult recorded before witnesses would have greatly increased Conrade's offence. Nevertheless, at Quarter Sessions the degree of the offence seems to have been considered more in proportion to the rank of the party injured, than with regard to the actual crime, since the fines imposed for insulting words spoken to, or of, a Justice are always heavy, while those for an attack on the constable seem comparatively moderate. The fines vary also in accordance with the political conditions of the time. In 1610 a man is fined 2s. "for breaking the Constable's head[2]," but in 1656 for "assaulting and threatening the Constable in the execution of his office" a yeoman and his wife have to pay 10s. each[3].

Since a broken head was only assessed at 2s. it behoved the constable to have a care for his own safety, and in 1632 one "Tho Williamson Constable of Bagby declared on oath that if any Justices' warrants come to him there is such disorder kept in Eliz[th] Simondson's house that he dare not execute them there," therefore the court ordered "the said Elizabeth to be disabled from brewing for three years, and a warrant, etc., to take her two sons Rob and John bound to appear, etc.[4]," they being evidently the persons known to have contributed to the disorder of the alehouse. Yet Thomas Williamson need not have entered alone into the said Elizabeth's unruly house, for in the execution of his duty the constable could demand help in his Majesty's name, or by showing his magistrate's warrant, from any person and could present such a one for trial at Quarter Sessions if he refused to give it.

[1] *Much Ado about Nothing,* Act IV. Sc. 2.
[2] *N.R.Q.S.R.* Vol. I. p. 93. Helmsley, July, 1610.
[3] *Ibid.* Vol. v. p. 218. Malton, July, 1656.
[4] *Ibid.* vol. III. p. 334. Malton, July, 1632.

In 1609 Richard Tiplady, late of Whitwell Super Monterre black-smith was presented at Helmsley for refusing to help Roger Cowper Constable of the same, when required to do so, in the apprehension of certain criminals, the warrant of Robt Hungate Esq being duly exhibited[1].

Richard Tiplady submitted and was only fined five shillings because he was a poor man, but two years previously

Robert Harrison of Middleton for refusing to assist the Constable, being commanded in his Majesties name, for the attacking of Raphe Newell was fined xx*s*.[2]

The constable was bound by his original oath to execute any writs, warrants, and precepts to him lawfully directed; moreover, Lambard, writing in the seventeenth century, declares that a constable must execute any warrant of a Justice even though the Justice may have exceeded his authority in giving it[3]. This may have arisen from the fact that the superior officers could not have their authority questioned by their inferiors, and indeed the Justices held all the cards, for the same Justice who issued the warrant could also present the unruly constable to be judged by his fellow-magistrates on the Bench. They would certainly up-hold his authority in case they experienced the like.

On the other hand the constable soon got into trouble if he exceeded the limits of his jurisdiction, or made mistakes in the time or place of executing warrants. He must not execute a warrant on a Sunday, nor must he enter a liberty. In 1680 a New Malton labourer was presented for executing warrants from the County Court within the liberty of Whitby Strand without the permission of Sir Hugh Cholmley. This part of his duty was evidently very disagreeable work and to be avoided if possible. A certain Raphe Awmond, con-stable of Thirsk in 1611, was given a warrant by Sir Henry Tankard, J.P., for the apprehension of one John Carter for

---

[1] *N.R.Q.S.R.* vol. I. p. 141. Helmsley, Jan. 1609.   [2] *Ibid.* vol. I. p. 91.
[3] Lambard, *Duties of Constables, Borsholders*, etc., p. 18.

misdemeanours by him committed, which warrant was not executed for six weeks. One day Sir Henry Tankard met the constable and Francis Cawton of Thirsk, a tanner. The matter came up and the constable boldly told Sir Henry that he would not go into men's houses to serve any warrant: moreover Cawton said, when questioned by Sir Henry, that if he were constable he would do the like; at which Sir Henry told the said Cawton that he would commit him for his boldness. Whereupon Cawton evidently lost his temper and replied saying "that Sir Henry would comitt a pudding" "using withal other disgraceful speeches to the further encouragement of the said neglectful and contemptuous constable[1]." Therefore both Awmond and Cawton were brought up for trial. The constable was fined 10s. and had to enter bond for good behaviour. His friend, the tanner, was ordered to be committed to York Castle, "there to remain without bail or mainprise for the space of 10 days," and before his delivery he also had to enter bond for good behaviour. As Cawton remained unsubdued he was not even given the option of a fine. However, before the court departed "the said Cawton by petition submitted himself and thereupon his imprisonment and good behaviour was released and he *only* fined 13s. 4d." Evidently an insult to a Justice was held to be a more serious offence than neglect of duty.

Thus the Justices wielded a strong hand over those under their jurisdiction and no constable could disobey their orders with impunity[2].

Not only fighting, but every murder, rape, manslaughter and felony whatsoever, and every affraying and putting in fear of the King's people, whether it be by unlawful wearing of armour, or by assembling of people to do any unlawful act; are taken to be disturbances or breaches of the Peace.

[1] *N.R.Q.S.R.* vol. I. pp. 216–217. Thirsk, April, 1611.
[2] *Ibid.* vol. I. p. 268. Northallerton, July, 1616. "That Will Haynes and Will Richeson, Constables of Allerton, be fined 5s. each for not executing a Warrant from Sir Arthur Dakins for the apprehension of John Wasse."
"That John Wasse of Allerton, on his submission, be fined 2s. 6d. etc."

The constable might take or arrest suspected persons "which walk in the night or sleep in the day," and carry them before a Justice of the Peace to find sureties for their good behaviour[1].

To avoid breaches of the peace, to prevent visitations of the plague through infected people, it was necessary that someone should always be on the look out to prevent suspicious characters from entering into the township; thus an important daily or weekly duty of the constable was the appointing of suitable people for the watch since he was the man to blame if anything went wrong[2].

The constable of Gilling was summoned before the court for compelling a poore old blinde man not able to see the light of a candle to watch the whole towne in his course of vicinitie this last summer, in the time of the visitation (*i.e.* the plague) of Newcastle and the Bishoppricke of Duresme, to the great dainger of the inhabs of Gillinge[3].

The duty of watch and ward as in the case of other parish offices seems to have depended on the occupation of houses or land[4].

A certain order was observed in keeping the watch, different well-known customs holding in different villages, and no man could refuse, when warned by the constable that the turn had come to his house[5].

[1] Lambard, *Duties of Constables, Borsholders*, etc., p. 11.
[2] *N.R.Q.S.R.* vol. v. p. 132. Thirsk, April, 1653. The constable of Egton for neglecting his duty in setting the watch there when Henry Jackson was slain is fined 6s. 8d.
   Vol. I. p. 199. Topcliffe, Oct. 1610. "Geo Sadler and Will Reade Constables of Yarme, for negligence in their office, viz. at diverse tymes neglecting the setting and keeping of the watch in the tyme of the visitation in diverse places &c since June 1st last; and for not punishing of rogues &c; and for that they have both bene absent many tymes when great occasion for his Maties service did happen, to the evill example &c."
[3] *Ibid.* vol. IV. p. 69. Richmond, Jan. 1637.
[4] *Ibid.* vol. IV. p. 225. Thirsk, April, 1642. "A Barmeby gentleman for not paying the sum of two shillings in which he was assessed by the inhabts of the said vill, according to an ancient custom of the said inhabts, called a Bylaw, for lands in his occupation there, as his proportion for the maintenance of the watch which they had been directed to keep by Order of the Justices of Peace at York lately assembled. A yeoman of the City of York for the like, for lands in his occupation at the same place, his asst. amounting to £12."
[5] *Ibid.* vol. I. p. 50. Malton, Oct. 1606. "Cuthbert Cowston of Normanby

It was incumbent on everyone, and an order from the court was necessary to free a man from this obligation[1]: in some places an assessment was made on lands to maintain the watch, and doubtless the richer people usually paid a deputy. All references to the watch tend to show that it was kept by men in a humble position; yet there are various entries of yeomen keeping (or not keeping)[2] the watch; Brian Stapleton of Bedale, who was of gentle birth, and evidently of good estate, on being presented for refusing to keep the watch in Bedale was ordered by the court "on lawful warning to do as the other inhabitants there."

Disputes concerning the liability of individuals or of hamlets in the same township to keep watch[3] were frequently referred to the Court of Quarter Sessions. When plague was over the land, watch had to be kept during the day as well as the night. In 1607 the Bench ordered the petty constables to be warned "that the day watch be forthwith diligently kept for the avoiding the danger of infected people and the suppressing of rogues and vagrant persons[4]."

Outbreaks of plague were so frequent in the early years of the seventeenth century that in 1604 the petty constable received by statute[5] governmental powers for one year, in

when commanded by the Constable to take the night watch, when it came to his course, refusing to kepe the night watch, in contempt &c and thereby no watch was kept that night."

[1] *N.R.Q.S.R.* vol. III. p. 121. Richmond, July, 1621. The court ordered "eight men to be discharged of their ordinary day and night watch in Brompton, by reason of their dwelling in new erected houses distant from the said towne."

Ibid. vol. VI. p. 63. Richmond, Jan. 1663. "The hamlets and outhouses of Holnaby and Warmire in the Constablery of Croft, to keep day watch and night watch proportionally in the town of Croft or pay according to the value of their estates as often as any watches shall be required."

[2] *Ibid.* vol. VI. p. 67. Richmond, July, 1663. "Six yeomen of Halnaby in the Constablery of Croft, for neglecting to keep the watch."

[3] *Ibid.* vol. I. "At Richmond Oct. 1610 the inhabitants of Little Busbie are presented for not keeping their watch within the Constablery of Busbies Ambo and it is agreed that the said inhabitants shall contribute in money with those of Great Busby for the keeping of the watch within the said Constablery for every third day viz for the third part of that Constablerie."

[4] *Ibid.* vol. I. p. 73. Thirsk, April, 1607.

[5] I Jac. I, cap. xxxi.

that he could order infected persons to keep within their houses. To carry out this order and to prevent people who had suffered from plague entering the township, the keeping of the day watch was strictly enforced and people who neglected it got into trouble[1].

In the North Riding the Justices issued charges from time to time to the high constables concerning the watch. In 1619 they order warrants to be made for the keeping of the day watch "as hath been accustomed for the three years last past sealed with the seal of the office and signed by the Clerk of the Peace[2]."

In 1642 the high constables were ordered to disperse copies of the Justices' warrant "for the diligent and carefull keepinge of the watch[3]." In 1665 most stringent precautions were to be taken to keep out of the Riding all people coming from London[4], and to watch the houses of persons who had received visitors from the infected city. Such diligent and careful keeping of the watch occupied many men and the plague took no heed of seed-time or harvest when it visited the land, therefore watchmen were specially hired, and received the wage of an ordinary day-labourer[5].

Usually the watch varied in number from four to eight, according to the size of the township. One of the four was appointed to take the lead and "bear the lantern," and was called the constable of the watch[6].

The watchmen received their charge from the "master constable." "You are to bid any man stand in the Prince's name"; if anything of importance occurred they called up "the right master constable."

---

[1] N.R.Q.S.R. vol. I. p. 9. Stokesley, July, 1605. John Hooge and Richard Rymer of Bagley are presented "for not keeping their watch in the day time."
    Ibid. vol. I. pp. 260–1. Leon Ruddocke of Loftus and Tho. Reave of Kinthorpe lab[r] presented "for not keeping the day watch."
[2] Ibid. vol. II. p. 202. Thirsk, April, 1619.
[3] See Appendix D.   [4] N.R.Q.S.R. vol. VI. pp. 92–3. See Appendix D.
[5] In 1637 and 1638, when the plague was raging the watchmen at Buttercrambe were paid 18d. a week for sixteen weeks each year. Ibid vol. IV. p. 99. Malton, July, 1638.
[6] Much Ado about Nothing, Act III. Sc. 3.

Taking into account that the humour of a situation to the generation for which it is written often lies in its nearness to, yet distance from, truth, the immortal Dogberry and his confrères give us much general information concerning the watch and its conception of its duties.

THE HUE AND CRY

The constable had not only to prevent affrays in his township but also to ensure that no breaker of the peace was allowed to escape. If a felon, or even a person suspected of felony, fled out of, or came into, the township, the constable was expected to take the initiative in raising the alarm, for he alone had legal authority to enforce his orders[1], he alone could and did present at the Quarter Sessions anyone who disobeyed him[2]. When the constable raised the hue and cry, all the inhabitants of the township had to take part in it on horseback and on foot[3]. They turned out of their homes with knives, bows and arrows—those weapons which they were expected to keep ready for such emergencies—and crying, "Out, Out," blowing their horns with shouting and uproar streamed after the fugitive. As the noise travelled over into the next township, so its constable must make his people take up the pursuit: thus "the hue will be horned from vill to vill[4]." If a murderer escaped, the township was fined for negligence[5], if a robbery was committed, and no township in the wapentake had captured the thief, the whole wapentake was held responsible and an assessment was levied on it to pay to the person robbed the value of

[1] 1 Ed. III, cap. ix.
[2] *N.R.Q.S.R.* vol. I. p. 215. Lawrence Poker of Lynton presented at Thirsk "for refusing to carry an hue and cry to Lynton being commanded by the Constable."
[3] 27 Eliz. cap. xiii.
[4] Pollock and Maitland, *History of English Law*, Bk. II. ch. ix. p. 576.
[5] *N.R.Q.S.R.* vol. V. p. 199. Thirsk, Oct. 1655. "The inhab[ts] of Warthill were indicted for suffering one Nick Oxard, a felon, to escape, and did not make fresh pursuite to apprehend him, whereby the felon escaped justice, the said inhab[ts] have appeared and submitted to the indictment, and were fined 100 markes, to be estreated and returned into the Exchequer."

the stolen goods: moreover every wapentake through which the thief fled had to take its share in making good the loss[1]. At the Thirsk Sessions, October, 1655, the following order (typical of many) is made[2]:

Whereas upon the 20th day of September last there was a robbery committed upon Mr Robert Berry within the wapentake of Allertonshire, who had £138 taken from him, and whereas also the Constable of Beedall did neglect to pursue the robers with hue and cry, who came through the town of Beedall...the inhabitants of Hallikeld and the inhabitants of Hang East shall pay £124 equally betwixt them which the said Mr Berry is willing to take in full satisfaction for the moneys taken from him as aforesaid.

The robbers evidently took a straight line from Allertonshire through the northernmost part of Hallikeld to Bedale, which is in the wapentake of Hang East, so they would probably only pass through one township of Hallikeld— Leeming Exelby-cum-Newton—nevertheless Hallikeld had to share with Hang East in making good the loss.

In days when there were no banks men travelled about with large sums of money and it was very necessary to enforce the local responsibility of maintaining security from robbery.

But while the township or the wapentake had to make recompense as a penalty for negligence, if a constable let a man accused of felony escape while in his custody he himself became a felon and "the judges of his fault may set his fine equal with the value of all his goods if in their discretions his defaults do so require[3]." Generally, therefore, an arrested person was placed for safety in the village stocks[4] until he could be taken before the nearest Justice or conveyed to jail. If he escaped out of the township, then the constable must seize his goods[5]: in any case so many of his goods

---

[1] By 27 Eliz. cap. xiii.
[2] In *N.R.Q.S.R.* vol. v. p. 96.
[3] Lambard, *The Duties of Constables, Borsholders*, etc., p. 22.
[4] *N.R.Q.S.R.* vol. III. p. 168. Helmsley, July, 1623. "A Thornton in le Moor woman presented for breaking the stocks and liberating a man arrested on suspicion of felony and placed in them for safe custody by Christopher Parkinson, Constable there."
[5] *The Exact Constable*, by E.W., 2nd ed. 1660, p. 24.

might be seized as would defray the cost of taking him to
jail. If, however, the offender had no goods, then a tax
allowed under the hand of a Justice of the Peace was to be
laid on the parish, township or tithing by the constables and
churchwardens, or in default of them by four of the principal
inhabitants, and if anyone refused to pay this tax then his
goods might be distrained[1].

Having apprehended an offender against the laws the
constable must forthwith take him before a Justice of
the Peace who examined him, and if he were guilty of a
petty offence, imposed the punishment, or if the case were
more serious committed him, either with or without bail, to
be tried at the Quarter Sessions or at the Assizes. In the
seventeenth century cases which at the present day would
be tried in the Petty Sessions of the magistrates, and in the
Middle Ages in the Courts Leet, were presented for trial at
Quarter Sessions owing to the fact that in many places Leets
had ceased to be held. Such offences were those committed
against the community by swearing, drunkenness, forcible
entry into land and houses, or into the pinfold, the cutting
down of wood or grain[2], the selling of goods on the Sabbath
day, the inordinate price of provisions[3], and the destruction
of game and fish[4]; also the enforcement of the laws concerning the provision of men trained to archery, the amendment of the highways, the laying down of four acres of land
to every cottage, the various regulations to ensure good husbandry, such as those for the preservation of the breed of
horses and all other statutes which affected the life of the
parish. The constable presented these offences, made returns

[1] Lambard, *The Duties of Constables, Borsholders*, etc., p. 27.
[2] 37 H. VIII, cap. vi. sec. iv (wood); 43 Eliz. cap. vii (grain); 15 Car. II,
cap. ii. sec. ii–iv. (wood).
[3] 32 H. VIII, cap. xiv; 7 Eliz. cap. v. Against great prices and excess of wines.
    [4] P. and M. cap. iii concerning butters.
[4] 14 H. VIII. cap. ii. Concerning tracing and killing of hares
    23 Eliz. cap. 10. Against taking of pheasants and partridges.
    1 Eliz. cap. 17 and 1 Jac. I, cap. 25 for the preservation of the spawn
and fry of fish.
    22 and 23 Car. II, cap. xxv. sec. vii. Not to use net, etc., without
consent of lord or owner of the water.

of wages, and of alehouses, and delivered over the assessments he had collected to the high constable at the statute
sessions held by the latter before every Quarter Sessions. If
he neglected his duties in any respect he was liable to be
presented himself by the high constable. The small township of Hackforth had its constable presented for three years
in succession and for a different offence in each case. The
first constable was presented because he did not meet with
the churchwardens in Easter week to appoint surveyors for
highways[1], the next "is so negligent that he will present
nothing[2]," and the third "neither punishes rogues nor
searches alehouses[3]." Nor was this the worst that befell;
three years later the constable of Hackforth was fined 20s.
"for making default when summoned to appear and make
presentments of such popish recusants and alehousekeepers
as remain within his constablery[4]."

On the constable also fell the unpleasant task of executing
summary punishment on offenders. He could demand assistance from anyone[5], but if he refused to perform this part of
his work he was heavily fined or sent to prison without the
option of bail[6]. Every parish had to keep in repair its instru-

---

[1] *N.R.Q.S.R.* vol. I. p. 171. Richmond, Oct. 1609.
[2] *Ibid.* vol. I. p. 201. Topcliffe, Oct. 1610.
[3] *Ibid.* vol. I. p. 234. Thirsk, April, 1612.
[4] *Ibid.* vol. II. p. 104. Richmond, July, 1615.
[5] *Ibid.* vol. I. pp. 71–2. "In 1607 Richard Seamer of Yarm, and Henry
Thompson a glover presented for refusing to help John Robinson the
Constable for the punishing of certain rogues and vagabonds resorting to
the market town of Yarm."
　　Ibid. vol. I. p. 133. Malton, Oct. 1608.
　　"Forasmuch as Thos. Stowpe and Will Fletcher of Gisbrough being
commanded by the Constable there to whipp a vagrant person or sturdie
beggar there taken, contemptuouslie refused, and for that Richard Yonger,
John Smith and Richard Atkinson, of the same being commanded in
default of the other to execute that service," did, "in neglect of justice
therein, strike their rods against the posts in the street, instead of the
rogue to give coulour as though they had cruelly beaten him, whereas
afterwards upon view there appeared no show of any stroak upon his
back or shoulders, that such remisness in officers may be punished...a
warrant be made to take them bound to appear etc."
[6] Dalton, *The Country Justice*, 1635, chap. lvii. Trespass, p. 139.
　　"If the Constable neglected to execute the Justice's warrant for drunk-
eness he forfeited ten shillings to the use of the Poor. If he refused to whip

ments of punishment[1], its whipping post, and ducking stool,
for

> there dwelt
> A potent monarch call'd the Constable
> That does command a citadel called the stocks[2],

into which the undutiful daughter[3], the wandering rogue or
cut-purse[4], the brawler[5], the thief[6], the traitor, were hustled
and padlocked by the orders of the amateur policeman,
aided by a shouting rabble[7] who held it no disgrace to be
"laid aside" for a few hours. Sometimes the offenders were
ordered to be taken to the nearest market town to sit in the
stocks there the whole market time with a paper on their
heads showing their offence[8].

a man who had been convicted before a Justice for keeping an alehouse
without license and who had not enough goods to pay the fine of twenty
shillings then the Justice could commit the Constable to the common gaol
without bail until he agreed to perform his duties or until he paid a fine
of forty shillings."

[1] *N.R.Q.S.R.* vol. I. p. 56. Richmond, Oct. 1606.
"That in the towne of Langthorne aforesaid there is neither stockes
nor cockinstole for the punishment of offenders."

[2] Massinger, *A new way to pay old debts*, Act I. Sc. I.

[3] *N.R.Q.S.R.* vol. III. p. 260. Northallerton, 1626.
"Margery wife of Miles Metcalfe of Cracall to be sett in the stocks at
Bedall, in full markett time, with a paper on her head written with great
letters: 'I SITT HERE IN THE STOCKS FOR BEATINGE MY OWNE
MOTHER,' and there to remaine until such time as she shall sitt downe
upon her knees and submitte herselfe to her mother, and crave her bles-
singe: [Rob. Storr and Chr. Smith, Cons^bles^ of Bedale, are to see this Order
performed]."

[4] *Ibid.* vol. I. p. 52. Malton, Oct. 1606.
"Will Worsley and Rob. Cootes being brought into Court for suspicion
of purses cutting and are noted to be wandring roagues, be sett in the
stockes at Malton, and there after soundly whipped and to have their
passport according to lawe, &c."

[5] *Ibid.* vol. V. p. 162. Malton, July, 1654.
"John Petch, for his cursing and execrating and rude carriage in the
face of the Court, to pay 3s. 4d. for the use of the poor of New Malton,
or to be set in the publique stocks the space of three hours, and enter bond
to appear etc., and meantime be of good behaviour."

[6] *Ibid.* vol. I. p. 67. Richmond, Jan. 1606.
"John Whitton of Langton, for sheep stealing shalbe sett in the stocks
in Richmond and to be well whipped from the waist upward."

[7] See *Perkin Warbeck*, Act V. Sc. 3. The rabble on the orders of the
Constable do the work.

[8] See note 3. The constable of Crakehall would have to conduct the
undutiful Margery to Bedale a distance of about three miles as appears
from the following order made at Huton.
N.R.Q.S.R. vol. II. p. 121. Bushell special Sessions in 1616.
"Isabel Grainge of Ruswarp, widdow, John Smith and Thomas Gage

Though ducking in the nearest stream was still the penalty inflicted on scolding women in the seventeenth century, instances of this punishment are rare in the Quarter Sessions records.

In 1658 the Court ordered Margery Watson of Whitby, being a scold, to be ducked by the constable "unless she within a month do ask James Wilkinson and his wife forgiveness in Whitby church publicly, and at the cross in the market town there[1]." The month was January; it is to be hoped that the said Margery Watson came to a humble frame of mind before its close.

But far worse than the stocks and the ducking-stool was the public whipping inflicted on men and women alike for petty larceny[2], and on all "rogues and wandering people[3]." Frequently after being whipped the unfortunate wretch was placed in the stocks as an additional punishment. Persons who had been detained in the House of Correction were sent back to their native places on their release by the assistance of the constables. One man is returned in this way to Garsin[4] in Scotland, another to a parish in Kent[5]. Thus the

of the same shalbe sett in the stocks in Whitby town on Sat. 13 April instant and these shall sitt from 8 of the clocke in the morning until 5 of the clocke in the afternoon and that they shalbe brought by the Constable of Ruswarp unto Whitby and there shalbe delivered by him to the Constables of Whitby to se execution done."
    N.R.Q.S.R. vol. I. p. 132. Malton, Oct. 1608.
    "Fr Booth of Egton, having beaten the Constable of Whitby, and being bound thereupon and being now in Court be fyned 5s., and to sit in the Stockes at Whitby upon some markett daie in full tyme of the markett."
    [1] *Ibid.* vol. v. p. 262. Helmsley, Jan. 1658.
    [2] *Ibid.* vol. I. p. 74. Thirsk, April, 1607. "Richard Shacklock of Yafford, found stealing a pair of shoes at Thirske, brought into Court with the shoes in his possession and confessing the theft, be sett in the stocks, (Sedente curia) be soundlie whipped, and bound over to good behaviour and to appear &c." *Ibid.* vol. I. pp. 140–141. Helmsley, Jan. 1609. "Agnes Egglesfield, late of New Malton for stealing there 'unum pheltrum Angl. a felt hatt' value 10d., the property of John Jackson &c. (Confessed: sentenced to be whipped and set in the stocks at Malton, with a paper on her head, &c.)."
    [3] *Ibid.* vol. I. p. 11. In 1605 the constables of Sutton are presented because "they allowed 4 women 'vagrantes more Egyptianorum' to stay n the said village and go forth unpunished though previously warned by the Chief Constable."
    [4] *Ibid.* vol. v. p. 180. Richmond, Jan. 1655.
    [5] *Ibid.* vol. IV. p. 58. Richmond, July, 1636. "A man who had been

North Riding got rid of undesirable characters but in every case at the cost of two or three hours taken from the working day of numerous petty constables.

The constable could not legally charge for the time spent in doing this part of his work until after 1662[1], though he was accustomed to collect "constable's lays" for his expenses long before this date, and if people refused to pay he generally got redress from the justices[2].

QUALIFICATION FOR THE OFFICE OF PETTY CONSTABLE

As the constable's office was unpaid and involved very disagreeable duties, properly speaking no qualification was demanded, and exemptions were eagerly sought after. The constable had to be a lay person but not a woman[3]. The manuals written to assist him in the performance of his duty lay stress on the fact that the constable should be "idoneus" which "in law means having honesty, knowledge, and ability[4]." He should also possess respectability of character, integrity, activity, firmness, discretion and humanity[5]. He

committed to the House of Correction for misdemeanours done and outrageous words to Sir Tho Posth Hoby, and abuseing his authority of Justice of Peace in a most indecent manner, has suffered eight weeks imprisonment and punishment, is now to be released and sent from Constable to Constable to the parish in Kent in which he had lived for six years last past."

[1] 13 and 14 Car. II.
N.R.Q.S.R. vol. VI. p. 111. Richmond, Jan. 1667. "The late Constable of Downeholme is presented for not paying to the late Constable of Hudswell 2s. for conveying certain persons from Constablery to Constablery."

[2] *Ibid.* vol. III. p. 356. Richmond, 1633. "Inhabts. of Bolton cum Ellerton and Whitwell for refusing to pay Sim. Somerside Constable, for keeping two women taken for breakinge a house at Richmond, two nights and one daie and for conveyinge them to York Castle 17s. being disbursed by him for that service."

[3] Yet a woman seems to have held the office at least once in the North Riding. *Ibid.* vol. VII. p. 153. Thirsk, April, 1695. "Ordered that Anne Sigsworth and her son be discharged from the Office of Constable for the town of Great Smeaton, and that Rob Glover of the same appear before some J.P. to be sworn Constable for the said town, and the inhabts of Great Smeaton to pay unto the said Anne Sigsworth such money as she shall fairly make appear she hath disbursed for the said town."

[4] *The Office of Constable*, J. Ritson, ed. 1791.
[5] *The Exact Constable*, E.W., 2nd ed. 1660.

should be able to read and write and have a sufficient degree
of bodily strength. James Gyffon who was constable of
Alburye in Surrey wrote a pathetic ballad about the trials
and troubles of a constable's life; how he was at everyone's
beck and call and could please no one. He, too, insists that
to perform his work adequately the constable must have
strong character and bodily vigour to enable him to get
through his strenuous year of office.

> A Constable must be honest and just,
> Have knowledge and good report
> And able to straine with body and brain,
> Ells he is not fitting for 't.

But James Gyffon realised that the work may enlarge a
man's mind and develop his political insight.

> The Constable's warned to the Sessions then
> Unwilling some goes alas!
> Yet there may he wit and experience lern
> If that he be not an asse.

It is possible that the worthy constable of Alburye knew
of a certain Dogberry who had made his office for all time
the "laughing stock of literature." The song ends by ex-
horting "you that are to choose"

> Put able men ever in place
> For knaves and fools in authority do
> But themselves and their country disgrace[1].

While all writers insist upon the ablest men being chosen,
one of them laconically remarks, "It is the common course
to put the office upon the poorest and weaker sort[2]."

Nevertheless the work had to be properly done, and if the
constable proved really unfit then the inhabitants of his
township were fined by the Court of Quarter Sessions[3], since
they, ultimately were responsible for the man whom they
had elected. Thomas Wighell, the constable of Osmotherley
allowed a prisoner taken for felony to escape. He was fined

---

[1] *The Song of a Constable*, by James Gyffon, Constable of Alburye,
Surrey, 1626.
[2] *The Exact Constable*, by E.W., 1660, p. 10.
[3] *N.R.Q.S.R.* vol. II. p. 48. Helmsley, July, 1614

12s., but the township had to pay 40s. for appointing an insufficient, that is an incapable, constable.

In 1609 a general order was issued by the Justices of the North Riding "that every township not having a sufficient constable shall be fined upon default[1]." This order was promptly enforced and in the following years various townships were presented by the high constable of the wapentake "for that they want a Constable[2]," and were fined more or less heavily[3].

ELECTION OF CONSTABLE

It has been already noticed that the constable was appointed and sworn at the Court Leet. The method of election varied in accordance with the custom handed down in the locality. In some places the constable was nominated by the bailiffs of the liberty[4], in others by the Leet jury[5], or by the freeholders[6].

---

[1] *N.R.Q.S.R.* vol. I. p. 171. Richmond, Oct. 1609.

[2] *Ibid.* vol. I. p. 196. Easby, 1610. *Ibid.* vol. I. p. 266. Easby; 1612. Easby had a constable in 1611, one James Andrew, who was evidently not "sufficient," for he was presented in April because he took no notice of a warrant duly sent by the high constable touching the punishment of rogues (vol. I. p. 212) and in July of the same year he was again in trouble because he did not appear at the Petty Sessions of the high constable (vol. I. p. 232).

[3] *Ibid.* vol. I. pp. 91 and 98. Richmond, Oct. 1607.

Inhabitants of Kepwich fined 10s. } for not having a constable.
,, ,, Newton Morrell 20s. }

In 1639 fine of £10 was threatened against Lofthouse if a constable was not appointed within ten days. See *N.R.Q.S.R.* vol. IV. p. 110. Helmsley, Jan. 1639. Lofthouse is near Guisboro' and was doubtless a thriving place on account of the alum works which were vigorously carried on by the Early Stuarts. See *Victoria County History of Yorkshire*, pp. 381–2, for account of alum industry in Yorkshire.

[4] *Ibid.* vol. II. p. 100. Helmsley, July, 1615. "Ordered that Humphrey Warton gent[n] and Ralph Smith, Baliffes of Biland shall nominate a Constable for the Libertie and shall appear &c and bring the said persons so nominated to be sworne."

[5] *Ibid.* vol. v. p. 29. Thirsk, April, 1649. "Wm. Williamson of Stillington having been chosen Constable by the Jury at the last Court holden there, to be sworn accordingly within ten daies upon paine of £10."

[6] *Ibid.* vol. IV. p. 186. Richmond, July, 1640. "The Homage of Melsonby according to their ancient custome hath presented a townsman to be sworn as Constable for the same but he refused therefore a warrant etc."

Vol. II. p. 100. Helmsley, July, 1615. Ordered "that a warrant &c to attach John Bowes and Oswold Win of Welbury &c and take them bound to appear &c and tender then and there an honest and able person to be

In some townships a definite order was kept, the office being served in turn from house to house[1]; in others it was held in connection with the occupation of a particular house[2], or farm[3], or even as the hereditary charge of a certain family[4]. Such a custom seems to indicate that the office may have been part of the feudal burden attaching to the tenure of that particular parcel of land.

All men were bound to serve in respect of residence; "I am a wise fellow," said Dogberry, "...and which is more a householder[5]." Though some manuals take the view that if

sworn Constable of the said towne..." (John Bowes was Lord of the Manor at Welbury).

[1] *N.R.Q.S.R.* vol. I. p. 25. The inhabitants of Newton Morrell presented for not having a constable gave the following reason: "And whereas the said inhabitants do object now in Court that the same defect is by means of one Tho Clemett refuseth to serve in that office alledging that he is priviledged being an attorney: nevertheless the Court hath thought good and so ordered that forasmuch as the Court is informed that the said Thomas Clemett hath two tenements in the said town subject to the said service, that he shall be priviledged from executing the said office of Constable in person: But for that the said Constable is usually chosen by their tenements (as is alledged) in course, and lest His Majesty's service hereafter should be neglected by the like occasions, that the said Thomas shall procure someone to serve in his place at such time as the said office shall (by turn) come to his tenement."

[2] *Ibid.* vol. V. p. 82. Richmond, July, 1651. "Wm. Williams to be Constable for South Cowton vice Mr. Weltinghall instead of the office being imposed upon one house as formerly, and afterwards the inhabitants to appoint a fit person to be Constable as other townships do."

[3] *Ibid.* vol. I. p. 248. Richmond, Jan. 1612. "That whereas there is no Constable for Coverham, and the occupiers of the farm belonging to the late Henry Dighton ought to find one, the tenants and occupiers of the said farm shall do so henceforth."

Ibid. vol. III. p. 257. Richmond, 162⅚. "Reference to an Order made at Richmond Qu. Sessions. Jany 14th, 1612, directing that the occupiers of a farm sometime belonging to the late Henry Dighton should provide a Constable for the townshipp of Coverham, Alice, the said Henry Dighton's widow, and Mary Dighton, widow, being now the tenantes and occupiers of the said farmhold: Ordered that they and all future occupiers shall yearly find and appoint a sufficient Constable according to the said Order, &c."

[4] *Ibid.* vol. VI. p. 167. Richmond, Jan. 1672. "Forasmuch as Tho. Warcope of East Tanfeild, gent., and his ancestors have for several years heretofore served as Constables of the Constablery of East Tanfeild, though they have not been possessed of the moyety of the lands in the said Constablery, the other half being in the possession of several persons inhabiting in the adjacent towns, who do not at all contribute to the charge the said Mr. Warcope doth expend in the execution of his office, nor have allowed him a deputy for his assistance therein, and therefore he hath petitioned this Court for relief."

[5] *Much Ado about Nothing*, Act IV. Sc. 2.

a man held land in one wapentake and lived in another, he need not serve for the place where his land lay, yet in the North Riding at any rate he was called upon to pay his share (according to the proportion of his land) of the expense of a deputy[1].

Any inhabitant householder was liable to be chosen by his fellow-townsmen, and unless he could plead that he was privileged[2], no escape was possible except by engaging a deputy to do the work. Otherwise he was fined and set in the stocks if he refused when duly elected to take up his duties[3]. Possibly it often happened as in the case of Elbow that when a constable had served his year and was willing to continue in office, he was paid by the man whose turn came next to act as his deputy.

"Alas it hath been great pains to you," said the ancient lord when discussing his office with Elbow. "They do you wrong to put you so oft upon't. Are there not men in your ward sufficient to serve it?"

"Faith Sir," replied Elbow, "few of any wit in such matters. As they are chosen they are glad to choose me for them: I do it for some piece of money, and go through with all[4]."

The piece of money was about £3 a year[5], being equivalent

---

[1] *N.R.Q.S.R.* vol. I. p. 3. Southolme presented for not having a constable. *Ibid.* vol. II. p. 41. Southolme presented for not having a constable. Vol. II. p. 101. The Court "ordered that there shall be a Constable for the township of Southolme the expense to be borne by the owners of the lordship according to their several proportions in the ownership, and if they cannot agree to chuse a Constable before the next Sessions then the Bench to appoint one." Southolme is a small rural township consisting of only 843 acres of land. At the present day there is no hamlet.

[2] S. and B. Webb, *Local Government. The Parish and the County*, p. 15, gives a list of privileged persons; also Ritson, *The Office of Constable.*

[3] *N.R.Q.S.R.* vol. I. p. 208. Helmsley, Jan. 1610. John Preston of Baxby is ordered to be set in the stocks and fined 6s. 8d. because "he did not take upon him the Office of Constable."

[4] *Measure for Measure*, Act II. Sc. I.

[5] *N.R.Q.S.R.* vol. VI. p. 242. Richmond, July, 1675. "The inhabitants of Bainbridge petition the Court for relief saying that 'of ancient custom they have yearly chosen a Constable within the town but that the execution of the office has become very chargeable in respect of the greatness of the Constablery,' therefore an order is made that a substantial able person shall yearly be chosen in Bainbridge to execute the office of Constable... and that such Constable shall yearly receive as a salary for his great trouble and pains in executing the said office £3, which is to be assessed upon the whole Constablery."

to the lowest wage given to the most unskilled labourer when the labourer also received his food; doubtless the constable's duties did not take up his whole time, but on the other hand he ran the risk of incurring heavy fines if they were not discharged correctly[1].

In thinly populated districts as is shown in the case of Ainderby Myers it was very difficult to find a man to serve. In October, 1609, an order was made at the Richmond Quarter Sessions "that Tho Smelt of Aynderby Myers gentⁿ. stand Constable of the same for this year ending at Michaelmas next[2]." However, in April, 1611, it appears that "there hath been usually a Constable in Aynderby Myers but is not now, through the default of Tho Smelte gentⁿ who hath refused to exercise the same himself or to send a sufficient deputy. Therefore a warrant is issued to bring Tho Smelt before the nearest Justice Sir Coniers Darcy (who lived at Hornby Castle two miles away) to take the oath of Constable[3]."

The township of Ainderby Myers consists at the present day of three farms; adjoining it and now united with it is the township of Holtby, consisting of one farm only, the whole comprising 953 acres of land. Thus the only inhabitants of the township who could take the office were the farmers, the occupier of Holtby Hall, and the labourers. Possibly the farmers would not care to invest labourers with the powers of the petty constable even if competent to fulfil the duties, and the occupier of Holtby Hall would be too great a man to serve, so that the whole burden fell upon

---

[1] *N.R.Q.S.R.* 1607. For not punishing rogues the constable of Ellerbeck is fined 10s. Vol. I. p. 92. *Ibid.* 1615. For not presenting recusants constables of five townships of the parish of Burneston, fined 20s. each. Vol. II. p. 104. For suffering prisoner to escape the constable of Sutton upon Goltres, fined 20s. Malton, 1656, for suffering prisoner to escape the constable of Egton fined 45s. Vol. v. p. 218. For suffering Lord's day to be profaned the constables of Middleham fined 20s. Thirsk, April, 1656. Vol. v. p. 212.

Vol. I. p. 229. Helmsley, 1611. Henry Humble, constable of Kirby Moorside, for having refused to carry a man to York Castle was ordered to pay 10s. or to be committed to the jail.

[2] *N.R.Q.S.R.* vol. I. p. 171. Richmond, Oct. 1609.

[3] *Ibid.* vol. I. p. 217. Thirsk, April, 1611.

the farmers. At that date moreover the township of Holtby
seems to have been separate from Ainderby Myers. In 1611
the difficulty was referred again to the Bench.

Forasmuch as great controversies have been between the townships of Aynderby Myers and Holtby whether the latter should be
chargeable to find a Constable or no, Ordered with the consent of
Henry Conyers of Holtby gent[n] and Tho. Smelt of Aynderby gent[n]
and others (parties therein) that Aynderby Myers shall for three
years together find a Constable and Holtby every fourth year, and
this order to remain firm for ever from time to time, Aynderby
beginning at Michaelmas as last past for the first three, and after
these three Holtby for one year[1].

It is probable, therefore, that the three occupiers of the
three farms of Ainderby Myers each had a turn at the office
and then the farmer at Holtby took up the work.

From the foregoing it is clear that when difficulties occurred touching the election of the petty constable, they
were referred to the Justices in Quarter Sessions. The Bench
insisted that every township, however thinly populated,
should be provided with a constable, and, while steadily
enforcing the custom of election, was ready in the last resort
to appoint a man[2] itself if the township failed to do so.

Indeed, to the Justices, sworn as they were to maintain
peace and order within their county, the petty constable
was indispensable.

Each individual Justice also by his commission was obliged
to see that the peace was kept in his locality; thus the custom grew up that, if a constable died while in office or while
out of the parish and the time for holding the Court Leet or
the Court of Quarter Sessions was far distant, then another
could be chosen and sworn by any two Justices of the Peace,
until the next Quarter Sessions, when the court must ap-
prove of the officer so made and sworn, or appoint another[3].

A treatise on the constable's duties, published in 1660,

---

[1] *N.R.Q.S.R.* vol. I. p. 241. Richmond, Oct. 3, 1611.
[2] As at Southolme above.
[3] *The Compleat Constable*, J. Paul.

declares that in an ordinary way no Justice of the Peace is to meddle in the choosing of a constable[1].

If a Justice should interfere concerning the election of a constable duly chosen by the Leet, then the court of King's Bench, not the Quarter Sessions, is to decide the case. Supposing, however, a miscarriage of justice be proved against the Leet, then the lord loses his Leet[2]. But if the Leet does not choose a constable then the Justice may do so[3].

During the Interregnum, the Courts Leet in several places either ceased or were only held at long intervals; while at the same time efficient constables were particularly necessary. The difficulty, however, in obtaining them increased on account of political factions and the Bench is found deposing a constable at South Cowton and ordering the inhabitants to appoint a fit person[4], by which, from the Justices' point of view, is evidently intended a Parliament man since only such an one would be desirous of keeping the peace for the Commonwealth. There is no indication of any attempt on the part of the Justices to usurp the privilege of the township as regards the election of constable, but it is clear that they carefully supervised the appointments, in order that no person who might be disloyal to the existing government should be chosen[5], and they entrusted difficult cases to the nearest Justice[6] to determine.

After the Restoration the custom which had been growing up became law. An act was passed allowing any two Justices of the Peace to appoint and swear in a constable "until the Lord shall hold a Court[7]," thus giving the Justices power to

---

[1] *The Exact Constable*, by E.W., ed. 1660, p. 95.
[2] *Ibid.* p. 98.
[3] *Ibid.* p. 96.
[4] See above, p. 107, note 2.
[5] *N.R.Q.S.R.* vol. v. p. 216. Thirsk, April, 1656. "Ordered in case any Papist or Delinquent be elected Constable, the next J.P. to appoint some other fitt person, and the said Papist or Delinquent to be at charge thereof."
[6] *Ibid.* vol. v. p. 177. Kirbymoorside, Jan. 1635. "Ordered Tho Savile to be Constable for Welburne or show cause etc and if he shew sufficient cause the next J.P. is to appoint a fit person to be Constable."
[7] 14 Car. II, cap. xii. sec. xv.

insist that petty constables should be both appointed and sworn[1]. Incidentally also the court gained the power to depose one constable and appoint another.

RANK OF CONSTABLE

During the seventeenth and eighteenth centuries the constable was apparently a man of the same social standing as the churchwarden, the overseer or the surveyor. Sometimes he performed at the same time the office of churchwarden[2]. In the early eighteenth century at Wensley the offices of constable, churchwarden and overseer of the poor were held in turn by a few men, evidently the farmers and some well-to-do labourers whose names recur in the parish books again and again. The churchwarden in 1731 was constable in 1734 and constable again as well as overseer of the poor in 1736. The overseers of 1739 became the constables of 1740[3]. It seems, therefore, that there was little to choose in dignity between these unpaid parish offices and the interchange of offices was probably conducive to amicable co-operation.

Possibly also, in a thinly populated district like the North Riding, the status of the person holding the office varied according to the locality. In one place a yeoman evidently a small freeholder is constable[4], in another a labourer, while Thomas Smelt of Ainderby Myers, who was ordered to be constable there, was designated "gentleman[5]". Though generally speaking there were not hard and fast class distinctions in the seventeenth century, yet these names stand for a definite social rank.

[1] *N.R.Q.S.R.* vol. VI. p. 84. New Malton, Jan. 1665. "Whereas the inhabitants of Thirsk have elected three Constables for this year and there was not a Court Leet held there since Michaelmas Ordered that they repair to two justices to be sworn for the said town or shew cause etc."

[2] *Ibid.* vol. I. p. 17. Malton, Oct. 1605. "John Whitton was Churchwarden of the Parish of Kirk Leventon and at the same time Constable of Picton one of its townships."
Vol. II. p. 57. Will Thompson is constable and churchwarden of Northallerton in 1614.

[3] Parish Book, Wensley.

[4] *N.R.Q.S.R.* vol. II. p. 35. Thomas Screwton of Screwton is constable in 1613. He serves on the Grand Jury: therefore is a freeholder.

[5] See above, p. 109.

Nevertheless the petty constable was considered the humblest member of the local government hierarchy. In 1659 when Mr Richard Collings, one of the coroners for the Riding was elected constable for Kirkeby-on-the-Hill, he petitioned the Court of Quarter Sessions, which thereupon ordered

that he be discharged of the place of Petty Constable of Kirkeby-on-the-Hill where he lives, and that the people there do elect another fit person for Constable there in his stead, in regard of his said place of Coroner, which is a place of great trust, and is inconsistent with the place of Petty Constable[1].

The usual times for the election of constables were at Easter or at Michaelmas, and the normal length of service a year[2], but there are instances of the constable remaining in office for a much longer period[3].

In 1647, Edward Topham had been constable of East Whitton for three years when an order was made that another man from the same place should act in that capacity[4].

However, in 1649 he was still in office[5], and it may be that in the general disorder he could find no one to take up the work; possibly also he remained in office in the hope of recovering money which he had paid out on behalf of the township.

The constable paid any money required for his actual expenses in the public service out of his own pocket; at the end of his year of office he produced his accounts and an

---

[1] *N.R.Q.S.R.* vol. VI. p. 19. Thirsk, April, 1659.
[2] *Ibid.* vol. I. p. 171. Richmond, Oct. 1609, Henry Loftus,
      vol. I. p. 201. Topcliffe, Oct. 1610, John Husband,
      vol. I. p. 254, Thirsk, Ap. 1612, Nicholas Place,
were constables for Hackforth for these years, showing that the office was at the time annual.
[3] *Ibid.* vol. IV. p. 249. Thirsk, Ap. 12, 1647. "The Constable of Pickton being much money out of purse for the Constablery and the inhabitants refusing to cast an assessment for his disbursements or to take his accounts he having served 4 years."
[4] *Ibid.* vol. IV. p. 266. Richmond, Feb. 1647. An order is made that "four inhabitants of the Constablery of East Whitton be appointed to take the accounts of Edward Topham, Constable of the said town, since his entrance into the office, and if any moneys appear to be due to him, the inhabitants to cast an assessment for his satisfaction."
[5] *Ibid.* vol. V. p. 37. Bedale, July, 1649.

assessment, "the Constable's lay," was cast to reimburse him.

Not until 1606 was this authorised by statute[1]; in 1662[2] he was empowered to assess on the township all the expenses which he incurred in connection with vagrancy. These assessments were made by four of the most substantial inhabitants, who in their turn were liable to be presented, if they apportioned the rate unfairly[3].

The "Constable's lay," however, was for actual expenses, the office itself was unpaid, except that in some places a local custom existed by which householders in outlying hamlets paid a small sum yearly to the constable of the largest village, in order to avoid undertaking the office[4].

During the disordered times of the Civil War various constables had a difficulty in recovering even their out-of-pocket expenses[5]. Doubtless in almost every village and town there were factions, and it was the party opposed to the Government who refused to pay.

In 1649 the Constables for Helmsley complain that they are £28. 2s. 3d. out of pocket and that several orders to the inhabitants to collect and pay this sum have been altogether neglected; the Court thereupon "Ordered the present Constables, with such of the inhabitants as shall be pleased to be there, to assess, collect and pay the said sum before Feb. 2nd next" (the date of the Sessions being

---

[1] 3 Jac. I, cap. x. sec. i.   [2] 14 Car. II, cap. xii. sec. xviii.

[3] In 1680 four Kirbymoorside men, the assessors, are presented "for making a Constable sesse unequally."

[4] N.R.Q.S.R. vol. IV. p. 58. Richmond, July, 1636.

"The inhabitants of Carlton in Coverdale allege that the said towne is overchardged by reason that they always choose two Constables and have done time out of mind, though the hamlettes and farmes called Camerskell, Horsehowses and Braidley belonging to the towneshipp of Carleton have always contributed to the Constables' Cessments and all the houses in the said hamlettes have, or ought to have, paid one penny to the said Constables, notwithstanding the aforesaid inhab^ts doe disyre that the said villages and out townes where diverse able men doe live, the places being lardge and spacious, may make choice of a Constable amongst them to doe the King's Service there, and soe the said towne of Carlton may be eased by the chardge of one Constable."

"The Justices are evenly divided in opinion on the question which is therefore referred to the decision of the Justices of Assize."

[5] Ibid. vol. v. p. 5. Helmsley, Jan. 1648. The constable of Stonegrave complains that he is £13 out of pocket.

Jan. 9th) "and in case of neglect the next J.P. to bind the offenders etc.[1]."

It is evident that whenever the Justices appointed a date for the execution of an order they were seriously in earnest. It cannot be wondered that men tried to avoid holding the office since every constable had to spend both time and money in the service.

While the churchwarden collected the assessments chiefly relating to the sick and poor of the parish, the prisoners and the maimed soldiers, the constable was responsible for the rates which each township must pay in connection with the county or the state, such as the Muster Master's fee, the Purveyor's Money, the rate for county bridges, the provision for the King's household, etc. These had to be collected from each township and paid to the high constable of the wapentake. The constable was no more popular than the modern rate collector, but whereas at the present day people know more or less certainly what rates they have to pay and when they are to be paid, in the seventeenth century the incidence of rating varied both as to time and amount. There was no fixed county rate; as money was wanted for some particular object, the repairing of a bridge, the building of a House of Correction, the fine payable by the township for some misdemeanour, etc., it was assessed by the ablest inhabitants and collected by the constable or churchwarden as the case might be.

Owing also to the fact that rating was very uncertain, to some minds it was always a grievance, and, as the man was identified with his office there are numerous instances of assault on the constable while executing this part of his duty[2].

Since the constables had difficulty in getting the money together, they were frequently presented for non-payment of

[1] *N.R.Q.S.R.* vol. v. p. 20. Helmsley, Jan. 1649.
[2] *Ibid.* vol. III. p. 281. Richmond, Oct. 1626. A warrant is issued against a man "for abusing Anthony Pearson Constable of Startforth when demanding lays and cessments of him."

or for refusing to pay assessments[1]. There are instances also of extortion by constables in collecting rates[2]. This was a matter over which it must have been difficult either for high constables or Justices to keep any check, for the constable knew his man, and doubtless imposed the extra payment, (which he pocketed), on the weakest or most ignorant of the ratepayers.

In Dull, Elbow and Dogberry, Shakespeare gives us a choice selection of utterly stupid officials, who, however, serve his purpose by emphasising the delightful humour of his plays; nevertheless a consideration of the functions imposed on the petty constable (many of which required a certain amount of intelligence) hardly justifies us in accepting Dogberry as a type, though he was an excellent target for Shakespeare's wit.

It is to be remembered also that Shakespeare wrote drama, not history, and that, whether from youthful recollections or from the impatience with which an acute intellect naturally views the dead level of the official, he was especially severe on every "pelting petty officer, most ignorant of what he's most assured[3]."

In estimating the constable's share in the parish government, it seems astonishing that a man untrained for the work could perform all these manifold duties with any degree of efficiency. It may be that the various meetings which the constables could not shirk were a considerable help to their public education. In Quarter Sessions they could "wit and experience gain" in many respects; they

---

[1] *N.R.Q.S.R.* vol. II. p. 57. Richmond, 1614.
"Will Thompson, Constable of Northallerton, for refusing to pay to the Head Constable monie due for the provision of the King's Household, for the prisoners in York Castle, and the Rates due for fower bridges according to a precept delivered to him by the Head Constables of Allertonshire; and the same man, as Churchwarden of Northallerton, for refusing to pay to the Head Constables monie due for the L.S. and Hospitalls."

[2] *Ibid.* vol. IV. p. 69. Richmond, Jan. 1637.
Thomas Lobley, constable of West Scrafton, presented "for injuriously and extorsively taking, in all, more by 6s. 6d. than the Cessments by the Cessors warranted, from three several persons."

[3] *Measure for Measure*, Act II. Sc. I.

could take warning when they heard their fellow-officers fined for neglect, and they could discuss one with another their difficulties or grievances. In the Petty or Statute Sessions of the high constables they received any new orders the Justices had made, together with much good advice and many salutary warnings: while they could refer disputed points to the high constable. This official was generally appointed for three years; on this account therefore, and because he was usually a man of superior judgment and education, he was fairly competent to advise his subordinates.

When the constable returned home from the Sessions, he would be expected to relate all the news he had heard to his fellow-townsmen, especially any matters directly concerning themselves. These topics would be discussed again in a more serious manner at the monthly meetings of the parish officers; since these men lived in the same little village where everything under the sun was talked over at the alehouses, it can be understood that amid all the conversation a certain amount of general information would be gained. Bearing in mind that, in an ordinary way, each of these parish offices was held for one year only, it follows that every capable man in the parish would eventually serve in one or all of them; thus, there were plenty of people to instruct a newcomer in his work. Moreover, the office of petty constable was one of the most ancient institutions of the race; is it not possible then, that, through the continual performance of their civic duties, as one generation succeeded another, men inherited from their fathers that instinct for government and order which is characteristic of the British people?

APPENDIX D

PRECAUTIONS TAKEN BY THE JUSTICES AGAINST INFECTION OF THE PLAGUE IN AUG. 1665

Whereas divers and sundry persons have for these three months last past removed and remove from the city of London, and other places infected with the plague, unto most parts of this kingdom of England, whereby divers towns and countries are infected with the plague, and in probability greater inconvenience will ensue to several parts of this Riding by strangers removing into the said Riding if present care be not taken for prevention hereof, and that the contagious sickness may not approach or spread abroad it is Ordered (189) that a strict and sufficient night and day watch be kept in every township within the said Riding to prohibit all manner of persons, as well travellers suspicious to have come from London, or other places infected, as vagrants and beggars, to stay, lodge, or inhabit within any township, grainge, or other places of habitation in the said Riding, and to this end that the respective watch and watches do convey from place to place such travellers, vagrants and beggars by sufficient guard and guards, until they be removed out of this said Riding, that thereby the said Riding may be by the blessing of God kept safe from infection, and that the respective C.C^s[1] weekly take a view, both night and day, whether the inhab^{ts} of the several townships within the respective wapentakes keep a sufficient night and day watch accordingly, and present the inhab^{ts} failing their watch to the next J.P., that the offenders may be bound over to the Sessions and receive condign punishment according to law, and that the C.C^s at their utmost perils give a personal acc^t upon oath to one of the next Justices, if there be not a sufficient night and day watch kept accordingly to the effect of this Order, and that a sufficient night and day watch be appointed in every Constablery and township by the C.C^s, and the said watchmen to have reasonable wages to be paid by way of tax upon respective Constableries, and it is further Ordered that the C.C^s issue out true copies of this Order to the several Constables in their wapentakes, and they and all persons are required to take notice of this Order and give obedience to the same; eight Forcett men to diligently watch the houses of Ann Firbancke, and Mr Tim Ivison of Forcett from time to time, as namely, two of the night and one of the day for forty days next coming, at the proper charge of the said Ann

---

[1] Chief Constables.

Firbancke and Mr Ivison, after the discretion of the Constables of Forcett, (190) to the end that none of their present families mix themselves or have any society with any other families or people during the aforesaid forty days, by reason of the great fear of the persons received by the said Ann Firbancke and Mr Ivison lately come from the city of London, and in case any persons inhabiting the said Constablery shall adventure to have society with the said families then the said Constablery to keep a strict and strong watch over any such persons for forty days: and it is further Ordered that if any trunks, etc., shall come to the said Anne Firbanke or Mr Ivison, or to any of their people, they shall be received only into their houses and there to lodge until they be sufficiently cleansed by a cleansor or cleansors.

N.R.Q.S.R. vol. VI. p. 92. Richmond, August 8, 1665.

CHAPTER VI

THE REPAIR OF HIGHWAYS AND BRIDGES
THE WORK OF THE SURVEYOR

THOUGH the parish succeeded in delegating to paid or unpaid officials the greater part of the duties imposed on it by statute or by immemorial custom, yet there remained certain obligations in which the state required that each parishioner should take a share; one of these duties was the maintenance and repair of the highways and bridges. By the provisions of an act passed in the reign of Queen Mary, the upkeep of the main roads was incumbent on the various parishes, while the bye-roads were still kept in order by private individuals.

Every year on the Tuesday or Wednesday in Easter week, the churchwardens and constables must summon a meeting of parishioners in the vestry to elect "two honest persons of the Parish to be Surveyors and Orderers for one year of the works for the amendment of the Highways in their parish leading to any Market town[1]." If a parishioner on being elected surveyor refused to serve, or if he neglected his duties while in office, he was summoned to appear before the Justices in Quarter Sessions, or he was liable to incur a fine of 40s. for every default[2]. The churchwardens and constables must also appoint certain days before the Feast of St John Baptist which all parishioners had to set aside for road-making; these days were to be openly proclaimed to the congregation in church on the following Sunday after the parish meeting: if the parish officers neglected to carry out any detail of the act they could be summoned to appear

[1] 2 and 3 Ph. and Mary, cap. viii.
[2] *N.R.Q.S.R.* vol. IV. p. 98. Malton, July, 1638. "A linen webster appointed Surveyor of common days works at Byland, for not fulfilling the duties of his office."

before the Justices in Quarter Sessions[1] and the records show us that this did happen[2]. At Thirsk in October 1632

Vincent Parvin, Phil Winde, Jas. Artis, and Rich. Wawburne, Constables and Churchwardens of Sigston, were presented for not appointinge six daies upon Tuesdaie or Wednesdaie in Easter weeke for the amendinge of the highwaies in the said parish, and for not publishinge anie daies upon the Sondaie followinge for the Common Woorke, according to the Statute etc., three Sigston men (Artis above-named being one of them) for not scouring the Beacon hedge-gutter adjoining on the common highway leading from Sigston to Thirsk Markett, being three-score roods in length and more, everie rood 12d. to the evil example of others to perpetrate the like.

As the time drew near for the roadmending the constable was expected to warn the parishioners; if they failed to attend or neglected to send workmen and draughts of horses[3], the surveyor presented them in their turn at the forth-coming Sessions. If he failed to do so he was himself pre-sented[4].

All men who possessed a plough-land in tillage or pasture and all who kept a plough or draught were to send "one wain or cart furnished with oxen, horses or other cattel upon pain of every draught making default, 10s." Every other householder, labourer or cottager of the parish (except ser-vants hired by the year) was to give his labour for the six days "upon pain of every person making default to lose for every day 12d." Moreover everyone was expected to bring the trowels, spades, picks and mattocks which he used for

---

[1] *N.R.Q.S.R.* vol. VI. p. 173. Stokesley, July, 1672. "The Constable of Ryton, and the Churchwardens of Kirby Misperton for not assembling the parishioners to elect 2 honest persons for Surveyors for highways."
[2] *Ibid.* vol. III. p. 337.
[3] *Ibid.* vol. I. p. 83. Richmond, July, 1607. "Will Collinson of Speny-thorne for refusing to come to the mending the highwayes with his draught."
Ibid. vol. II. p. 23. Helmsley, July, 1613. "Margaret Dakins of Fryton widow for not coming to the common work at the times limited by the Surveyors of the highways within the Constabulary of Hovingham having lawful warning given her."
[4] *Ibid.* vol. VI. p. 103. Stokesley, July, 1666. Presentment: "The Supervisors for Highways for Sutton-under-Whistin-Cliff for neglecting to present the names of such persons as have made default in not sending sufficient persons or carriages to the Common day's work."

his own ditches, and to do whatever work the surveyor appointed for him[1]. When the roads of a parish were in bad condition the inhabitants were presented at the Quarter Sessions by the high constable of their wapentake or the Justices of the neighbourhood[2]. The people of Middleham, that hilly little town which lies high up in Wensleydale were summoned in 1640 "for not repairing their several streets leading from Midleham Moor to the Eastern boundary of the hill and from the Marketplace at Midleham to St Awkell's Well." There was also the informer, a person who took upon himself to present any bad roads and received a gratuity from the Bench for doing so. In 1662 the Justices at Helmsley ordered the treasurer of the Lame Soldier Fund to pay a certain James Calvert of Swaineby 40s. because he "hath done this Riding very good service in presenting the decays in common highways, which tend so much to the general advantages of the inhabitants of this riding[3]." Four years previously the same man had received 40s. from the court for "his great service about the repairing of highways." Frequently, when summoned, a parish was given a further period of grace; if it then failed to make good its delinquency a fine was levied by the chief constables and handed over to the surveyor (or to two people appointed by the Bench) to be used for the repair of the highway[4]. The fine was distrained on the goods of some member of the parish who had to get it back from the various individuals as best he could;

---

[1] From the entry in the Wensley Parish Book it seems that people were allowed to pay a sum of money instead of performing their statute work upon the highways; see p. 128.

[2] *N.R.Q.S.R.* vol. v. p. 60. Thirsk, Oct. 1650. "Col. Lascelles presents the highway from North Kilvington to Knayton." "The Inhab. of Wykeham for not making large and broad the common highway leading from Scarbro' to Pickering and Kirbymoorside."

[3] *Ibid.* vol. vi. p. 50. Helmsley, Jan. 1662.

[4] *Ibid.* vol. v. pp. 120–121. Thirsk, Oct. 1652. "The sum of £40 estreated this Sess. against the inhab. of the precincts and parish of Scarbro' for not repairing the highway between Faulsgrave and Seamey Yeate before June 24 acc. to order, to be levied upon the said Inhabts by the C.Cs of Pickering Lythe who are to pay the same to two gentlemen who are to receive and employ the same in the repairing of the said highway and give an acct. from time to time at every Session of their proceedings therein."

if a parish had no conscience and refused to pay then the unfortunate person appealed to Quarter Sessions. An order made at Northallerton in 1674 reads:

Forasmuch as Leon Hartley and John Robinson of Barton have complained unto this Court that they have their goods distrained by vertue of two several estreates issued out of the Crown Office against the inhabts of Barton for not repairing their highways, one of £8. 10s. which was levied of the goods and chattels of the said Leon Hartley, and another of £3. 10s. which was levied of the goods and chattels of the said J. Robinson, which sums the said Leon Hartley and John Robinson were forced to pay and lay out for the said inhabitants before they could have their goods restored and since have several times desired that they might be reimbursed by making an asst. or putting it into a Constable cart which the said inhabts refuse to do: This Court doth therefore think fit and so order that the said sums of £8. 10s. and £3. 10s. be put into a Constable cart and that the Constable of Barton aforesaid do collect the same of the inhabts there and reimburse the said Leon Hartley and John Robinson the moneys by them disbursed for the said inhabts[1].

Sometimes when the fine had been paid the inhabitants set about repairing their roads and got their penalty remitted, upon which the money was repaid to the contributors.

Whereas an estreat of £16 or thereabouts was issued out of the Exchequer against the inhabitants of Marton for not repairing their highways and upon certificate of the way being repaired, the said money was repaid to the Constable there, he is forthwith to pay over the same etc. to be paid back to the contributors etc.[2]

Quite considerable sums of money were imposed[3] as fines; the inhabitants of New Malton were ordered to pay £100 for not repairing their streets, the penalty doubtless varying in proportion to the amount required to be spent on the street or pavement. What between the surveyor, the high constable, the local Justice, and the man in the street who turned informer, the highways of England should have been worthy of the time and trouble spent on them.

[1] *N.R.Q.S.R.* vol. VI. p. 221. Northallerton, July, 1674.
[2] *Ibid.* vol. V. p. 133. Thirsk, Ap. 1653.
[3] *Ibid.* vol. VII. p. 16. Thirsk, Oct. 1678. "£100 to be estreated upon the goods of the inhabitants of New Malton for not repairing the pavement in the said town."

Yet this method of road-making was not successful for the labour was forced and the work that of amateurs: parishes were continually being summoned until under threat of a heavy penalty they patched up the piece of condemned road, probably doing the minimum of work on it, and very soon its condition was as bad as ever.

The surveyors, being weavers, tradesmen, farmers, etc., had little technical knowledge of road-making; the writer of a paper read before the Royal Society in 1736 declared that the system followed in the country was both expensive and unsatisfactory. The roads were made in summer when labour was dear and water difficult to obtain. No foundation was prepared, the gravel being merely laid on the loam; moreover the mud which was taken out of the ditches on either side was thrown on the roads and therefore worked its way back to fill up the ditches again.

In many places the roads were merely broad tracks through the open fields. In 1615, on the testimony of John Fosse of Marriforth, a yeoman on the jury,

The Town and inhabts of Spennythorne are summoned for not re-payringe a waie, being the Kinges Strete in Spenithorne field betwixt Bedall and Laburne[1].

Sometimes when the field was enclosed an attempt was made to stop up these pathways. A Carlton-in-Cleveland man is summoned at Helmsley in 1623

for plowing up the Kings high Street leading betwixt Helmesley and Stokesley in a place there called the Ladiebecks Closes-side etc., the same for stopping an ancient foote waie lying within his lofte at Carlton being an usual footpath between Allerton and Stokesley for 8 years last past[2].

"Ploughing up the highroad[3]," that is encroaching on either

---

[1] *N.R.Q.S.R.* vol. II. p. 89. Thirsk, Ap. 1615.
[2] *Ibid.* vol. III. p. 188. Helmsley, Jan. 1623-4.
[3] *Ibid.* vol. I. p. 142. Helmsley, Jan. 1609. "Rog Garbut of Faceby husbn. for ploughing forth the Streetway from Gowton Howes that men cannot passe with their waynes. (Per Will Bayte et Marke Lyell Cap const.)"

side to gain additional land for corn, and "making pits in the street[1]" by carrying away the soil, were common offences.

Even when the roads were mended, the ditches which were intended to drain them were soon allowed to get stopped up[2], and again the roads, being continually under water, became almost impassable. The only fences were those which divided off the open fields belonging to the village from the surrounding commons, or those round enclosures. They, also, were frequently neglected both by parishes and by individuals[3] with the result that cattle went astray and were lost, and corn crops were spoilt. In 1658

the owners and occupiers of Tollerton Acres are summoned for want of repairing hedges and fences whereby the inhabts. of Newton-on-Ouse have lost some of thar goods (cattle)[4].

The tendency to enclosure shows itself throughout the century in attempts to prevent a right of way being used. Freeholders would lock the gates leading into their land and so block up the road; forthwith a protest was lodged at Quarter Sessions. When the matter came before the court the freeholder was ordered to appear and show cause for his proceeding. If he failed to come then the inhabitants of the parish might pull down the gate or fence "so they do not the same roughly but in a placable manner[5]"; if he traversed and was unable to justify his action, then he had to open

---

[1] *N.R.Q.S.R.* vol. v. p. 169. Thirsk, Oct. 1654. "The inhabts of New Malton for digging pits or hoes in the common highway between Malton and Thirske (to be amended by Dec. 31 upon pain of £10). The inhab. of Barton in the Street for the like (£5)."

[2] *Ibid.* vol. IV. p. 50. Thirsk, Ap. 1636. "The inhabitants of Gt Broughton for suffering their hedges and fences to lye down and open betweene that lordshipp and the Lordshipp of Kirkby nere Dromonby for three years and a halfe by reason whereof the water for want of scoureing their gutters runneth over the Kirkby meadows."

[3] *Ibid.* vol. v. p. 219. Malton, July, 1656. "The inhabts of Haxby for not making their fences between Haxby grounds and the grounds of Slingsby Bethell of London, merchant, called Sewett Carr."

[4] *Ibid.* vol. VI. p. 5. Thirsk, Ap. 1658.

[5] *Ibid.* vol. v. p. 119. Thirsk, Oct. 1652. "A warrant against a man of Atlay Moore to enter bond to traverse an indictment preferred against him for stopping up a highway between Whitwell and Darrington in a parcell of Atlay Moor and for that he did not appear to plead to the said indictment the inhabts of Whetwell in the Whenns to pull down such ditches and stopps as have been and are made to stop the way aforesaid,

the road under pain of a fine. In 1656 an order is made at
Kirbymoorside as follows:

A presentment having been preferred against an Acklam man at
Allerton Ap. 24, 1655, for stopping up a highway betwixt Midles-
brough and Stoaxley in a place called East Field, and he being
found guilty upon traverse at Thirske Oct. 2. 1655, to forfeit £3. 6s. 8d.
for every month till he open the said highway from the date of this
order, a J.P. to call the parties concerned in this petition before him
and to do therein as to justice appertaineth[1].

Whenever a pathway could be proved ancient it was kept
open. In 1632 a Crakehall yeoman is summoned "for stopping
up a footway at Kirkbrigg Closes, being an ancient footway
between Langthorne and Bedall for church and markett[2]."

The King's highway had to be repaired by parishes; but
the occupiers of land abutting on bye-roads were obliged to
maintain such roads, and were often summoned for negligence[3] in this respect.

Very rarely did the King pass over his highway in Yorkshire. In 1633, however, when Charles I went to see his
Northern Kingdom for the first time, an effort was made to
prepare a suitable way for him. The order ran:

All bridges and highways in Richmre. and other parts of this
Countie that are within the roade where His Matie. is to passe on
to his Highnes Kingdome of Scotland shall be sufficiently repaired
before May 10 on paine of £40 upon every parish making default.

This was not difficult, for he travelled through the Riding
along the Great North Road, so well built by the Romans,
that it is still the easiest road to mend and the best to keep
in repair of any in the district. It pursues its long straight

for their necessary passage that way, so they do not the same roughly,
but in a placable manner."

    [1] *N.R.Q.S.R.* vol. v. p. 205. Kirbymoorside, Jan. 1656.
    Ibid. vol. v. p. 151. N. Allerton, Jan. 1653–4. "A Tunstall yeoman
for inclosinge up part of the common street or towngate there."
    [2] *Ibid.* vol. III. p. 335. Richmond, July, 1632.
    [3] *Ibid.* vol. III. p. 163. Thirsk, April, 1623. "A highway leading be-
tween Ripon and York lying between the lordship of Miton on Swale
and Ellingstringe Ings commonly called Miton Great Close as in great
decay and that Tho. Caley of York gentn. and Jas. Woodburne of York
butcher by reason of their tenure of the said close ought and have been
used to repair the said way."

course with rarely a bend and passes through comparatively few villages, and in the seventeenth century it was a resort of highwaymen. Consequently strict watch seems to have been kept over the landlords of the Coaching Houses on the road. In 1608 one Robert Suttle of Leeming Lane was summoned: for that he doth kepe a very badd house for the reteyning and releeving of badd fellowes, who very suspiciously ryde in the high street called Leeming Lone, as we suspect for robbing, as we have some suspicion from circumstance[1].

Leeming Lane is a part of the Great North Road which is still called "the High Street" by the people in the neighbourhood.

The bridges were by far the most expensive county item. The rivers in the North Riding are swift and liable to sudden flood[2], the Swale being a great offender in this respect. In 1673 "The Court orders relief for a man at Brompton on Swale who has had his house carried down by the late great floods." Arrangements are made for a new road at Easby, in July, 1677, along the banks of the Swale because the old one was undermined by the river[3].

In the seventeenth century many of the bridges were still built of wood and these required almost constant repair. The smaller bridges were left to the care of the parishes, the larger ones and the beacons were looked after by the county. Regulations were made ordering heavy wagons to use the fords so as not to be drawn over the bridges, many of which were secured at night against further traffic by a lock and chain[4].

In 1615 an order is made that the bridges at Normanton and Newsom which had been seriously damaged by a recent flood should be repaired at the cost of the county.

[1] *N.R.Q.S.R.* vol. I. p. 147. Northallerton, Jan. 1608–9.
[2] *Ibid.* vol. II. p. 88. Thirsk, Ap. 1615. "Normanby Bridge as in decay and ruinated now more than it was att anie time before or since the building thereof by force of this flood and ought to be repaired by the country; Newsom Bridge now greatly weakened by the force of the late flood whereby the same is likely without spedy releife, to be caried away: to be repaired by the county."
[3] *Ibid.* vol. VI. p. 181. Richmond, Jan. 1673. Vol. VI. p. 279. July, 1677.
[4] *Ibid.* vol. I. p. 205, and vol. V. p. 78. Helmsley, July, 1651. "A Pickering man who disbursed 18s. 4d. for How Bridge to be paid from the money that remained of the buying of a chaine for Ayton Bridge."

When sudden floods arose endangering the safety of the bridges it seems to have been the custom for private individuals to repair the damage, claiming expenses later from the court[1].

In conclusion the following account of Whitby bridge and the entry in the Wensley Parish Book about statute work give some idea of the careful arrangements made by these amateur architects and the cost of the repair of highways and bridges.

THE REPAIR OF WHITBY BRIDGE

The Survrs of Whitby Bridge, appointed by Rog. Radcliffe, Esq., J.P., are these,—Rob. Sneton, Tho. Yeoman, Chr. Yeoman.

We think fortie oke trees are as few as we can judge to serve for that purpose, which will be worth £20. Also we thinke that the workmanshipp of the same will not be made wainemeete under the value of £20.

And likewise we thinke that the cariage thereof will lie in £20, because wood is farr from us that must serve for our purpose.

Further we do thinke that the timber, when it is laid on the ground, the workmanshipp thereof to be sufficientlie done, will not be under the sum of £50.

The totall summe whereof is £110.

Signed in the presence of Geo. Anningson, Will. Blenkorne, John Fisher and Chr. Blenkorne, with others.

£40 is assd upon the Countie, whereof twentie markes is to be assd of Whitby Strand.

Tho. Layton. John Sayer. Roger Radcliffe. Antho. Tailboys.

ENTRY IN THE WENSLEY PARISH BOOK

20 May, 1767. *Memorandum*

It is agreed & thought reasonable by all present that those persons who cannot or do not chuse to perform their Statute Work upon the High Ways shall pay in manner following:

For a single horse cart	0	11	0
A two horse cart	0	15	0
An Ox Gang or 50lb a Year	1	0	0
A Labourer	0	5	0
A Woman	0	2	0

20 May 1767

[1] See note 4, p. 127.

20 May 1767

A cess made for Wm Burneston & Wm Humphrey Overseers of the High Ways at sixpence in the pound for which they must be accountable.

Present	J. Costobadie	Robert Ward
names all	Chris Tennant	James Coates
signed	Michael Glenton	Peter Pearson
		Robert Pearson

14 April 1768. Examined & stated the accounts of Wm Burniston & Wm Humphrey late Surveyors of the Highways & there remains in their hands £0. 8. 7 which is to be paid to the present surveyors Andrew Bell & Robert Pearson & James Coates & more in Andrew Bell's Hands £0. 7. 9

(*Signed*)   Wm Burniston
Wm Humphrey
Andrew Bell

CHAPTER VII

THE LABOURERS AND APPRENTICES

WHILE much of the constructive legislation of the Tudor period has left its mark deep in the customs and institutions of the race at the present day, the Statute of Labourers and Apprentices passed in the fifth year of Queen Elizabeth's reign may now be considered obsolete. For, although it repealed all previous laws relating to the subject, as being out of date, and although it showed desire on the part of the legislators to benefit the hired servant and the day labourer, nevertheless, in spirit and in substance, it belonged entirely to the Middle Ages, and ultimately proved to be a hindrance rather than a help to progress.

For two hundred years after the passing of this act, the individual effort of the worker was bound down by the various enactments as rigidly as it had been for two hundred years previously by the feudal tenure, since a fixed standard of wages (always assessed by the employers and more or less strictly enforced) prevented that healthy competition which has some share in the production of the skilled workman, while the law of settlement impeded the fluidity of labour.

Though the act ensured that every person should learn a trade, and be thereby made capable of earning his own living, yet through its provisions a man, apprenticed in his undeveloped youth to an uncongenial trade, could not leave that trade in later life and take up another more to his liking and ability, unless he was prepared to serve another seven years' apprenticeship.

By such restrictions on the liberty and initiative of the worker, it seems not unlikely that the Statute of Labourers and Apprentices, though it redressed the evils of the time, was nevertheless itself one of the causes of the continual increase of poverty in the seventeenth century. It may be well to consider briefly the particular difficulties which the statute was intended to meet. In the middle of the sixteenth century chaos existed in the industrial world. The guilds which regulated industry in the Middle Ages had lost much of their power by the legislation of Edward VI's reign; new industrial centres had sprung up which recognised no guild authority. In an age when most manufactures were wrought by hand (there being little machinery), if any standard of efficiency was to be maintained it was essential that artizans should thoroughly learn their trade. Only in this way could they produce good work, and pass on their knowledge to the next generation. But the town artizans were endeavouring to establish themselves in villages and were converting their land into pasture in order to breed sheep and produce their own wool for spinning and weaving. The result was that corporate towns decayed and villages increased, but, owing to the fact that the holdings which the artizans occupied had formerly belonged to the workers on the land, servants in husbandry became scarce. The standard of work also of the artizans, being freed from the competition prevalent in towns, was likely to depreciate; therefore the Tudor statesmen aimed at providing enough servants in husbandry for the rural districts, while reviving industry in the corporate towns and making sure that every man learnt his trade, so that he should not fall into poverty through inability to earn his own living. For always in the background of Elizabethan England was that army of rogues and vagabonds, recruited in part, at any rate, from men who were poor and out of work.

Therefore, by insisting on the seven years' apprenticeship (which had hitherto been the custom only in London and some towns) everywhere, and for all trades, better handicraft was ensured, and the rural districts ceased to have any advantage over the towns[1], also by regulations regarding the apprentices[2] whom clothiers in market towns could take, these latter places were restricted in favour of the corporate towns. Such regulations, however, were very arbitrary and were perhaps only justified by the fact that they seem to have arrested the decay of corporate towns[3].

Industry being thus reorganised throughout the country a national standard could be maintained in contradistinction to local, separate customs, which had obtained in the Middle Ages. Labour also became more stable, by the enforcement of a definite length of service, though it seems probable that the regulations always tended to act in favour of the employer rather than of the employed.

The aim of the Elizabethan statesmen, however, was sound. They desired "to banish idleness, advance husbandry, and yield unto the hired person, both in time of scarcity and in time of plenty, a convenient proportion of wages[4]."

The act sets forth that the wages and allowances limited by previous statutes regarding labourers are in divers places too small in proportion with the advancement of prices, and therefore such laws "cannot conveniently without the greatest grief and burden of the poor man and hired labourer be put into execution."

The idea, however, that a saleable commodity like labour should find its own market price was incomprehensible to the economic thought of the age, therefore it was still conceived necessary to fix the rate of wages. Under this system, the good and the bad workman received alike the same sum of money, with the certain result that the unskilled artizan or labourer would be dismissed by his master as soon as possible, and might eventually take to "roguery" or become

---

[1] Cunningham, *Growth of English Industry and Commerce*, Part II. p. 30. "The rural artificer was no longer able to train boys in a briefer period than the townsman."

[2] Clothiers, etc., in market towns could only take the sons of 60s. freemen to be their apprentices. 5 Eliz. cap. iv. sec. xxii. Sons of 40s. freemen must be apprenticed in the corporate towns. Sec. xx.

[3] Cunningham, *op. cit.* p. 32.   [4] 5 Eliz. cap. iv. sec. i.

chargeable to the community. This, it was necessary to prevent; therefore labourers in certain specified occupations were required to remain a year with one master[1].

The act may be considered from two points of view according as it concerned

1. Labourers,
2. Apprentices.

In an agricultural district such as the North Riding of Yorkshire, labour is chiefly concerned with the land. The labourers may be divided roughly into three classes:

1. Farm servants receiving board and lodging in their master's house.

2. Day labourers each having his own holding.

3. Handicraftsmen who undertook piece-work, *e.g.* masons, thatchers, etc.

No hard and fast rule is intended in this classification; men continually passed from the first class into the second, occasionally from either of the first two classes into the third.

We have an invaluable record of agricultural work in Yorkshire in the farming book written by Henry Best, who lived at Elmswell in the East Riding. From it the following details concerning the agricultural labourer have been taken.

The farm servants started as stubble-boys, and drove the ox-plough, then gradually rose to be swineherd, neatherd, cowman, shepherd, or first man in husbandry, according to their aptitude for tending animals or working on the land. So long as they were unmarried they were boarded in their master's house and received annual wages.

The stubble-boy began at 20s. a year, which was advanced to 30s. when he was able to plough, and as soon as he was strong enough "to carry pokes[2], or fork hay or corn on to a waggon," he received 35s. or 36s. As his agricultural education advanced, and he became "a goode mower and a goode

---

[1] 5 Eliz. cap. iv. sec. ii.
[2] *Poke* is the word generally used at the present day in Yorkshire for sack.

fower horse-man, and one that can goe heppenly with a
waine, and lye on a loade of corn handsomely," then he was
third man on the farm and was worth seven nobles. The
second man in husbandry received 50s. to 54s.; he should be
able to "sowe, mowe, goe well with a draught, and bee a
good ploweman"; if necessary he accompanied the foreman
to market.

The foreman understood the whole business of husbandry,
the sowing of the right kind and amount of seed (which in
those days was always done by hand) on the right soil,
mowing, stacking, the manuring of the land, etc. He was
sent to market with the farm produce and in the absence
from home of the master he was in charge of the men; he
received "five marks per annum, and perhapps 2s. or halfe
a crowne to a godspenny[1]."

For when he was hired, each labourer or servant received
a godspenny, that is, earnest money, in token of the bargain
made between him and his master[2]. At the present day the
godspenny is usually given only when the servant is first
hired, but in the seventeenth century, the labourer received
a godspenny every year or every two years, whether he went
to a fresh place or remained with his old master. The godspenny seems to have remained stationary in spite of the
difference in the value of money; it is generally 2s. 6d. at the
present day as it was in the middle of the seventeenth century. In addition to their wages, or perhaps as part of them,
the farm servants were allowed to keep stock of their own[3];
they were also given, sometimes in lieu of wages, sometimes

[1] See Best's Farming Book for Hyringe of Servants, *Surtees Soc. Pub.*
vol. LXXXIII. pp. 132–3, from which this account of farm servants and
their wages is taken.

[2] *N.R.Q.S.R.* vol. III. p. 254. Helmsley, Jan. 1626. The following order
shows that the fact of giving the godspenny decided the obligation to
serve. "That a woman professedly hired as a servant by a Snainton man,
shall be the servant of Sam Stockton, Clerke, Vicar of Snainton, who
proves that his wife had formerly hired the said woman and given her a
Godespenny, and that he himself had duly obtained her testimoniall from
her last master."

[3] Best's Farming Book, p. 152, 1618. "William Crosswood to have
50d., and 12d., I gave him for a godspenny and a pigg oute."

as a perquisite, apparel for which their master had no longer any use; "an olde suite, a payre of breeches, an olde hatt or a payre of shoes[1]." It was a convenient method by which the employer could get rid of misfits. The Master of Elmswell gave Christopher Parson for his wage in 1642 £4. 6s. 0d., "and a pair of my boots which are too strate for mee, and a pair of old shoes[2]." Such articles of clothing were expensive at the time, and being made of better material than the labourers could afford to buy, were doubtless acceptable[3].

No man could leave service without giving his employer a quarter's warning, nor on the other hand without such warning could the master dismiss his servant[4]. While there are frequent instances of servants being presented and fined for leaving service without their master's leave[5], very seldom is the employer presented[6], and this seems to show that servants were no more plentiful in the North Riding in the seventeenth century than they are to-day.

If any special occasion arose on account of which either master or servant desired to terminate the agreement, then it was necessary to appear and explain the reason before two justices, who were to settle the matter "according to the equity of the cause." In 1605, John Turner, late servant of John Welles of Heworth, was presented "for leaving his service before his term without cause for it duly assigned before some justice." John Turner had gone to Huntingdon, probably his native place; at the same sessions Seth Stott, the

---

¹ Best's Farming Book, p. 134, also p. 153, 1619. "Robert Jefferson to have 40d. wages besides the godspenny I gave him, and an old hatt, and a pair of old showes."
² *Ibid.* p. 164.
³ *Ibid.* p. 153. Henry Best notes in his account book: hat costs 8s. 6d., pair of shoes 2s. 6d.
⁴ 5 Eliz. cap. iv. sec. iv.
⁵ *N.R.Q.S.R.* vol. IV. p. 232. "A man duly hired to service for a year for leaving his service without his master's leave." *Ibid.* vol. IV. p. 75. Malton, July, 1637. A woman "for leaving her master she had hired herself unto (fined 10s.)." See also vol. I. p. 180, vol. VI. p. 59.
⁶ *Ibid.* vol. I. p. 143. Helmsley, Jan. 1609. "Robert Stable of Sillery for putting away from his service before the end of his term and without reasonable ground, Will Lasynby, etc." See also vol. IV. p. 43.

constable of Huntingdon is presented "for permitting the said John Turner to stay in the said vill, notwithstanding the above offence. (Per Rich. Spofforth and Tho. Wait Cap. Constab.)[1]" Seth Stott is presented by the chief constables, to whom evidently John Welles of Heworth, the master, applied. It was the business of the petty constable to know when a fresh inmate came to any house, therefore Stott should have found out if Turner had received his discharge before allowing him to remain at Huntingdon.

In actual fact, even if a servant gave his quarter's warning, he could seldom leave his situation unless his master was willing, because if he desired to go out of the parish he had to obtain a testimonial from the constable[2].

In the first half of the century this regulation was constantly broken, so frequently in 1611 that at the Special Sessions for Pickering Lythe and Whitby Strand, the chief constable seems to have been nonplussed, for he sent the following memorandum to the Court of Quarter Sessions.

That there are presented in this presentment divers servantes who are departed from their maisters to other places without testimonials, therefore quere what shal be done y^r in. (Per Pollard Cap. Const.)[3]

This testimonial seems to have depended so greatly upon the employer's recommendation that presently it became the custom for the chief constable at his Sessions to ask the masters "if they will sett such and such a servant at liberty[4]," before making out the testimonial. If the master refused then the servant had to remain with him and the constable arranged "a reasonable and indifferent wage between them[4]."

"In hyringe of a servant," says Henry Best, "yow are first to make sure that hee bee sette att liberty...and soe soone as yow have hyred them, yow are to call to them for their ticketts, and thereby shall yow be secured from all future dainger[4]."

---

[1] *N.R.Q.S.R.* vol. I. pp. 11–12. Stokesley, July, 1605.
[2] 5 Eliz. cap. iv. sec. vii.
[3] *N.R.Q.S.R.* vol. I. p. 222. Pickering, April, 1611.
[4] Rural Economy in Yorkshire, Best's Farming Book, *Surtees Soc. Pub.* pp. 134–135.

Those people who were not as cautious as the Master of Elmswell and who did not ask for testimonials, found themselves summoned by the high constable to appear at Quarter Sessions. The regulation was entirely in favour of the employer. A man having a useful servant would refuse a testimonial being unwilling to set him free; if, however, in spite of this, the servant hired himself to another, then his former master summoned the new employer. Such a regulation took no account of favourable or unfavourable conditions of service, the servant was almost as completely at the mercy of an unscrupulous employer as the serf at the mercy of his lord.

There are few presentments of offences against the statute of labourers after the outbreak of the Civil War, but the case of Ellinor Bellass in 1656 illustrates the foregoing remarks and shows that the Act was still rigidly in force.

"Whereas Ellinor Bellass," the entry runs, "was by her own confession, hired servant with William Parker of Easingwold the last year and departed from her master's service about Martinmas last, without giving him a quarter's warning, or a testimonial certificate as the law directs, and that one Brian Thompson of Thirkelby hired her to be his servant in Easingwold Market without the consent of the said William Parker or seeing a testimonial certificate, the said Ellinor Bellass to be commit to the Sheriff for one and twenty days for her offence and afterwards to be sett at liberty without paying of fees and the said Brian Thompson for his offence to forfeit £5 to the Commonwealth for hiring such a person without testimonial from her master[1]."

When a farm labourer wanted to marry he left his master's house and tried to hire a cottage in the neighbourhood. This was not easy to obtain, for every house must have its four acres of land[2], and there was only a limited number of such small holdings.

Enclosure had made possible better methods of agriculture

---

[1] *N.R.Q.S.R.* vol. v. pp. 205–6. Kirbymoorside, Jan. 1656. See also vol. II. p. 239. Helmsley, July, 1610. "A Pickeringe husbandman is present for hiring another man's servant without his license etc. (fined £5)."

[2] 31 Eliz. cap. vii. The penalty for breaking the law was £10, but the fine usually inflicted was 40s. See *N.R.Q.S.R.* vol. I. pp. 92–93.

with the result that more labour was required; but though the farmers were willing to build cottages, they did not wish to give up any land to provide the necessary acres[1]. They built cottages or divided a larger house into two dwelling-places hoping the lack of the four acres might escape notice; there were, however, too many local officials who knew everybody's business; consequently yeomen are frequently presented for "building a cottage without laying four acres of land to it contrary to the statute[2]."

This unwillingness to provide more small holdings accounts for the reason why so many of the farm servants were boarded in their master's house[3], from which service some were never able to rise; consequently in old age they went to swell the ranks of the poor. "It is as usual," says Fuller, "to see a young serving man an old beggar, as to see a light horse...come to the hackney coach[4]." Possibly it is responsible also for the slow increase in population in the North Riding.

When, however, a man made up his mind to settle down, and there were no houses available, the obvious remedy was to obtain work near some village where he could find a suitable habitation. Here the law stepped in, and forbade him to leave his parish, unless he obtained a testimonial "under the seal of the Constable or other head officer, and of two other honest householders of the city, town, or parish where he last served, declaring his lawful departure[5]." The testi-

---

[1] Sometimes freeholders are presented for taking away the four acres, e.g. N.R.Q.S.R. vol. I. p. 106. "Will Rymer of Morton super Swale for contynuing a cottage wherein John Markson dwelleth, and taking that from it which did belong to it; and also for another cottage in like manner, wherein Rob Wright dwelleth."

[2] N.R.Q.S.R. vol. I. p. 68. Thirsk, April, 1607. "Rob Thompson of Alne, Yoman, for building a cottage or habitation for John Joye of Alne, Laborer, now occupied by the same, without assigning to it four acres of land etc., contrary to the Statute, 31 Eliz. etc."

[3] The custom is still very general in the North Riding and for the same reason, that there are not yet enough cottages on the farms for the labourers required.

[4] Fuller, *Holy and Profane State*, p. 17.

[5] 5 Eliz. cap. iv. sec. vii.

monial had to be registered by the curate or churchwardens and the legal charge for it was twopence.

The desired permission hinged on the interpretation of "lawful departure" in the minds of employers and officials. It is easy to conceive that if the employer wished to retain his servant he could so represent the matter to the constable, churchwardens or parson as to prevent the testimonial being given, and registered; thus it came about that by the middle of the seventeenth century no servant was able to leave his place without his master's leave.

Whenever the farm servant was fortunate enough to obtain a cottage in his own parish, he took unto himself a wife and continued his work as a day labourer.

The day labourers formed a considerable proportion of the inhabitants of the parish. Their position in the seventeenth century does not seem to have been an unfavourable one. They were not wholly dependent on their wages, indeed every labourer might be called a farmer on a small scale.

He grew on the four acres of land which was laid to his cottage[1] enough barley or maslin[2] to provide bread for his family. He had rights on the common for his cattle and a small enclosed garth or croft at the back of his cottage for his young stock. In the spring he could tether his cows on the balks, of the common fields[3] and turn them out on the stubble in the autumn. When his stock increased and he required more land he could buy cowgates or calfgates[4] from a neighbouring farmer. In some places the labourers received part of their

---

[1] 31 Eliz. cap. vii.

[2] *Maslin*, mixture of wheat and rye usually grown together.

[3] Best's Farming Book, *Surtees Soc. Pub.* vol. XXXIII. p. 118. "Our townesfolkes first on St Hellen day being the 3rd of May, beginne to teather theire draught cattle viz: theire horses and theire oxen abroade; in the field, on the heads, common balkes, boarder of fields,...and on such places, I have knowne poore folkes beginne to teather their kyne, the 20th of April."

[4] *Ibid.* p. 120. "Mrs Salvyn her gates on the Greets are allwayes att a rate viz: 5s. 4d. a cow-geast...on the Greets poore folkes putte on theire kyne and seldome speake to her for them to knowe what they shall pay till theire time be expired beinge that they knowe her usuall rate."

wages in kind[1]. The shepherd had the right to pasture so many sheep on his master's land[2]; the husbandman had a measure of corn and so much land allotted on which to sow it[3]; the neatherd had the milk of a cow and pasture for her[4].

From Henry Best's Farming Book, which gives a picture of life on a Yorkshire farm in the middle years of the seventeenth century, it would appear that considerable perquisites were allowed to trustworthy labourers. In 1622 the Master of Elmswell made the following agreements with two of his men: John Bonwicke, who was probably the foreman, was to receive for his wages "£6 in money, 8 bushells of barley, 2 bushells of oates and a pecke of oatmeale and a frise coate and a stooke of strawe every weeke from Chrissmas to Lady Day in Lent[5]." Symon Hewetson the shepherd who had 26s. wages in 1620 was to have two years later, "£5 in money and 10 sheepe wintered and the rent of his howse and garth the next yeare[6]; and I to pay for his cowes cost on the Greets the next somer[7]."

When labourers who lived in their own houses did not receive a fixed sum of money a year, they were hired by the day; in winter they received 2d., in summer 3d., a day as well as their food (without food 5d. or 6d.). Especially hard work, such as mowing grass or reaping corn, was paid at a higher rate[8].

The day was a long one; in winter "from the spring of

---

[1] Best's Farming Book, p. 134. "Some servants will condition to have soe many sheepe wintered and sommered with theire maisters, and looke how many sheepe there is, we account that equall to soe many eighteene pences."

[2] *Ibid.* p. 151. "Symond Huson to have 26s. 8d. per annum, and winteringe (1617) of 9 sheepe."

[3] *Ibid.* p. 151. "John Bonwicke senior hyred for £3 wages per annum (1617) and the sowinge of a matte of barley in the claye besides 12d. I gave him for a godspenny."

[4] *Ibid.* p. 120. "(Mrs Salvyn above) her nowtheard's wages is 20s. in money, the milke of a cow and a cow-geast." Fuller in his Essay on The good Servant mentions the servant trading for himself, as if this were a common custom.

[5] Henry Best's Account Book, *S.S.P.* vol. XXXIII. p. 154.

[6] Henry Best's Farming Book, *S.S.P.* vol. XXXIII. p. 125. The rent was 15s.

[7] Henry Best's Account Book, *S.S.P.* vol. XXXIII. p. 154.

[8] See Appendix E, scale of wages in 1658.

the day in the morning until the night of the same day, while between March and September from five of the clock in the morning, until betwixt 7 and 8 of the clock at night." The meal times were not to exceed 2½ hours and for every hour's absence the worker forfeited one penny of his wages[1]. There is no entry in the Quarter Sessions records referring to this regulation and it is difficult to believe that it was ever put in force. The fine for absence is excessive in proportion to the wage given which was not so liberal that labourers could afford to lose one penny of it.

In the seventeenth century, however, the labourer was not yet divorced from the land; and in this respect he was in a more favourable position than at the present day.

A hard-working man with a thrifty wife who looked after the homestead in his absence might under favourable conditions hope to become a farmer or even a small freeholder. But no occupation is more dependent for success on external circumstances than agriculture. A series of bad harvests, or an outbreak of cattle plague, might sweep away the savings of many years and reduce a man almost to beggary. In such a case the law stepped in and hindered him still further in the effort of making good his losses by restricting his personal action and tying him down to his native place. For, if he desired to mend his fortunes elsewhere, no parish would receive him, unless he proved satisfactorily that neither he nor his family would ever become chargeable to it[2]. Back he must go to his old home, whether there was work for him or not.

There remains the class of occasional labourers; handicraftsmen, such as masons, carpenters, thatchers, etc., who earned their living by an occupation, but were able in slack times to do other work, and whose labour rate was fixed by the Justices of the Peace.

These men, being more independent, frequently showed discontent with "statute wages."

---

[1] 5 Eliz. cap. iv. sec. ix.   [2] See ch. iv. p. 63, note 4.

At the Special Sessions held for Birdforth and Allerton-shire in October, 1610, before three Justices only six persons were presented. Of these two were men who refused to work for the wages allowed[1]. One would not thresh under 4*d*. a day, the other would not thatch at the statute rate. Almost all living-houses had thatched roofs in the seventeenth century and thatching was amongst the better paid work, the rate being the same as that of mowers of grass, carpenters and masons, *i.e.*, in 1658, 6*d*. a day with food and 1s. without. The same proportion as regards food holds good for all "day taile" men. Reapers of corn receive 4*d*. a day with food, 8*d*. without[2]; possibly the Justices never asked themselves why reapers of corn should be expected to eat less than mowers of grass. Henry Best explains why his thatchers have 4*d*. a day though in most places 6*d*. "and theire meatee...if they meate themselves they have usually 10*d*. a day."

"Because," he remarks, "theire dyett is not as in other places; for they are to have three meales a day...and att each meale fower services, viz: butter, milke, cheese and either egges, pyes, or bacon, and sometimes porridge insteade of milke[3]."

Moreover thatchers did not work in the coldest weather, therefore they could not earn a regular wage all the year round; they usually stopped thatching for the winter about Martinmas, "for it is an occupation that will not gette a man heate in a frosty morninge, sitting on the top of an house, wheare the winde commeth to him on every side."

Thatching is an occupation which requires skill, and a man who could do his work really well was in great request; doubtless there was plenty of temptation for such a man to demand higher wages[4]. People must have a dry roof over their heads, yet by the enforcement of statute wages, the

---

[1] *N.R.Q.S.R.* vol. I. p. 220. Thirsk Special Sessions, 29 Oct. 1610.
[2] See Appendix E, Rate of wages assessed by the Justices in 1658, *Ibid.* vol. VI. pp. 3–4.
[3] Best's Farming Book, *S.S.P.* vol. XXXIII. p. 138.
[4] *N.R.Q.S.R.* vol. II. p. 171. "Will Bartman of Askrigg, Thatcher, for taking wages contrarie to the statute etc. (per ad Thomlinson Cap. Const.)."

man who could efficiently produce this roof received the same wages as the man whose thatching let the rain water come in.

The carpenters, masons and tailors usually took their apprentices with them and if the apprentice had served two or three years of his term and knew his trade, his master received half wages for him with or without food; thus the apprentice was expected to eat half as much as his master, while as actual fact he probably ate more. Just as in medieval times a man had to work so many days in the busy seasons on his lord's land even if he owed no other service[1], so in the seventeenth century each parish expected its joiner or tailor or cobbler to give it the benefit of his labour, in the haytime or the harvest. Thomas Ledell of Ampleforth, a rough waller, was presented at Quarter Sessions in 1614 for "refusing to work for statute wages beginning divers woorkes and leaving them unfinished going forth of the North Riding into other countryes to worke in sommer so as his neighbours cannot have his worke in haytime and harvest[2]"; he was let off without a fine because he was poor but he might have been put in the stocks "by the space of two days and one night," for this was the penalty imposed by law on anyone who refused to work in hay time or harvest "for the mowing...or inning of corn, grain, and hay[3]," when requested to do so by a Justice of the Peace or the petty constable. Only when not wanted at home and armed with a testimonial under a Justice's hand, might men go harvesting into other parishes[4]; otherwise they were liable to be presented at Quarter Sessions[5].

The feeling that a man's labour should be at the disposal

---

[1] See Appendix F, where in 1641, at Watton, the tenants were still "tyed" to go to Lord Finch's sheepshearing.

[2] *N.R.Q.S.R.* vol. II. p. 53. Malton, Oct. 1614.

[3] 5 Eliz. cap. iv. sec. xv.

[4] *Ibid.* iv. sec. xvi.

[5] *N.R.Q.S.R.* vol. I. p. 202. Topcliffe, Oct. 1610. Three men of Cayton presented "for denying to worke amongst their neighbours in Harvest and for departing forth of the Libertie for greater wages."

of his farming neighbours still lingers in country districts in
the North Riding. The village mason, the joiner, the innkeeper, invariably hire themselves out to the surrounding
farmers in hay time and harvest. In the wide moorland
parishes the large farmers send their mowing machines to
cut the little grass fields of the cottagers and in return the
whole village turns out to help the farmer gather in his
larger crop of hay. The essential difference lies in the fact
that such labour is entirely voluntary on both sides. In the
seventeenth century much of the agricultural work was let
out by piece to labourers, *e.g.* the threshers were paid by
the amount threshed[1]; whatever bargain was made with
such pieceworkers or with bricklayers, carpenters, etc., they
received a godspenny[2]. Part of their wages, also, was frequently paid in kind[3].

The high constable was responsible to the Justices for the
administration of the Statute of Labourers.

"Aboute a fortnight or tenne dayes before Martynmasse," says
Henry Best, "the chiefe constable of every division sendeth abroad
his precepts to all pettie constables, willinge them to give notice to
all masters and servants within theire severall constableries howe
that hee intendeth to sitte att such a place on such a day, command-
inge everie of them to bringe in a bill of the names of all the masters
and servants within theire severall constableries[4]."

These Sessions became the fixed public hiring days still in
vogue in the North Riding. The high constable's Sessions,
however, was not the origin of the hirings; for there is

[1] In 1641 4*d*. a quarter for oats, 8*d*. a qr for winter corne, viz. wheat
and rye, 5*d*. a qr for barley, 6*d* a qr for pease. Also each man had a threave
(2 stookes or 24 sheaves) of straw a week of whatever kind he thrashed.
[2] See Best's Farming Book. Carpenter receives 3*d*. godspenny, p. 156.
Brickmaker, executing an order to value of £73. 6*s*. 8*d*., receives 12*d*. godspenny, p. 161.
[3] Best's Farming Book, p. 156. "Bargained with...carpenters to digg
up a walnutt tree of myne and to saw it into 2 ynch and a half plankes,
and the rest of the small peeces into such peeces as it is fittest for; and to
make mee two chaires one for myselfe and the other a lesser, well turned
and wrought, and I am to give them for doing these things above mentioned
workmanlike 10*s*. in money, a bushell of barley and a pecke of oatemeal
and give them in money 3*d*. for their godspenny."
[4] *Ibid.* p. 134.

mention of them so early as the fourteenth century. After the disastrous Black Death the Statute of Labourers of 1351 ordered all labourers to appear, tools in hand, in the market towns, there to be publicly hired. It is possible, however, that the hirings became fixed and settled institutions through their intimate connection with these special Sessions of the high constable.

When the high constable had received the bills he called the masters separately before him in the order in which they were set down and asked them if they would set such and such a servant at liberty, and, if the master was willing, the chief constable made out the ticket or testimonial "and the servant giveth him 2d. for his paines."

If the master agreed with his servants that they should remain in his service, then neither he nor they were obliged to go to the high constable's Sessions, but the master had to pay 1d. to the high constable for every servant who remained two years in a place. He also gave his servant another godspenny. Henry Best in his advice to young farmers about hiring servants gives a picture of the hirings in the Yorkshire of his day. So strong is the force of custom in rural districts, so conservative is the cold North, that the same picture can be seen in most of its details on the market days in the small rural towns just before Martinmas and May-day at the present time.

The farm labourers and maid servants still go to the hirings, having "putte on theire best apparrelle that theire masters may see them well cladde." They do not stand in the churchyard as formerly but at the market cross or in the town hall; nor does their prospective employer "call them aside and walke to the backe side of the church, and there treat of theire wage," but little groups of people may be seen standing in the broad open square seriously discussing such matters.

They still receive their godspenny, which is considered as binding as formerly, and come to their new quarters after two or three days with their friends. If, however, the masters should "say to a mayde when they hire her that if shee have but beene used to washinge, milkinge, brewinge, and bakinge, they make no question but shee can sweepe the howse and wash the dishes[1]," it is to be feared that they would not receive a very satisfactory answer; indeed they have to be content with fewer qualifications at the present day. Only the high constable is absent, together with the vexatious legislation it was his business to enforce.

The petty constables in producing their bills of all the masters and servants in their township entered also the names of those employers who would not register their servants, nor the wages they gave, and such people were presented by the chief constable at the next Quarter Sessions[2], together with the names of those who were giving wages in excess of the rate set down by the Justices[3].

There was considerable opposition to this part of the act even though it had been in existence already more than forty years. In 1607 the inhabitants of Thirkleby (Great and Little) are presented "for refusing to give the names of their servants and their wages to the Constables of the said townes or to the High Constables." Likewise also the inhabitants of Kilbornes, Over and Nether; in their case the high constable seems to have divined the reason, since, though they refused to disclose the wages, he presents them "for giving their servants more wages than the statute doth allow[4]." Sometimes the petty constable refused "to make

---

[1] Henry Best's Farming Book, *S.S.P.* vol. XXXIII. pp. 134–6.

[2] *N.R.Q.S.R.* vol. I. p. 65. "Richard Mennell of Dalton Gent. for refusing to record his servants, etc., and Isaac Pilkington for the like." *Ibid.* vol. I. p. 69. Thirsk, Ap. 1607. "Tho. Orange of East Harlesey for refusing to give a note of his servantes and their wages, etc. (Per Will Hodge Cap. Const.)"

[3] *Ibid.* vol. I. Helmsley, Jan. 8, 1607. "Cuthbert Ibyson of Awdwarke, Husbn, for reteyning Tim Johnson servant at husbandry for 46s. contrary to the rates assessed by the Justices, etc." Vol. I. p. 207. Helmsley, Jan. 8, 1610. "Widowe Nesse of Fryghton for giving to her servant £4. 6s. 8d. wages."

[4] *N.R.Q.S.R.* vol. I. p. 60. Helmsley, Jan. 8, 1607.

presentment of the maisters and servants and their wages[1]."
The high constable, who, unlike the Justices, received no
remuneration for his time spent at the Hiring Sessions, was
accustomed to charge the masters one penny for registering
each servant, and this also was resented[2]. Gradually, however, the law asserted itself and after a few years there are
no further presentments of this kind[3].

As soon as a servant was hired his master was expected
to record his name and the salary given[4], and the servant
had to show his testimonial to the constable, curate or
churchwardens of the parish in which he was going to live;
otherwise he was liable to imprisonment until he obtained
his testimonial and if he failed to obtain it within twelve
days he was to be whipped as a vagabond[5]. Though it is
dangerous work for one century to criticise the methods of
another, yet it may be suggested that Tudor legislation
took, unknowingly perhaps, the surest way to produce
rogues and vagabonds.

That hardworking sons of the soil should have been so
treated for what was mere negligence or at worst a certain
conservative obstinacy against new fashions, shows clearly
enough that their position in the eyes of the state was not
far removed from serfdom. It must be noted, however, that
the records of the time show that it was the employer who
generally got into trouble for not showing testimonials[6], at
any rate with regard to servants living in the house.

[1] N.R.Q.S.R. vol. I. p. 248. Richmond, Jan. 14, 1612.
[2] Ibid. vol. I. p. 60. Helmsley, Jan. 8, 1607. "In 1607 Rob Bossal
of Huby is presented...for refusing to pay 1d. to the head Constable for
entering his wages in their booke according to the custome." Also at
the same Sessions, "John Gelderd of Wigginthorp, for refusing to pay
pence for 5 servantes for entering their names and wages."
[3] After 1611 very few, the latest regarding wages is 1621; "Marm:
Wilde of Hunton, gentn, for refusing to register his servantes names,"
Ibid. vol. III. p. 111. Evidently there was no respect for persons for he was
one of the county treasurers.
[4] Ibid. vol. I. p. 69. Thirsk, Jan. 17, 1606. "John Bulmer of West
Cottam, husbn, for hiring servants without recording their names and
salaries before the chief constable contra formam statutis; and also Rob
Harrison and Will Keldell both of the same for the like."
[5] 5 Eliz. cap. iv.
[6] N.R.Q.S.R. vol. I. p. 69. Thirsk, April, 1607. "John Rymer for re-

Moreover, since the Elizabethan legislators recognised that all men had a right to work, they would not allow that any one should be idle. Only those who could show that they had enough money to keep them might retain this privilege. Any man who "had not a convenient farm or other holding in tillage on which he might employ his labour," and who was not an apprentice, could be compelled to serve in husbandry by any person "that keepeth husbandry," or, if he knew a trade, by any master in that trade[1]. Parents were summoned if they kept their children at home out of service[2]. Unmarried women between the ages of twelve and forty could be compelled to go into service by the year, week or day[3]. It is quite evident also that many women were employed as day labourers, as indeed they are at the present day, but not for such hard work as formerly. Two women were always employed to help the thatcher; one drew the straw, the other served the thatcher by carrying the "bottles[4]" of straw and forking them up to him; she also tempered the mortar and carried it up. The handling of the heavy damp straw and the heavier mortar seems very hard work for a woman. This was recognised, for she earned 4d. a day, while the drawer only received 3d.[5] Women were also employed to spread manure or scatter mole-hills, to gather stones, to pull peas, and to work in the hay and the harvest. They were not paid well; a man got 4d. a day for reaping corn, a woman 3d. The domestic servants were probably paid the best. Dairymaids seem to have been in great demand, and were frequently offered and accepted

teyning unto his service one Jayne Taylour without showing any testimonial to the Constable Curate or Churchwardens contrary etc." *Ibid.* vol. I. pp. 206–7. Helmsley, Jan. 1610. "Will Jenninge of Cornborough for reteyning in his service John Pope without shewing testimonial to the Constable Curate etc."

[1] 5 Eliz. cap. iv. secs. iii and v.

[2] *N.R.Q.S.R.* vol. I. p. 220. Thirsk Special Sessions, Oct. 29, 1610. In 1610 a certain Ann Milner is presented at Thirsk Special Sessions "for keeping Will Gainesby her son at home out of service."

[3] 5 Eliz. cap. iv. sec. xvii.

[4] A "bottle" was as much as a person could carry; in this case the sheaf of straw drawn ready for thatching. Cp. the proverb A needle in a bottle of hay.

[5] Henry Best's Farming Book, pp. 138–9.

more than statute wages. In 1681 an Eppleby yeoman was presented for agreeing to give his dairymaid £2. 10s. 0d. per annum, "which was more than he ought to give or she ought to receive[1]."

In 1680 the Justices had ordained that a dairymaid should not receive more than 40s. a year and any other maid not more than 33s. 4d.

These wages were an advance on those given at the beginning of the century when an ordinary maid received 26s.[2] Henry Best notes that formerly maids could be hired for 18s. per annum, and 12d. or 1s. 6d. for a godspenny, but that in 1641 "wee cannot hyre a good lusty mayd servant under 24s. wage, and sometimes 28s., and 18d. or 2s. for a godspenny[3]."

Frequently, however, the girls seem to have entered service quite young and to have received small wages which were raised yearly. This was the case with Priscilla Browne, one of those "lusty maids" who lived at Elmswell.

Priscilla Browne had (the first yeare shee dwelt heare) 18s. wage and 12d. to a godspenny, the next year 24s., the 3rd year 28s. and 2s. to a godspenny, and might have had the fowerth yeare 38s. and 12d. to a godspenny[3].

Maid servants in the farm houses needed to be lusty for they must have worked hard; not only was there the brewing, milking, churning, and washing to do, the house to keep tidy, but also the cooking for all the men-servants, five and six in number, and the preparation of meals for them.

The life of the farm labourer and the domestic servant was never monotonous. Each season brought with it its different occupation, and as one strenuous course of labour after another was accomplished—the sowing of the corn, the shearing of sheep, the gathering in of the harvest—a general

---

[1] *N.R.Q.S.R.* vol. VII. p. 47. Bedale, Jan. 1681.
[2] *Ibid.* vol. I. p. 130. Malton, Oct. 1608. "Anth. Pubons of Thirske, tanner, presented for hiring etc Margaret Sewghell from May 3 to Martinmas, engaging to give her 13s. wages, for paying her no more than 8s. &c."
[3] Best's Farming Book, p. 133.

merrymaking took place with dancing and bagpipes and a hearty supper[1]. Except for the few days at Martinmas when the servants went to see their friends, the only holidays were Sundays and festivals; when, however, the Puritans held sway, Parliament ordained in 1647 that all festival days should be abolished and that apprentices, etc., were to be allowed every second Tuesday in each month.

The legislators anticipated the Shop Hours Act by commanding that on such holidays all shop windows were to be shut from eight in the morning until eight at night. The constable, however, was ordered to search the alehouses and if he found any servants or apprentices there after eight in the evening they were to be punished[2].

The only time when games were allowed was at Christmas, but woe betide those who attempted to continue the Christmas festival after Twelfth Night. Will Bretton of Thornton Beanes is presented on January 12th in the year 1613 for "playing at cardes with other men's servantes for money in his house out of Christenmas, viz. on Sonday 10 Jany inst.[3]" After they had been to church on Sunday lawful games were allowed, but few were within that category. The servants might even be required to work on Sundays during harvest for the Queen's Injunctions ordered parsons to teach their parishioners "that they may with a safe and quiet conscience, after their common prayer in the time of harvest labour upon the holy and festival days and save that thing which God hath sent[4]."

The Statute of Labourers and Apprentices was placed under the administration of the Justices, who

at every general sessions first to be holden after Easter...calling unto them such discreet and grave persons of the said county or city as they shall think meet and conferring together respecting the plenty or scarcity of the time, and other circumstances necessary to

[1] See *Winter's Tale* for sheep shearing feast, Act IV. Sc. 4; also Appendix F.
[2] J. Huntingford, *The laws of Masters and Servants*, 1790.
[3] *N.R.Q.S.R.* vol. II. p. 13. Richmond, Jan. 1613.
[4] Queen's Injunctions, xx.

be considered, have authority within the limits of their several commissions to rate and appoint the wages[1].

This governmental function of appointing the rate of wages was the greatest power ever delegated to local magistrates, because the fortunes of many men were dependent on the faithful discharge by the Justices of this part of their work. In the North Riding the wages seem to have been rated at regular intervals[2], but there is ground for believing that they were always lower than they would have been if assessed by the economic need of the time in an open labour market[3]. Employers were frequently in trouble for giving "unreasonable wages," which in the eyes of the Justices undoubtedly meant higher than the rate assessed by them[4]. In April, 1680, the wages seem to have been regulated much under the market price, for in the January Sessions of 1681 after the Michaelmas hirings, there are numerous presentments, of which the following is a type; it throws some light on the domestic service of the time.

"At Thirske Sessions[5], April 20, 1680," the entry runs, "before Sir Richd Grahme of Nunington, Sir Will Frankland, Sir Will Chaytor, Tho. Metcalfe Esq., and their associated Justices, the majority of the said Justices had limited and rated and appointed among other wages of servants and labourers that a maid able to take care of brewing, baking and a dairy, being retained by a gentn, widow or yeoman, should not receive for her salary with food and drink, more than 40s. per annum, and that any other maid should not receive with food and drink, more than 33s. 4d.; and Richd

---

[1] 5 Eliz. cap. iv. sec. xi.

[2] There are many presentments for giving wages "contrary to the rates assessed by the Justices," see *N.R.Q.S.R.* vol. I. pp. 60, 99, 143. In vol. VI. pp. 3–4 the rates for 1658 are given, see Appendix E. In vol. VII. p. 33 there is a reference to the rates assessed by the Justices at the Quarter Sessions held at Thirsk in April, 1680. In April, 1692, an order is given at Thirsk for "the same rates of wages for servants and labourers to stand for this year as they were appointed and settled by order of this court for the last yeer." Vol. VII. p. 128.

[3] Miss Leonard shows in her book on *The Early History of English Poor Relief* that the Privy Council interfered with the Justices' ruling on behalf of the workers.

[4] *N.R.Q.S.R.* vol. IV. p. 270. Thirsk, April, 1647. Warrant issued against a man "for paying unreasonable wages to a labr contrary to law."

[5] *Ibid.* vol. VII. p. 45. Helmsley, Jan. 11, 1680.

Melton of Hemsleys Ambo, gentleman, retained a certain Mary Benton to be his domestic servant for dairy work and agreed to give her and she, well knowing the premisses, agreed to accept, for her wages, £3, which was a larger wage than he ought to give or she ought to receive, according to the rates of servants wages appointed as aforesaid."

The penalty for giving wages higher than the rate allowed was a fine of £5 and ten days' imprisonment, for receiving the same twenty-one days' imprisonment[1]; it is to be hoped that Mary Benton, who was evidently such a clever servant that she could obtain half as much more salary than the legal wage for dairymaids, did not suffer the extreme penalty.

In 1680 the Justices issue a special order in July and October to the petty and high constables enjoining them to make returns of the names of masters and servants "what services they are in, what wages they have, and when their terms expire[2]." Again the next year, in January[3] and July[4], they order the constables "to make return of all servants that remain at home and are able to work[3]," and they allow 30s. which is to be paid by the Treasurer "for the charges of printing the rate of servants wages and rules for the better observation of the Statute of the 5th of Elizth touching servants and labourers[5]." Thus more than a century later, when the battle of individual liberty had been fought, and won, the domestic legislation of the Tudors still remained in force.

From the records it is clear that the act was regularly administered in the North Riding throughout the seventeenth century. The chief constable held his Statute Sessions twice a year, before May-day and Martinmas, consequently the presentments were more numerous at the July and January Quarter Sessions, and offences against the statute were tried at both Special and Quarter Sessions.

---

[1] 5 Eliz. cap. iv. sec. xiii.
[2] *N.R.Q.S.R.* vol. VII. p. 38. Richmond, July, 1680.
[3] *Ibid.* vol. VII. p. 48. Bedale, Jan. 1681.
[4] *Ibid.* vol. VII. p. 51. Richmond, July, 1681.
[5] *Ibid.* vol. VII. p. 50. Stokesley, July, 1681.

The earliest record of the North Riding Quarter Sessions contains a presentment of one "Wilfrid Fewster of Byland, for retaining in his service Christopher Blacke without the license or certificate of the said Blacke's late master[1]," showing that the act was in good working order in 1605.

APPRENTICES

The Justices were enjoined to hold two Sessions[2] "to make especiall and diligent enquiry" of the good execution "of the act, and for each day on which they sat to administer it they received 5s. paid out of the fines levied for offences against it[3]."

On the other hand every Justice was liable to a fine of £5 if he neglected to attend[4]. But such Special Sessions of Justices in different divisions of the Riding were not limited to offences against this particular statute; they also took cognisance of any infringement of other social legislation. Out of Sessions also the Justices were called upon to witness the signing of indentures for apprenticeship. When a boy became of an age to be apprenticed, that is any time from seven to fourteen years old, as soon as the trade was selected and arrangements duly made, the parties had to appear before two Justices in whose presence the indenture of apprenticeship was signed[5].

The indenture sets forth that for seven years the apprentice must serve his master "as a true and faithful servant ought to behave himself."

It enjoined on the master to teach his apprentice "and in due manner to chastise him, findynge unto his said servant meate, drinke, linnen, woollen, hose, shoes and all other things to him necessary[6]."

[1] *N.R.Q.S.R.* vol. I. p. 2. Thirsk, April, 1605.
[2] 5 Eliz. cap. iv. sec. xxx.   [3] *Ibid.* sec. xxxi.   [4] *Ibid.* sec. xii.
[5] People were summoned if they neglected to get indentures. In July, 1613, a carpenter was presented at Helmsley for entertaining a person as his apprentice for six years and never had indentures, etc., and the latter for working as a carpenter and not having served for seven years, etc. *N.R.Q.S.R.* vol. II. p. 23.
[6] See Appendix C for Indenture of Apprenticeship.

Thus the bond is not one between teacher and pupil but between servant and master, more nearly approaching the bond which existed between the lord and his serf. Though the indenture could be signed before two Justices, four magistrates were required by law to cancel it[1]. Sometimes two Justices arbitrate between a master and his apprentice, but their award had to be read and confirmed at the Quarter Sessions[2], where causes of dispute were generally signed by the four Justices[3].

Since almost all legislation can be traced to some existing custom it is interesting to notice that though serfs and villeins had almost disappeared from the land, yet the power of the feudal lord is shown in the complete sway the master is allowed to exercise over his apprentice.

If an apprentice ran away neither his parents nor his friends could receive him without being liable to be summoned[4] at Quarter Sessions. Very seldom was there any inquiry why the apprentice left his master; he was sought out, brought back[5], and generally severely punished[6]. The premium paid by the parents when the indenture was signed, in money or labour or both, was forfeited for any misbehaviour on the part of the apprentice. In 1622 "Will Huntrodes of Filingdale, weaver, makes complaint that his apprentice Will, son of Chr. Browne, of the same place, has run away from his service; which is admitted."

---

[1] 5 Eliz. cap. iv. sec. xxviii.

[2] *N.R.Q.S.R.* vol. vi. p. 152. New Malton, Jan. 1671.

[3] *Ibid.* vol. vi. pp. 189–190. Richmond, July, 1673. There is a long entry about an apprentice who had not been properly taught by his master, therefore the Justices discharge him of his apprenticeship; "the said indenture of apprenticehood notwithstanding; in witness whereof we have hereunto set our hands and seals at the Sessions aforesaid, the day and year abovesaid; Rich. Grahme, Will Robinson, Henry Calverley."

[4] This is shown in the following presentment at Thirsk, April, 1608: "Tho. Smelt of Gilling labr for enticing John Smith apprentice to Chr. Wilson of Ampleforth, from his service and receiving him into his house."

[5] At Richmond, July, 1667: "a woman of Well for taking her son away from his master before the time of his apprenticeship had expired."

[6] *N.R.Q.S.R.* vol. iv. Helmsley, July, 1641. A warrant is issued "to enforce the return of an apprentice to a tailor, who had served 3 years out of his 7 and then run away."

The Court Ordered that the Indentures be cancelled, that Hunt-rodes keep all moneys paid to him on account of the lad, that Chr. Browne shall still plowe Huntrode's land as he had agreed to do but gratis, and that he shall enter bond to deliver his son to one of the Constables of Whitby by 9 o'clock on the following Saturday morning, to be set in the stockes in the Market place for 4 hours, the boy to be kept in the custody of the constable of Filingdale in the mean time.

For seven years the apprentice was handed over to his master, who, so long as he taught him his trade, exercised over him very full powers, even to transferring him to another master against his will[1].

If the apprentice misbehaved himself he was sent to the House of Correction. In 1670 an order was made for

an apprentice who was in the House of Correction for departing from his master to be received again as an apprentice by his said master, according to the form of his indentures, and the said master not to be too cruel with him, but use him accordingly as an apprentice ought to be[2].

It would be interesting to know what degree of cruelty the Bench allowed to a master. Even in cases of ill-usage, the utmost penalty which is imposed on the master is the cancelling of the indenture and the return of part of the money paid as a premium. A particularly bad case of ill-treatment occurs in 1658,

upon petition of Will Thompson of Osmotherley whereby it is testi-fied that John Johnson useth the son of the said William, his appren-tice not after the manner of an apprentice, beating him, pulling the haire of his head, by dragging him about the house thereby and almost strangling him in a bridle raine, and other great and unhand-some usage. The said John Johnson to appear to show cause why his said apprentice and he should not be parted and abide the end of the court[3].

---

[1] N.R.Q.S.R. vol. III. p. 131. Malton, Jan. 9, 1622. In 1622 the Court issues a warrant to appear at the next sessions against "John Binninge of Tirrington, apprentice to Stephen Hogg of the same, cordwainer, having divers years of his apprenticeship to serve and having been assigned by his master to serve those years with one Lawrence Peacocke of the same place, cordwainer, and a sufficient workman, but obstinately refusing to serve the said Peacocke."

[2] Ibid. vol. VI. p. 143. Thirsk, April, 1670.

[3] Ibid. vol. VI. p. 6. Thirsk, April, 1658.

In July the Court

ordered with consent of Will Thompson of Osmotherley and John Johnson of the same, about parting of Thomas Thompson, apprentice to John Johnson, the said apprentice having been examined of his master's ill-usage towards him and the parties having referred themselves to this Court, that the said master and apprentice shall be parted, and Johnson to repay of the 50s. with his apprentice 35s. back to Will Thompson by Aug. 24th next[1].

The premium paid for an apprentice varied according to the trade and the circumstances of the parties. John Johnson who used his apprentice so "unhandsomely" received 50s. with him, and this is a very usual sum; in 1673 the Court allows £5 for the apprenticeship of a child born in the county gaol[2]. No man without reasonable cause could refuse to take an apprentice[3]. Indeed the position of the master was so favourable that possibly the only cases of refusal were the children of paupers or felons[4]. Regulations, however, were made to ensure that the apprentice was instructed in his trade. Only people who were householders[5] and who had half a ploughland at least in tillage might take apprentices. Moreover, for such trades as that of cloth-maker, tailor, shoemaker, etc., they were to employ for every three apprentices one journeyman[6], who had also learnt his trade and was therefore capable of teaching it to his master's apprentices.

If a man became incapacitated for work[7] or if he died[8]

[1] *N.R.Q.S.R.* vol. VI. p. 9. New Malton, July, 1658.
[2] *Ibid.* vol. VI. p. 185. Thirsk, April, 1673.
[3] *Ibid.* vol. II. p. 309. Stokesley, March, 1630. A Marton man is presented "for refusing a widow's son to be his apprentice for seaven years being desired thereunto."
[4] Many of the parish children (*i.e.* those supported by the poor rate) were apprenticed to the farmers and became agricultural labourers or domestic servants.
[5] 5 Eliz. cap. iv. sec. xviii; cp. *N.R.Q.S.R.* vol. II. p. 231. A Pickering tailor is presented at Ebberston Special Sessions for "(being no householder) keeping and maintaininge two servants or apprentices, etc."
[6] *Ibid.* cap. iv. sec. xxvi.
[7] *N.R.Q.S.R.* vol. VI. p. 159. Richmond, July, 1671. A certain tailor becomes blind, the court orders that he shall assign his apprentice to some person "being a sufficient workman" of the same trade, "or otherwise deliver up to his said apprentice his indenture of apprentice."
[8] *Ibid.* vol. V. p. 120. Thirsk, Oct. 1652. A widow is ordered "either

arrangements had to be made by his widow or his friends to teach the apprentice. Indentures, which were so rigidly adhered to, were allowed to be cancelled if the apprentice could prove that he was not learning his trade[1].

The law demanded that every man exercising "the art or mystery" of any trade should have served an apprenticeship to that trade for seven years[2]. It was not difficult for the local authority to carry out this regulation, since under the act, half the fine (forty shillings, a month default) went to the person giving information "to him that will sue for it[3]"; commercial jealousy was ever ready to keep out intruders, especially those who had not even benefited the trade to the extent of giving their services free for seven years while learning it.

In 1607 Will. Watson of Sheriff Hatton is presented for "exercising the misterie of a taylor not having served any master as an apprentice[4]."

In 1610 an order of the Court of Quarter Sessions speaks of neglect on the part of the Justices in keeping their Special Sessions to administer the Statute of Labourers and Apprentices within their several divisions, and desires them to hold such Sessions twice yearly as enjoined by the act[5].

Consequent on this order in October, 1611, "9 butchers, 4 bakers, 4 glovers, 1 chandler, 2 slaters and 4 badgers are presented for using their trade without having served seven years[6]."

Presentments of this nature appear intermittently all through the century, though more numerous in the early years.

to repay the money her husband had with his apprentice, or to take care the apprentice be taught his trade of butcher."

[1] *N.R.Q.S.R.* vol. v. p. 111. Malton, July, 1652. "A Wiggington pewterer having failed to teach his trade to an apprentice bound to him, to th'end the said apprentice may not lose any of the time he is to gain his trade in, he is to be permitted to leave his said master and apply to anyone else he is able to arrange with."

[2] 5 Eliz. cap. iv. sec. xxiv.

[3] *Ibid.* cap. iv. sec. xxxii.

[4] *N.R.Q.S.R.* vol. I. p. 69. Thirsk, April, 1607.

[5] *Ibid.* vol. I. p. 204. Topcliffe, Oct. 1610.

[6] *Ibid.* vol. I. pp. 235–6. Malton, Oct. 1611.

Contemporary plays[1] show us that the apprentices were a happy rollicking set, generally treated by their master as members of the family, and fully deserving his confidence; often, however, getting into trouble because they persisted in courting his daughters.

Shakespeare, who was country-bred, portrays the Justice and the constable, while Dekker, who was of the town, gives a picture of the life of the apprentice. But in the records of the Quarter Sessions there are comparatively few references to the apprentice, since the North Riding contained no large towns, being almost wholly agricultural, and in the seventeenth century possessing even fewer trades and industries than at the present day.

THE CONDITIONS OF SERVICE OF WORKERS IN THE SEVENTEENTH CENTURY

Many of the regulations relating to contracts were settled by the Justices out of Sessions. If this method failed then the matter was referred to the Court[2]. If a servant could not obtain his wages from his employer he appealed to the Court of Quarter Sessions[3], which, however, frequently appointed one or more Justices to arbitrate in the case[4].

[1] E.g. *The Shoemaker's Holiday.*

[2] *N.R.Q.S.R.* vol. I. p. 33. Thirsk, April, 1606. In April, 1606, "Thomas Hargate of Bulmer, gentleman, is summoned for keeping in his service without any certificate one Ursula Fitchet from Martinmas last till now. The said Ursula being a duly contracted and hired servant with Ths. Bamburgh of Cramb, and although she, the said Ursula being brought on a warrant before Sir Wll. Bamburgh, J.P., owned the contract and was ordered to return to her former service."

[3] *Ibid.* vol. V. p. 188. Malton, July, 1655. "Upon complaint made by John Taylor that whereas he was the legal hired servant of John Worsley Esq. in the year 1654, nevertheless he detains and withholds his wages; these are therefore to require you the said John Worsley to pay the said servant his wages acc. to covenant or appear before the two next J.P.s to shew cause wherefore you detain the said wages."

Ibid. vol. VI. p. 87. Thirsk, April, 1665. "A New Malton man found guilty of detaining his servant's wages, and fined £3."

[4] *Ibid.* vol. IV. pp. 4–5. Helmsley, Jan. 1664. "A New Malton yeomn. for refusing to pay £3 of lawful money to his servant for one whole year's service. The difference between the yeoman and his servant was referred to a gentn. of New Malton and a gentn. of Kirby Misperton who ordered the New Malton man to pay his servant £2 of the wages which was in arrears."

Some curiously detailed orders are made[1]. One master refuses to pay wages because the servant has lost some tools, he is ordered to deduct their value[2]; an apprentice is allowed to count the time he served as a soldier in the Parliament's service in the time of his apprenticeship[3].

The legislation regarding labourers and apprentices took away from the Lord of the Manor the ancient customary right of arranging the price of labour, and gave it to the Justice of the Peace; it also deprived the lord of exclusive right to the labour of his tenants; nevertheless it still endeavoured to bind down the labourer to the soil, by restrictions on his freedom of movement.

So long, however, as Queen Elizabeth's act of four acres of land to every cottage remained in force, it is probable that the fixing of the wages rate was not an insupportable grievance, for the whole maintenance of the labourer was not dependent on his money-wage[4]. In almost every village the subsidiary employment of spinning and weaving was actively carried on, especially by women, together with the agricultural work. So long as the labourer, or the handicraftsman, kept his holding and his commonable rights he had an economic motive. He was perhaps in as good a position financially as the small freeholder, who was obliged to pay many lays and assessments levied on his land.

Nor was the labourer oppressed and downtrodden. To the young, the strong, the energetic, life was very tolerable and

---

[1] *N.R.Q.S.R.* vol. v. p. 151. Allerton, Jan. 1654. "Elias Hutchingson of Kilvington, Clerk, for not paying his servant his wages—the Minister traverses and upon traverse is found guilty for not paying the same, a J.P. to mediate an end thereto if he can, otherwise to see Justice done."

[2] *Ibid.* vol. II. p. 38. Helmsley, July, 1614. "That an Ellingthorpe gentn pay his late servant in husbandry the wages yet due to him for last year's service, and also the like proportion of wages from Martinmasse last to Christenmasse now past, deducting the value of a hatchet and a spade alleged to be lost by the said servant."

[3] *Ibid.* vol. v. p. 119. Thirsk, Oct. 1652. "The tyme Percivall Trewhitt, a shoemaker, served as a soldier in the Parliament's service to be allowed him in the time of his apprenticeship. as if he had continued with his master."

[4] Thorold Rogers suggests that working for money was a by-employment.

contained infinite possibilities. His four acres gave each man a certain position in the village hegemony; he graded off into the small farmer, or the freeholder, who augmented his scanty income by working for day wages. Labourers are found undertaking the office of petty constable, and even churchwarden; together with yeomen they get into trouble for forcible entry, for poaching, for playing unlawful games, or for breaking those other social statutes enacted for their benefit and improvement, and they seem to have been able to pay the considerable fines imposed for these offences. But the labourer had no political rights, therefore the movement in favour of enclosure, which was against his interests, went on steadily. Prices advanced though wages remained stationary. At last, when by some means or other, the labourer lost possession of his holding, so that he found himself dependent entirely on his money wage, still rigidly fixed, when he realised he was absolutely bound down to his native place, when through sickness, old age, or misfortune he had to accept the parish alms, then, losing both his self-respect and all hope of bettering himself, he sank to the dead level of apathy, to "that fatal attitude of immobility impervious to economic motive which is characteristic of the pauper habit[1]."

In the seventeenth century, however, this condition was not yet realised. The Tudor legislation sowed the seeds of it, the Civil War with its attendant evils prepared a fertile ground, but it was not until the eighteenth century that the evil was in full fruition. It is, however, possible to trace the downward path of the labourer's career by the steady increase in the orders for poor relief during the century.

[1] *Public Relief of the Poor*, by Thomas Mackay, 1901.

APPENDIX E

Table of wages showing the rate paid in 1658, assessed at the Thirsk Quarter Sessions, April 20, 1658.

To the carpenter by the day	With meate	6*d*.
	Without meate	12*d*.
To his apprentices by the day	With meate	4*d*.
	Withoute meate	8*d*.
To a mason by the day	With meate	6*d*.
	Withoute meate	12*d*.
To his apprentices by the day	With meate	4*d*.
	Without meate	8*d*.
To a taylor by the day	With meate	4*d*.
	Withoute meate	8*d*.
To his apprentices by the day	With meate	2*d*.
	Withoute meate	4*d*.
To a theaker (thatcher) by the day	With meate	6*d*.
	Withoute meate	12*d*.
To a man servant able to take the charge of husbandry	For the yeere	£4
An ordinary man servant	For the yeere	£3
To a cooke maide	For the yeere	£2
To a maid servant able to take care of a dairy	For the yeere	£2
To an ordnarye maid servant	For the yeere	30*s*.
To a maid-servant between fourteen years of age and one-and-twenty	For the yeere	20*s*.
To a mower by the day	With meate	6*d*.
	Without meate	12*d*.
To a man for reaping of corne	With meate	4*d*.
	Without meate	8*d*.
To one between fourteen and eighteen yeeres of age	By the day	4*d*.
To a woman for reapeing of corne	With meate	3*d*.
	Without meate	6*d*.
For working in the hay by the day	With meate	2*d*.
	Without meate	4*d*.
To a maid betwixt fourteen and eighteen yeeres of age	By the day	4*d*.

To a man for ordinarye labour betwixt May 1st and Sept. 29	By the day	With meate	3d.
		Without meate	6d.
From Sept. 29th to May 1st	By the day	With meate	2d.
		Without meate	5d.

(*Signed*) Luke Robinson, Fr. Lassells, Chr. Pearcehay, Will. Aiscough, Geo. Smithson.

ORDERED that the Sheriff of the county of Yorke do forthwith cause the rates of artificers' and labourers' and servants' wages hereto annexed to be proclaimed in and thorow the North Riding and especially in every markett towne in the said Riding.

N.R.Q.S.R. vol. v. p. 3.

APPENDIX F

THE LABOURERS AND APPRENTICES

My Lord Finches Custome att Watton for Clippinge Hee hath usually fower severall keepinges shorne alltogeather in the Hallgarth, *viz*: two from Hawitt; one keepinge from the Court-garth; which is on the west side of South Dalton as wee goe to Weeton; and the fourth from a place adjoyning to Huggett field. Hee hath had 49 clippers all at once, and theire wage is, to each man 12d. a day, and, when they have done, beere, and bread and cheese; the traylers have 6d. a day. His tenants the graingers are tyed to come themselves, and winde the woll, they have a fatte weather and a fatte lambe killed, and a dinner provided for their paines; there will bee usually three score or four score poore folkes gatheringe up the lockes, to oversee whome standeth the steward and two or three of his friends or servants with each of them a rodde in his hande; there are two to carry away the woll, and weigh the woll soe soone as it is wounde up, and another that setteth it downe ever as it is weighed; there is 6d. allowed to a piper for playinge to the clippers all the day; the shepheards have each of them his bell weathers fleece.

Best's Farming Book, *S.S.P.* vol. XXXIII. pp. 96–97.

CHAPTER VIII

THE ROGUES AND VAGABONDS

AUTOLYCUS: Every lane's end, every shop, church, session,
hanging, yields a careful man work.
The Winter's Tale, Act IV. Sc. 4.

ONE of the features of the sixteenth century common alike to England and other countries was the existence in large numbers of rogues and vagabonds.

These vagrants were a terror to rich and poor; in an age when the larger half of mankind was emerging from a state of serfdom, when passions were fierce and uncontrolled, the bands of wandering beggars were as great a terror to country districts as if they had been brigands. The cause of their existence was in large measure due to unemployment.

The sixteenth century saw the rise of that spirit of nationality which was opposed to and finally destroyed feudalism. In England the Sovereign gained the upper hand over the baronage with the result that great lords were forced to disband their mercenaries. But the King kept no standing army, into which the private soldiers could be absorbed, and these therefore had no longer any occupation. About the same time also landowners began to appreciate the possibilities of their estates as profitable enterprises on account of the lucrative wool trade, so that, instead of welcoming new husbandmen in the disbanded soldiers, their chief desire was to get rid of more of the small holders in order to turn arable land into sheep farms.

Employment indeed could be obtained in the towns owing to the growth of commerce, but as manufactures were developed by capitalists so the labour market became unstable and in times of bad trade men were frequently thrown out of work.

The ranks of the unemployed were not lessened by the indiscriminate charity of the monasteries and the houses of great noblemen, no distinction being observed between the really deserving poor and those who were able to work.

But gradually throughout the century the fact that these two classes existed side by side became more clearly recognised and various expedients were adopted to distinguish between them. The impotent poor were licensed to beg, while the able-bodied vagrant was publicly disgraced; and as time went on the penalties on the latter became increasingly severe. A law passed in the reign of Henry VIII ordered that vagabonds were to be whipped and sent back to their native place with a testimonial; for a second offence they were to lose part of the "grisel of the right ear[1]." In Edward VI's reign they were to be branded by a hot iron with the letter V in the breast, and to be reduced to the condition of slaves[2]. By the Statute of 1572[3] they were to be "grievously whipped and burnt through the gristle of the right ear"; if apprehended a second time to be considered felons, and for a third offence to be hanged.

But the Elizabethan legislators were beginning to recognise that roguery was produced largely by unemployment, therefore they enacted[4] that Houses of Correction must be provided where rogues should not only receive due punishment but also should be set to work.

Finally, in the same year that Parliament drew up the great Poor Law (by which help was given to those who were willing but unable to work) it also enacted as a sequel the statute for the punishment of rogues and vagabonds[5] and sturdy beggars, in order to repress those who were able but unwilling to earn their own living.

This statute marked an advance in humanity. Branding was abolished and the punishment was whipping; if the

---

[1] 22 H. VIII, cap. xii. and 27 H. VIII, cap. xxv.
[2] 1 Ed. VI, cap. iii.   [3] 14 Eliz. cap. v.
[4] 18 Eliz. cap. iii.   [5] 39 and 40 Eliz. cap. iv.

native place or last settlement of the rogue could not be discovered, he was to be sent to the House of Correction[1], there to be employed until he could be placed in some service. Dangerous rogues, however, were to be sent at once to the House of Correction or to the gaol until the next Quarter Sessions when they were to be banished the realm or sent to the galleys.

This statute was re-enacted and amended in James I's reign[2], the chief alteration being the return to branding, since it had been found that rogues with no mark on them escaped punishment by going into other parts of the realm where they were not known. Therefore they

were to be branded in the left shoulder with a great Roman R upon the iron...and...if any rogue so punished shall offend again...the party so offending...shall suffer as in cases of felony, without benefit of clergy[3].

The law also provided that all people should be fined 10s. if they did not apprehend and carry to the constable rogues who came begging to their houses[4].

The administration of the statute was given into the hands of the Justices of the Peace, any two or more of whom had full power to hear and determine all causes[5].

They were ordered to build Houses of Correction, appoint governors and provide stock for them, and to meet twice a year in their divisions for the due execution of the statute.

In the North Riding the Justices also tried rogues and vagabonds at the monthly meetings, which they held in their separate divisions, to consider questions of poor relief. But it was not until after 1607 that they set about providing the House of Correction. The matter came up at the Sessions from time to time, and a building was rented at Richmond[6].

---

[1] 39 and 40 Eliz. cap. iv. sec. iii.
[2] 1 Jac. I, cap. vii. and 7 Jac. I, cap. iv.
[3] 1 Jac. I, cap. vii. sec. iii.   [4] 1 Jac. I, cap. vii. sec. iv.
[5] 39 and 40 Eliz. cap. iv. sec. xii.
[6] N.R.Q.S.R. vol. II. p. 110. Richmond, Oct. 1615. "That a house of Correction shal be erected within the N.R. which is thought fyttinge by

Finally in 1619[1] Geo. Shaw of Leeds, a clothier, was appointed as master, or governor, and in 1620 money for furnishing and stock was granted[2].

The House of Correction was designed by Government for the "setting of the poor on work, for the avoiding of idleness," thus it occupied an intermediate position between an alms-house and a gaol. Idle people[3], beggars, lame soldiers, were taken to the House of Correction if found without a licence, and suspicious characters were detained there until they could be tried at the Sessions[4]; if convicted of roguery they were sent back to be treated according to their deserts, if vagabonds they were whipt and sent to their homes[4]. The true character of the rogue could be discovered; he was given employment and if he refused to work he was punished. Persons sent to the House of Correction were brought again to the Quarter Sessions when their term was completed and if their report was good were set at liberty.

Gradually, however, the House of Correction became less

this Court (for the tyme beinge) to be the house called The Frieries in Richmond, for the which house Sir Tim. Hutton is to have the rent of £8 per annum."

[1] *N.R.Q.S.R.* vol. II. p. 229. Richmond, Jan. 8, 1619–20. "Forasmuch as the House of Correction at Richmond is now almost finished,...it is therefore Ordered that Geo. Shaw of Leeds, clothier, shalbe maister or Governour of the said House, who hath put in securities etc., and that he shall have allowed him for his paines and care, for the first yeare £60, and yearlie after, £50 to be paid at each Quarter Sessions..."

[2] *Ibid.* p. 235. Thirsk, Ap. 1620. "In reference to the Order made at Richmond Sessions touching the £60 to be paid to the Governour of the House of Correction...it is now Ordered that it be forthwith estreeted etc., and be made ready for payment at the next Sessions: and it is further Ordered by consent of the said Governour, that he shall furnish the said House with beddinge, and maintenance of meate and drincke and such like necessaries to those which happen to be committed, convenient for a House of Correction...loomes and yrons for imployinge and ruling from time to time, those who shalbe committed."

[3] *Ibid.* vol. IV. p. 17. Richmond, July, 1634. "Geo. Shawe Master of the House of Corrn. at Richmond, for letting a prisoner committed to his custody until the next Sessions go free."

[4] *Ibid.* vol. V. p. 57. Richmond, July, 1650. "A man in the Ho. of Corrn. to be sent to Wharton in Northumberland, where he was borne, and another to Yearme in this Rideing, where he last remained, after they be stript from the midle upwards and whipt."

a workhouse and more a gaol[1]. Irons and fetters[2] were provided and in 1680 the inmates are spoken of as prisoners. Yet Houses of Correction were evidently considered to be useful institutions and the Justices in Richmondshire complain of the increase of vagrants in the shire after the House of Correction was removed to Thirsk[3]. Houses of Correction were established for the North Riding at Richmond, Thirsk[4], Whitby[5] and Pickering[6].

The chief burden of administering the act fell on the petty constable and the main difficulty of the Justices of the Peace was to keep him up to his work. Four or five days before the half-yearly meeting of the Justices of the Peace, the constable, assisted by sufficient men of the township, had to institute a privy search in one night for rogues and idle persons, and bring such to the meeting. But at any time it was his duty to take in charge persons found wandering about, or those who were brought to him for begging within his township, put them in the stocks or keep them in custody, until he could carry them before the Justices.

If convicted of roguery, the constable had to whip the man, and either take him to the House of Correction or provide him with a testimonial, subscribed and sealed by himself, the minister and another parishioner, and then give him in charge of the next constable on the road to be passed

---

[1] *N.R.Q.S.R.* vol. VII. p. 31. Middleham, March, 1680. "Mr Tho. Lightfoot Jr. to pay an additional sum of £3. 10s. od. unto Peter Hood Gov. of the House of Correction at Richmond for buying of irons to secure his prisoners and amende a sink and the doors, bolts and locks of the gaol."

[2] *Ibid.* vol. VI. p. 132. Richmond, Jan. 1677. "Mr Tho. Lightfoot Jr. for Richmondshire to pay 26s. to Mich. Harrison gent. for reimbursing him for fetters for Ho. of Correction at Richmond."

[3] *Ibid.* vol. VI. p. 249. Richmond, Jan. 1675–6. "Whereas complaint hath been made unto this Court by the Grand Jury on the behalf of the inhabts of Richmondshire that for diverse years last past there hath been great increases of idle vagrant persons there...it is therefore Ordered that from and after February 6th next, there shall be a Ho. of Corrn. at Richmond for the five wapentakes of Richmondshire aforesaid..."

[4] *Ibid.* vol. VI. pp. 115, 119.

[5] *Ibid.* vol. IV. pp. 55, 67.

[6] *Ibid.* vol. V. p. 132.

on to his native place or last settlement. The Form of Testimonial was as follows:

A.B. a sturdy Rogue, of tall stature red-haired and bearded, about the age of 30 years, and having a wart near under his right eye, borne as he confesseth at East Tilbury in Essex, was taken begging at Shorne in this County of Kent, the 10th of March, 1624, and was then there lawfully whipped therefore and he is appointed to go to East Tilbury aforesaid the direct way by Gravesend over the River of Thames; for which he is allowed one whole day etc., no more at his peril: subscribed and sealed the day and yeere aforesaid,
By us

C.D. Minister }
E.F. Borsholder } of Shorne aforesaid.
G.H. Parishioner }

The necessary arrangements for the dispatch of every rogue involved a considerable outlay of the constable's time; thus it is no matter of surprise that constables did not eagerly search for rogues, and they were frequently summoned by the chief constable either for not punishing rogues or for allowing vagrant persons to wander and beg[1].

Every village was expected to keep its stocks in repair for the punishment of rogues[2], and no one was allowed to take any wanderer into his house without informing the constable[3]; nevertheless presentments of people for harbouring rogues frequently occur[4].

In 1650 the high constables were ordered by the Justices of the Peace

to give timely notice to the Petty Constables to meet at such times and places as shall be thought convenient and diligent search to be

---

[1] N.R.Q.S.R. vol. I. p. 92. Richmond, Oct. 8, 1607. "Geo. Watson, Constable of Ellerbeck for not punishing Rogues according to the Statute fined 10s."

Ibid. vol. I. p. 228. Helmsley, July, 1611. "Rich. Dawson the younger, Constable of Stokesley for suffering vagrant persons to wander and beg." (Per C.C.)

[2] Ibid. vol. II. p. 196. Richmond, Jan. 12, 1619. The Justices order "the inhabitants of Goversett (Gowersett?) to provide a pair of stocks for the punishing of rogues."

[3] Ibid. vol. I. p. 11. Stokesley, 1605. "Fr. Simpson of Whitwell, laborer, is presented for harbouring in his house rogues and vagabonds without notifying the same to the Constable."

[4] Ibid. vol. v. p. 57. Richmond, July, 1650. "A Melmerby woman for harbouring vagrants etc. (fined 10s.)."

made for the apprehension of vagrants and rogues and to bring them to the said monthly meetings to be punished according to law;

The high constables throughout the North Riding are to issue out warrants to all Petty Constables in their severall Divisions requiring them to put in execution the laws and statutes against Vagrants and Sturdy Beggars, and in case any within the severall Constableries shall harbour any such or releive them by almes at their doors, the Petty Constable where such offence is committed, to present the same to the next J.P. who is desired to inflict the statute against such offenders.

If the petty constables fail in the performance of their duties the high constable is to certify this to the nearest Justice of the Peace who is to put the laws in execution against them[1].

The statutes might have had good effect in reducing the number of rogues and vagabonds, but the political troubles of the century were not conducive to their extinction, and in 1662 Parliament again attacked the subject. The Court of Quarter Sessions received power to transport to the plantations incorrigible rogues[2]. A Justice could give a warrant to anyone apprehending a rogue to authorise him to demand 2s. from the constable of the last parish through which the rogue had passed unapprehended[3], and since the laws and statutes for oppressing of rogues and vagabonds had not been duly executed, sometimes for want of officers because Courts Leet had not been held, the Justice was empowered to appoint a constable in certain cases[4].

Parliament at last recognised that the execution of the statutes had demanded from the petty constable considerable expenditure in time and money, therefore these officers received power to levy a rate to reimburse themselves for their expenses[5]. After the Restoration the Justices in the North Riding made vigorous efforts to repress vagrancy; they recognised, however, that one chief cause of it was destitution, or lack of employment, and that another was negligence on the part of parish officers.

[1] *N.R.Q.S.R.* vol. v. p. 44. Richmond, Jan. 1650.
[2] 14 Car. II, cap. xii. secs. vi. and xxiii.   [3] 14 Car. II, cap. xii. sec. xvi.
[4] 14 Car. II, cap. xii. sec. xv.   [5] 14 Car. II, cap. xii. sec. xviii.

In 1675 vagrancy was rampant throughout the North
Riding and the Bench issued a general order to be sent to
the petty constables and parish officers, in the preamble of
which they declared that

many poor persons within these parts, for want of sufficient relief
and work at their own homes, do wander abroad, begging and leading
an idle, and disorderly and, some of them, a thievish course of life,
to the evil example of others and scandal of our Government, which
cometh to pass through the great neglect of the several Parish
Officers for these parts in not giving sufficient maintenance to such
as are impotent, and not providing work for such as are able of body
and have not wherewith to keep themselves imployed in labour[1].

Therefore they ordered the parish officers to repair to
their nearest Justices and to give an account of what they
were doing in relieving the poor; and (among other regulations) particularly desired them to apprentice the children of
paupers, so as to prevent their wandering abroad and begging
out of their respective parishes, " by which means many of
them turn rogues and lead a lewd and wicked course of life[2]."

The Justices showed an evident desire to go to the root
of the matter and prevent another generation of rogues
growing up[3].

They reminded constables and others of the rewards[4] for
apprehending beggars and showed themselves quite ready
to pay liberally for this amateur police work[5]. At times
they even exceeded the statute by ordering more townships

---

[1] *N.R.Q.S.R.* vol. VI. p. 247. Helmsley, Jan. 1676.

[2] *Ibid.* vol. VI. p. 248.

[3] *Ibid.* vol. VI. p. 245. Thirsk, Oct. 1675. "A boy to be sent to Tollerton,
the place of his last legal settlement, and the Parish offrs. there to provide
for him and to bind him apprentice to prevent his rogueing upon the
penalty of £10."

[4] *Ibid.* vol. VI. p. 247. "If any Constable or any other person shall
apprehend any wandering beggar and carry him before a J.P. he is to have
as a reward for his pains 2s. for every such beggar, to be paid him by the
Constables of that place where he passed through unapprehended by the
Statute of the 14th of Chas. II, cap. xii."

[5] *Ibid.* vol. V. p. 248. "Constable to have 2s. for apprehending Rogue
or wandering beggar."

Ibid. vol. VI. p. 252. Thirsk, Ap. 1676. "The Thrs. to pay 20s. as a
gratuity to Will. Cassen of Ripon for his good service in taking diverse
rogues."

than the last one through which the vagrant passed to pay the fine of two shillings[1].

The Quarter Sessions records show indeed that a great number of rogues were apprehended in the North Riding, but there is reason to believe that the statutes were not so enforced throughout the country, since a vagrant taken in the North Riding is ordered to be sent by testimonial "to Battel in Sussex near Hastings[2]," and another to Wisbridge (? Wisbech) in the Isle of Ely[3]. It seems extraordinary that a man could wander from the South of England to the North through such a number of townships without being apprehended by a constable in any one of them.

In actual practice a distinction was made between rogues and vagabonds—the latter term implies a wanderer, such as an unlicensed player of interludes, who might be expected to corrupt the morals of the King's liege people, and who did not "put himself to labour as a true subject ought to do." The term was wide and included "all persons being whole and mighty in body and able to labour, having not land or master, nor using any lawful merchandise, craft or mystery," labourers, who refused to work for statute wages and scholars from Oxford or Cambridge, who begged without the seal of the University. Moreover, all the numerous people who were accustomed to wander about the country, earning their living by amusing the inhabitants, and carrying news from village to village—bearwards, fencers, common players in interludes, jugglers, pedlars, tinkers and chapmen, had to obtain a licence from two Justices of the Peace or else they were liable to be classed as vagabonds[4].

---

[1] *N.R.Q.S.R.* vol. vi. p. 266. Helmsley, Jan. 1677. "Whereas Mr Henry Gilling did cause a man and his wife with four children being idle vagrants to be apprehended, and whereas the said man was suffered to pass through and relieved at Brafferton, Myton and Cundall and was not apprehended, Ordered that the several Constables of the townships aforesaid do pay the sums following for their neglect therein, viz: Brafferton 2s., Myton 4s. and Cundall 4s., and that they pay the said several sums unto the said Henry Gilling for his good service therein."

[2] *Ibid* vol. vii. p. 17. Helmsley, Jan. 1679.

[3] *Ibid.* vol. vi. p. 190. Richmond, July, 1673.   [4] 14 Eliz. cap. v. sec. v.

A rogue, however, was a person who led a wicked and thievish course of life. Rogues were branded, generally in the presence of the court[1]. Sometimes women were whipped[2] instead of being burnt in the shoulder, but they did suffer this penalty also[3]. After branding they were sent from constable to constable back to their homes, or to the place where they were last settled.

If they had been already branded then they were "incorrigible" and were sent to the House of Correction or to the gaol, from which latter place they only came out to be transported to the plantation or to be hanged[4].

Benefit of clergy was still given in the seventeenth century, for a first offence, to the felon who could read, but the con-

---

[1] *N.R.Q.S.R.* vol. v. p. 69. Richmond, Jan. 1651. "Whereas John Watson of Gigleswick in this county as he pretends in the Ho. of Corrn. whither he was committed as a wandering rogue was brought into this Court, appears upon his own confession to be dangerous to the inferior sort of people, and not fitt to be delivered or sett at libertie without branding in the left shoulder with a hott iron in manner and form sett downe in the statute etc. and intending to brand him upon baring his shoulder, the Court conceives he hath been branded already, and therefore by law a felon, these are to require you to receive the said John Watson into your gaole, where you are to keep him in safe custody, till he shall be from thence delivered by due course of lawe. Faile not hereof att your perill. To the Sheriff of the County of Yorke and to the Keepers of the Common Gaole, their Deputy or Deputies and to every of them."

[2] *Ibid.* vol. I. pp. 195–6. Northallerton, July, 1610. "Rob Duckdale, late of Carliell, glover, Geo. Harrison, late of Belgrave. co Lancashire, labr. Rob. Melmerby, late of Richmond, butcher, Elizth. Gryme, late of Lincolne, spinster, Anne Gryme, late of Nottingham, spinster, Anne Latham of Brunton, spinster and Andrew Lawson, late of...labr. as being rogues and vagabonds etc. (Side-note: Sentence of the Court the three men to be branded, sidente curia with the letter R. on the left shoulder, and the women to be whipped at the same time in Northallerton.)"

[3] *Ibid.* vol. v. p. 1. Richmond, Jan. 1658. "Two men and a woman for being persons that will not be reformed of their roguish way of life contrary to the statute (all branded in the left shoulder with the letter R. as rogues)."

[4] *Ibid.* vol. VI. p. 220. Northallerton, July, 1674. "A Brumpton man who was at these Sessions indicted and convicted as being an incorrigible rogue and hath received punishment by being burnt in the left shoulder: Ordered that he be committed to the gaole at the Castle of Yorke, there to be kept in safe custody until he shall be transported into some of the English plantations beyond the seas, according to a statute."

victed person was branded in the thumb[1] so that he or she should not escape punishment a second time[2].

In the sixteenth century "clergy" was taken away for piracy[3], rape[4], highway robbery, horse-stealing and theft from churches[5]. Quite considerable sums of money were paid out of the county funds to such persons as assisted to apprehend and prosecute felons[6].

The punishment of these wanderers gives a glimpse of the pitiless severity of the age. A woman of Hutton Rudby being a wandering beggar was ordered to be whipped by the constablery of Thirsk and sent to the next constable to be whipped, and so from constable to constable to Rudby. Hutton Rudby is in Cleveland and if the inhuman sentence was really carried out, this unfortunate person would be whipped at least seven times before she arrived at her destination.

Another instance of the curious lack of feeling of the times appears in the case of a woman committed to the House of Correction and found to be insane. Yet this unhappy creature is ordered to be sent from constable to constable to the town of Sandbridge in Chester, where she was born[7].

[1] *N.R.Q.S.R.* vol. IV. p. 57. Richmond, July, 1636. "The convicted person, a woman, claims benefit of clergy and is sentenced to be branded on the left thumb which is done by the Gaoler in presence of the Court." *Ibid.* vol. III. p. 225. Helmsley, 1624–5. "Tho. Faceby of Huby, labr. for stealing a whie (32s.)" "Tho. Faceby also guilty to 15s. (sentence to be hanged by the neck). Faceby claims to be a clerk and to have benefit of clergy. The Ordinary is called and a book being handed to the prisoner, he reads as a clerk. Therefore to be branded and suffered to go at large. Branded by the Gaoler in open Court in the presence of the Justices."

[2] By statute passed in 1487.

[3] In 1536.   [4] In 1576.   [5] In 1547.

[6] *Ibid.* vol. VII. p. 1. Thirsk, Oct. 1677. "20s. to be paid to Jas. Darling as an additional gratuity towards his charges in prosecuting a felon who was hang'd at last Assizes."

Ibid. vol. VI. p. 254. Thirsk, Ap. 1676. "Whereas Peter Coates was bound to prosecute against four persons at these Sessions and whereas they are committed to the Castle of Yorke, and the said Peter shall there further prosecute against them: Ordered that Mr Bell, Thr. shall pay the said Peter Coates 3s. 4d. towards his charges already expended, and 6s. 8d. more at the next Assizes to hear his charges there."

[7] *Ibid.* vol. V. p. 171. Thirsk, Oct. 1654. "Forasmuch as a woman taken wandering in the Constablery of Pickering, who saith she was born at Sandbridge in Chester, and was the daughter of a carpenter

A healthy public opinion existed regarding these outcasts from society, for it was an indictable offence to call a man a rogue[1], or to use any words to the same effect[2].

In the seventeenth century the wandering players of interludes, who were very popular in the North Riding, were rigidly suppressed by the Justices. Anyone who received them, or gave them hospitality, was heavily fined.

To the Puritans all stage plays were anathema, but it is possible that interludes like other plays of the Elizabethan drama had a highly political[3] flavour, and were on that account specially tabooed. Recusants appear among two bands of players in the North Riding[4].

In 1615 when the Justices were taking stringent measures against recusants, many gentry and yeomen were summoned for giving bread and drink to wandering players[5], while petty

there, being committ to the House of Correction as a rogue and a vagrant doth appear to be a person under distraction and distempered in her senses, and nothing appearing to require further detention to be conveyed from Constable to Constable to the town of Sandbridge aforesaid there to be provided for: to the Constables of Pickering, Malton, Hutton upon Darwent, Whitwell, Flaxton and all other Constables in the way leading to Sandbridge."

[1] N.R.Q.S.R. vol. III. p. 135. Thirsk, April, 1623. "John Noble of Whitby to be bound and to be committed to the Sheriff until so bound for speakinge these wordes in the markett putting of his hat and turning to the people (sainge) 'I do proclaime open proclamation against Chr. Newton that he is an arrant Rogue.'"

[2] Ibid. vol. VI. p. 181. Richmond, 1673. "An Askerigg Yeomn. for false and scandalous words that he would prove that a certain man was burnt in the shoulder."

[3] See "The Topical Side of Elizabethan Drama," by S. Lee; New Shakespeare Society's Transactions, Series I, II.

[4] N.R.Q.S.R. vol. I. p. 204. Topcliffe, Oct. 1610. "Whereas Tho. Pant apprentice to Ch. Simpson of Egton, Shoemaker, complains that he has not been employed in his occupation...but hath been trayned up for these three yeres in wandering in the country and playing of Interludes...and for the said Simpson is an obstinate convicted popishe Recusant, hiding himself so as lawe cannot be executed against him though diverse warrants have been awarded for his apprehension...the said Pant shalbe freed of his apprenticeship notwithstanding the Indenture (dated 4 March 1607) unless the said Simpson shall appear at the next Quarter Sessions and show cause to the contrary; and a copy of this Order to be left at his house at Egton etc."

[5] Ibid. vol. II. p. 110. Helmsley, Jan. 1616. "Geo. White, weaver (24 years of age) John Rich and Cuthbert Simpson cordiners (24, and 18) all of Egton and Recusants...as players of enterludes vagabonds etc., and Ralph Rookby Esq., of Marske for receiving them into his dwelling

constables had been in trouble for not suppressing them[1]. In 1616 no less than twenty-seven gentlemen or yeomen from different villages visited by players were summoned and fined, while the leader of the players was sentenced to be whipped[2].

When the Puritan Justices were supreme on the Bench any kind of minstrel or player was severely treated and held to be a rogue[3]; heavy recognisances were taken from people who were better off, binding them not to act stage plays[4], and constables were summoned if they neglected to apprehend all who took part in them[5].

Players, however, could make their occupation lawful by obtaining a licence from two Justices. Possibly this was seldom granted during the Commonwealth and some persons had recourse to forged certificates[6]. Scholars from Oxford or Cambridge had to show a licence to beg under the

house giving them bread and drink and suffering them to escape unpunished etc."

[1] *N.R.Q.S.R.* vol. I. p. 260. Helmsley, July, 1612. "Rich. Dawson of Stokesley, tanner and Constable there, for knowingly suffering Rob. Simpson of Staythes, Shoemaker, Rich. Hudson of Hutton Bushell weaver, Edw. Lister of Allerton, weaver, common players of Interludes, wandering up and downe etc. to escape unpunished."

[2] *Ibid.* vol. II. p. 122. Thirsk, April, 1616.

[3] *Ibid.* vol. V. p. 209. Richmond, Jan. 1656. "Eight men to be whipt, being, on their own confession convict for being common Players of Interludes and rogues by the Statute and to have certificates and to be sent from Constable to Constable to the places of their severall abodes. A warrant against the Constables of Sneipe and Beadall and all other Constables where any common Players of Interludes have acted or played any common plays since last sessions for not apprehending of them, they being rogues by the Statute and have them before the next J.P. to be proceeded against for the neglect of their office, this to be directed to the C.Cs."

[4] *Ibid.* vol. V. p. 187. Malton, July, 1655. "Recogn. Simon Arnett of Sowerby in £10, not to act stage plays or interludes during their lives in this Commonwealth."

[5] *Ibid.* vol. V. p. 221. Malton, July, 1656. "A Kirbymoorside man indicted for being a petty minstrel to be whipt etc."

[6] *Ibid.* vol. V. p. 260. Helmsley, Jan. 1658. "A man of Midlewith in Cheshire and another of Macklin in the county of Relsmoore in Scotland, for wandering in the country as players and counterfeiting Gen. Moncke's hand to the deceit of the people, to be stript from the middle upwards and whipt in the market place of Helmesley and afterwards to be conveyed from Constable to Constable etc."

seal of the University; occasionally their passes also came under suspicion[1].

Undoubtedly the seventeenth century inherited a train of vagabonds who were the product of the sixteenth; but while the measures taken to redress them protected society, they were a palliative rather than a cure. The period was one of transition; the growth of capitalism in manufacture and the system of enclosure of land were hurtful to the small farmer or trader, though possibly beneficial to the community. The restrictions on trade and labour made it difficult for a man once out of work to obtain it; and the picture which Sir Thomas More gives of the gradual decline of the countryman ousted from his holding and sinking to a state of beggary[2], though written in the sixteenth century, had its parallel in the seventeenth.

On the other hand there were among the vagrants many who never intended to labour and who made a trade of begging. They collected in the low taverns, herded together, bringing infectious diseases in their train. Throughout almost the whole century there was an undercurrent of revolt against authority, and these wanderers were suspected of carrying messages for disaffected persons. Gentlemen vagabonds of the type of Barnardine also existed in whose philosophy of life labour had no place; "careless, reckless, and fearless of what's past, present, or to come; insensible of mortality, and desperately mortal[3]."

Such an attitude of mind made them disturbing elements in any society, and their approach two or three together was feared and dreaded. The occupants of a lonely farmhouse gave food as a means of getting rid of them, but a very different treatment was meted out by the constable of

---

[1] *N.R.Q.S.R.* vol. IV. p. 183. Malton, July, 1640. "A man, calling himself by the name of a Scholler, having been taken begginge by colour of a passe which appears to be counterfoote, and he himself a wandering rogue, having already been in the Ho. of Corrn. to be sent from Constable etc. to Cheswicke in the Co. of Cumberland, where etc."

[2] More's *Utopia*, p. 64 (Routledge), 1899; Morley's Universal Library.

[3] *Measure for Measure*, Act IV. Sc. 2.

the village; and a reminiscence of them lingers at the present
day in the nursery rhyme:

> Hark! hark! the dogs do bark; the beggars are coming to town;
>
> .   .   .   .
>
> Some gave them white bread, some gave them brown,
> And some gave them a good horse whip and sent them out of the
> town[1].

[1] Quoted by Sir W. Ashley, *Economic History*, pt II. p. 352.

CHAPTER IX

THE SOCIAL LIFE OF THE VILLAGE COMMUNITY

HAVING considered the work delegated by Parliament to the parish officers, and the degree of efficiency with which these duties were performed by them, it may be interesting to take some account of the social life of the community.

There was little which could be concealed in the seventeenth century: the most intimate family relationships must be laid bare at the request of the churchwarden or the constable, the overseer or the Justice of the Peace: people were frequently accused on mere suspicion; men were held responsible for their wives' misdeeds[1] and were expected to see that their children behaved circumspectly[2]. No one was allowed to waste his estate by card playing or riotous living, no feasts or banquets were to be given after nine o'clock at night, and no person might behave in such a manner as to cause inconvenience to the community[3].

Edward Moore of Cowborne was summoned in 1608 "for using plaie and thereby hindereth his estate[4]." Also George Davison, butcher "for that he is a gamester at cardes and doth waiste his estate thereby[4]." Government regulated the life of the ordinary Englishman to a surprising degree:

[1] *N.R.Q.S.R.* vol. I. p. 8. "John Jackson of Birdforth, brewster, for that his wieff would not sell ale under 5*d.* a gallon to Dan. Bell and John Hutchinson travelling from York with two loads of merchandize."

[2] *Ibid.* vol. I. p. 215. Thirsk, April, 1611. "John West of Normanby for harboring men of evill demeanour, and suspected persons; and also for keeping his son Clement, who is an idler and of lewd behaviour and evill disposed, nather wilbe ruled."

[3] *Ibid.* vol. I. p. 147. Northallerton, Jan. 1609. "James Cootes of Barton...for that he doth not live within the compasse of lawe but is often drunken and doth lye harkening under men's windowes as an evsndropper."
Thirsk, Oct. 1684. "A Pickering dyer for throwing a coloured liquid into Pickering beck."

[4] *Ibid.* vol. I. p. 111. Thirsk, April, 1608.

during six days of the week the Statute of Labourers decreed that everyone must work: on Sundays all those whose religious tenets were suspected of not being in conformity with the religious thought of the day must attend church in the morning or pay a substantial fine, while in the afternoon men must assemble to practise archery at the butts and teach their sons to shoot.

In the Middle Ages it was a custom to play games and practise shooting at the butts on Sunday afternoon; in the sixteenth century Government woke up to the fact that the games were more popular than the shooting and thereupon endeavoured to prevent its decay by statutes forbidding "unlawful Games[1]." In Henry VIII's reign almost all games were designated unlawful, both those in use at the time and those "which would hereafter be invented."

Parishes were ordered to keep the butts in repair. All the King's subjects moreover "within the age of three-score excepting only spiritual men, the Justices and the Barons of the Exchequer," were to exercise shooting in the long bow, and to have a bow and arrows continually ready for use; also to teach their children "from the age of seven years until they come to the age of seventeen, having for each of them in the house a bow and two shafts." In the early years of the seventeenth century this statute was still in force[2], but in spite of legislation, archery went steadily out of fashion as the more exciting hand gun came into use.

Many were the restrictions laid upon people for Sunday observance, especially during the Interregnum. Yet in spite of the laws for the due keeping of the Sabbath, small respect

---

[1] 33 H. VIII, cap. ix.
[2] *N.R.Q.S.R.* vol. 1. p. 93. Richmond, Oct. 1607.
"Rich. Howme, son of Tho. Howme of Katterick, for default of bowe and arrowes contrarie etc. fined 6s. 8d. to be paid by the father; also Will. Howme another son, Rog. Metcalf and John and Christopher his sons, Will. Haule and John his son, all of Katterick, for the like all fined 6s. 8d. and in each case the son's fine to be paid by the father."
Ibid. vol. 1. p. 265. Northallerton, July, 1612. "The inhabts of West Wittin for not making of the buttes according etc."

was paid to the day; men bought and sold[1], wrestled[2], played football and other games even in the churchyard and during service time[3]; they sat drinking and feasting in the alehouses[4], or danced and sang there to the tune of the bag-pipes[5].

A yeoman of Healey Park is summoned "for playing at bowls and other unlawful games and selling tobacco upon the Lord's Day." He is fined 15s., to be given to the poor of the parish.

King James indeed in his Declaration of Sports gave his sanction to Whitsun Ales, Morris dances, and other sports which did not come within the category of unlawful games. Bowling, however, was prohibited "at all times to the meaner sort of people[6]," as also games of skill, such as foot-ball, trippet, backgammon and play at cards or dice.

It must be remembered that in Roman Catholic England games and dancing and all other amusement were the cus-tom on Sundays after the attendance at Mass in the morning. The Reformation brought in the idea that such amusements were not suitable for the Sabbath day, but doubtless in the country districts this Puritan idea penetrated slowly and was perhaps received unwillingly in many places. It must be admitted, however, that at times the people who broke

---

[1] *N.R.Q.S.R.* vol. v. Richmond, July, 1652. "2 Aperside yeomen for buying and selling wool on the Lord's Day, a Bainbridge man for selling soap and tobacco, a Sedbuske man for selling suits of apparel."
Ibid. Richmond, July, 1654. "A Reeth yeoman for selling oatmeal pease and tobacco on the Lord's Day."

[2] *Ibid.* Malton, July, 1656. "A Stonegrave man for making a bet to wrestle on the Sabbath Day."

[3] *Ibid.* vol. III. p. 199. Whitby, Ap. 1624.

[4] *Ibid.* vol. v. p. 129. Richmond, Jan. 1653. "John Swan of Little Danby and Tho Cooke of Bowes committ to the Sheriff, Cooke for suffering Swan to tiple in his howse on the Lord's Day and Swan for tiplinge on the Lord's Day in Cooke's howse and to sitt 6 hours in the stock according to law in that case for refuseing each of them to pay 10s. apeece."
Ibid. vol. I. p. 192. Helmsley, July, 1610. "Thomas Atkinson of Urebie, theaker for brewing without license and making of feastes upon the Sabboath daies and holydaies, betwixt Penthecost 1610 and the Feast of S. John Baptist next following."

[5] *Ibid.* vol. I. p. 50. Malton, Oct. 1606.

[6] *Declaration of Sports*, 1618, Somers Tract.

the law did so in a somewhat aggravated form. One Frances Milnes of Aislaby was presented

"for that he with divers others unknown, did, on Easter day last, in the time of afternoon Service, play in the Churchyard there, at a game called Trippett and did molest and disturbe the Minister there, readinge Diverse Service togither with the parishioners there etc." The Bench "Ordered that a warrant to the Constable of Aislaby to whipp Fr Milnes for playing at Trippet on Easter day last in time etc.[1]"

Dancing and football were evidently very popular. Christopher Knowles of Exilby gets into trouble because he keeps a common football for the young men of the town to play with, while Cuthbert Cowson of Normanby "on two several Sundays allowed people to assemble in his house with pipes and drums and dancing all the time of Divine Service."

Sundays and festival days were the only occasions when people took holiday, but Puritan ideas were tending not only to prevent holidays on the church festivals, but also amusements on Sunday[2], while the strict legislation against Roman Catholics caused investigation into every absence from church.

Consequently men were frequently in trouble for playing unlawful games[3]. The animal spirits which should have found outlet in football[4] and trippet spent themselves in forcible entry or in illegal games at cards[5] and dice, behind the alehouse doors.

---

[1] *N.R.Q.S.R.* vol. I. p. 265. Northallerton, July, 1612.
[2] *Ibid.* vol. I. pp. 100–101. Malton, Jan. 1607–8. "John Williamson of Bagby tanner, for playing 11th Oct. last at Shoule-bord (shovel-board) in the Evening prayer-time it being the Sabbaoth daie...Richard Fawcett of New Malton for keeping unlawfull games or play at cardes and tables in his house &c."
[3] *Ibid.* vol. I. p. 231. Richmond, July, 1611. "Chr Sadler and Will. Hewitson, both of Exilbie, for playing at unlawfull games being forbidden by the Constables so to doe."
[4] *Ibid.* vol. II. p. 34. Richmond, Oct. 1613. "Chr. Knowles of Exilby for suffering unlawful games, viz: cardes, to be used in his house on the Sabaoth day, and keping a common football for the young men of the towne to play with, contrary &c."
[5] *Ibid.* vol. I. p. 108. Richmond, Jan. 1608. "Henry Rowe of Scruton for being a gamester at cardes and thereby doth waste his estate: Will Bolmar

The seventeenth-century Puritan spirit tried hard but found it impossible to quell the sporting instinct of Englishmen. In spite of the severe game regulations men continued to hunt rabbits and shoot pigeons[1], to prefer horse racing[2] to Petty Sessions and games to compulsory prayers. Football survived in spite of the pains and penalties inflicted on those who played it.

As the century rolled on the authorities began to realise that they were powerless to combat the love of sport, that elemental characteristic which is inherent in the British race.

Though at no period in English history had so many laws been in force regulating the conduct of alehouses, yet all writers alike speak of the amount of drunkenness among men which existed everywhere[3]. "For a quart of ale is a dish for a king[4]," sang Autolycus, and so greatly did the English people agree with this sentiment, that the charge was brought against them in the early eighteenth century of spending all their money on drink.

The Government was fully sensible that alehouses were a disturbing element; the King in the Star Chamber spoke of them as "haunts for robbers, thieves and rogues[5]," and during the reigns of James I and Charles I many regulations were made by Parliament concerning them[6].

The innkeeper had to obtain a licence and in addition responsible people who were not alehouse keepers to stand as

of Scruton for keeping plaie in his house in time of service on the Sabbaoth day."

   N.R.Q.S.R. vol. I. p. 112. "Tho. Gaile of Scruton for playing at cardes for money."

   [1] *Ibid.* vol. VI. p. 216. New Malton, July, 1674. "A Middleton labr for discharging a hand-gun, charged with powder and hail shot, and killing a pigeon."

   [2] *Ibid.* vol. I. p. 232. Richmond, 1611. "Henry Bursey of Brignell for obstinately refusing to make a presentment at a Petty Sessions at Neusham by reason he was to goe to a horserace."

   [3] Cp. Burton, *Anatomy of Melancholy*, Evelyn's and Pepys's Diaries.

   [4] *The Winter's Tale*, Act IV. Sc. 3.

   [5] In 1616, see Dalton, *The Country Justice*.

   [6] 1 Jac. I, cap. ix. 4 Jac. I, cap. v. 21 Jac. I, cap. vii. and xxviii. 1 Car. I, cap. iv.

sureties for him. The Justices held special Brewster's Sessions for reviewing these licences, but at any Sessions an alehouse keeper might be "suppressed from brewing" for an infringement of the law such as selling ale above the lawful price, harbouring vagrants or allowing disorder in his house[1]. Sometimes he went on brewing after his licence was taken away and thereby incurred a further penalty. The alehouse was distinguished by a long pole set up in front; and if wine could be obtained a bush was placed on the top of the pole[2]. When an innkeeper was discharged from brewing, his sign was pulled down by the constable; and not always without protest; Michael Jackson's wife, of Cockeswold, was before the Bench in 1613 "for cominge forth of her house with a pitchforke and beating awaie a man that was cutting down her Ale-rodd, he being soe commaunded to doe by Sir H. Belassis Knt. Barronett[3]."

The innkeepers were expected also to supply food; moreover if people asked for their ale and offered lawful money they were bound to sell it. Robert Driffield of Easingwold and his wife transgressed many of these rules. He was summoned for suffering unlawful games to be played in his house, and his wife, who seems to have been rather a cantankerous party, is before the Court

for that she will not sell anie of her ale forth of doores except it be to those whom she likes on, and makes her ale of two or three sortes, nor will not let anie of her poore neighbours have any of her drincke called small ale, but she saith she will rather give it to her swyne then play it for them[4].

[1] *N.R.Q.S.R.* vol. I. p. 91. Richmond, Oct. 1607. "Lawrence Fermary of Disforth for selling ale for 5d. and 6d. the gallon. Fined 10s. Helen Casse of the same for the like (similar fine)"; and also "for harboring of idle vagrant persons and also being suspected to have roasted hennes eaten in her house at unlawfull tymes of the night. Fyned on the originall &c 6s. 8d. (Per Will. Raper Cap. Const.)"

[2] *Ibid.* vol. II. p. 31. Note by Canon Atkinson quoting ballads of the time.
"I rather will take down my bush and sign
Than live by means of riotous expense."
Good Newes and Bad Newes, by S.R. Lon. 1622.

[3] *N.R.Q.S.R.* vol. II. p. 31. New Malton, Sep. 1613.

[4] *Ibid.* vol. II. p. 54. Malton, Oct. 3, 1614.

Women took a considerable share in the life and labour of the time. They worked at many occupations, which, to-day, are exclusively undertaken by men; such as brewing, drawing straw for thatch, tempering mortar, etc.; doubtless such work made them capable and self-assertive. They certainly appear in the records to be strong-minded and vigorous in speech and action. One woman got into trouble for "chasing sheep with dogs," probably out of her own land; many were summoned for assault, and quite a number were presented for "seditious words."

A woman must not be called a witch[1], nor a man a rogue; public opinion decided that such terms were scandalous. At this time magic arts, incantations and charms were a part of the creed of superstitious country folk. Such arts were only learnt of the evil one, and people who set forth that by this knowledge they could tell fortunes[2] or declare where lost or stolen goods were to be found[3], and those who banned their neighbour's goods ran the risk of being presented at Quarter Sessions or at the Assizes. Elizabeth, wife of John Cooke of Thirsk, had to appear before the Justices in July, 1611, on the charge of being "a common scold and disquieter of her neighbours with continual banning and cursing of her said neighbours and their goods, inasmuch as the said goods and themselves whom she curseth oftentimes presently die (as they verily think) by her said ill-words."[4] There is nothing in the records to show what happened to Elizabeth Cooke;

---

[1] *N.R.Q.S.R.* vol. IV. p. 182. New Malton, July, 1640. "A New Malton mason and his wife for uttering opprobrious and scandalous words against one Eliz. England saying she was a witch and they would prove her so."
   Ibid. vol VII. p. 55. Richmond, Jan. 1682. "A Scargell yeomen for scandalous words to a woman viz: "Thou art a known witch."
[2] *Ibid.* vol. VI. p. 133. Thirsk, Ap. 1669. "A Thirsk woman for telling fortunes by charms and incantations and magic arts."
[3] *Ibid.* vol. IV. p. 20. Thirsk, Oct. 1634. "4 women of West Aiton for taking upon themselves to tell one Barbara Temple by witchcraft charm or sorceries where and by whom stolen or taken from her certain clothes were to be found."
[4] At Thirsk, July, 1611. Note in the above the Elizabethan use of "goods" to mean living creatures, also "presently" as implying immediately; both usages are found in the Book of Common Prayer.

the charge was probably dismissed, otherwise an order would have been given to the constable to inflict punishment.

Although some might be punished for their cursing and banning, many escaped owing to the constable's or the informer's fear of their power. In Court it appears that various people still insisted on their magic arts, possibly thinking they might be less severely dealt with, as in the case of the woman before Lord Chief Justice Tanfield[1]. The punishment of Elizabeth Creary gives a picture of the severity meted out to witches; she was accused of "exercising certain most wicked arts in English enchantments and charmes on a black cow (value 50s.) belonging to Edw Bell of Northallerton, by which the cow was sorely damaged and the calf in her totally wasted and consumed." She was tried by a jury (all yeomen) who found her "guilty of most wicked and diabolical arts called inchantements and charms." She was sentenced "to be committed to prison for a year and once in each quarter to stand in the pillory in some market town in the Riding upon some fair day or market day," when released "to be bound to the good behaviour for a year and then to appear at the next Sessions to stand to such further order as the Court shall set down therein[2]."

Yet in spite of the almost universal belief in them, very few witches were prosecuted at the Quarter Sessions. With the exception of Elizabeth Creary, almost all the presentments occur in the Interregnum[3], when both men and

---

[1] "Ask her whether she ill-wished John Symonds and caused his death?" said Elizabeth Tanfield to her father when he was trying a woman accused of witchcraft. The woman said she did. John Symonds was in Court; the woman then declared that she thought she might be less severely dealt with if she confessed she was a witch. *The Lady Falkland, her life*, quoted by E. Godfrey Home, *Life under the Stuarts*.

Fuller, *The Profane State*, The Witch. "Many are unjustly accused for witches, sometimes out of ignorance of natural...causes; sometimes out of their neighbours' mere malice...sometimes out of their own causeless confession."

[2] *N.R.Q.S.R.* vol. III. p. 177. Thirsk, Oct. 1623.

[3] *Ibid.* vol. V. p. 227. Thirsk, Oct. 1656. "Bills ignored: one against Rob. Gayle of Thruntofte for taking upon him to inkant and charme."

Ibid. vol. V. p. 259. Helmsley, Jan. 1657. "Rob. Conyers, late of

women were summoned, for "the days of the Commonwealth were the worst days for witches in England[1]." Many reputed witches, however, were presented at the Assizes but they were acquitted by the jury[2]. Yet though the hard practical sense of the Justices and juries in the North generally refused to convict witches, they listened to extraordinary stories told by informers about them; how a witch rode with a magic bridle, and received every choice dish she desired by touching a magic rope; how she "turned into the shape of a catt and a hare, and in the shape of a greyhound and a bee, letting the divell see how many shapes she could turn herself into[3]."

Such stories indeed were firmly believed by the mass of the people, as also the power of the evil eye which made horses and cows pine away. The witches themselves were partly to blame for their treatment; they made money at the business and endeavoured to surround their calling with fear and mystery.

Each house stood in its own toft or yard[4]; at the back stretched the croft, which was generally enclosed grass land and was called in Yorkshire a garth[5], the word most commonly used at the present day for a small grass field. Since the houses were mostly built of wood and roofed with thatch an outbreak of fire was not an uncommon occurrence, so much so that in the churches buckets of water were hung up as a provision against it[6]. Donations out of the county

Gisborough gentn. being charged with certain detestable arts called witchcraft and sorcery wickedly to practise the same."

Ibid. vol. VI. p. 22. Thirsk, Oct. 1659. "An Askrigg man for practising certain devilish arts called charms and sorceries."

[1] Pollock and Maitland, *History of English Law*, vol. II. p. 556.

[2] Depositions from York Castle, *S.S.P.* vol. XL. p. 30. See Introduction by Canon Raine, "in no instance have I discovered the record of the conviction of a reputed witch."

[3] *Ibid.* vol. XL. p. 191. For Witchcraft Ann Baites and others.

[4] *N.R.Q.S.R.* vol. II. p. 53. Malton, Oct. 1614. "A man...and his wife for stealing in a certain toft at Cuckwold...thre harden shirst value 6*d.*"

[5] *Ibid.* vol. II. p. 37. Helmsley, July, 1614. "A man for stealing a gimmer, worth 12*d.* from a garth at Sheriff Hutton."

[6] Vestry Book, St Nicholas, Durham, *S.S.P.* vol. LXXXIV. p. 256. 1686–7. "Md. that there is by us the present Churchwardens Mr Robson

fund for lame soldiers and hospitals were given to people whose houses and goods had been "spent by fire[1]"; such compensation being allotted at the discretion of the Justices and in proportion to the loss. When the damage was very considerable a licence was granted to the distressed person allowing him to ask for relief from parish churches[2] in his neighbourhood and ministers were ordered to exhort people to give alms[3].

The four acres of arable ground belonging to every cottage lay out in the common fields. In the seventeenth century much of the land in the North Riding was unenclosed. The team for ploughing was made up by each villager contributing an ox or a horse[4]. Thefts of corn[5] and hay[6] out of the common fields were frequent; every one kept stock, and

and Mr Trotter for a seate in the pew adjoyning to the West end of the wall for Arthure Ridley, being under the new bucketts there hanging, received twelve pence."

[1] *N.R.Q.S.R.* vol. I. p. 43. July, 1606. "To Mr Roland Hudson, Clerk, Vicar of Welwang (in respect of my Lo. President's letter) who had his houses and goodes in them spent by fire the sum of £6. 13s. 4d."

Ibid. vol. VI. p. 139. Thirsk, Oct. 1669. "Forasmuch as upon the 17th June last there happened a sad and lamentable fire, which in short time consumed the dwellinghouse of a Hornby man and great part of his household goods, and he being since dead and having left a wife and 6 small children very poor and destitute of a habitation, Ordered that Mr J. Pybus Tr. pay unto his widow £3. 6s. 8d."

[2] *Ibid.* vol. VII. p. 25. Northallerton, July, 1679. "A Wasse man to have licence to go to every parish church and chapel within this Riding and (in the behalf of himself and his two poor neighbours) to ask and receive the charitable benevolence of well-disposed people towards the repair of their late great loss by a sad and lamentable fire."

[3] *Ibid.* vol VI. p. 118. Richmond, July, 1667. "The respective ministers in Richmondshire to read this certificate and Order in their churches in the time of Divine Service, and to move their parishioners to contribute their charitable benevolence to the subject of the same, Jas. Blyth, for his loss by fire." (See Appendix F.)

[4] *Ibid.* vol. I. p. 212. Thirsk, July, 1611. "Two horses and four oxen yoked in a wain."

[5] *Ibid.* vol. II. p. 31. New Malton, Sep. 1613. "Will Loftus of Skelton for stealing from the common field of the said vill two stooks of wheat value 3s. 4d. of the goods of one John Knagges."

[6] *Ibid.* vol. III. p. 113. Thirsk, April, 1621. "William Lee of Northallerton for stealing a bottle of hay, value 1d."

Ibid. vol. III. p. 128. Thirsk, Oct. 1621. "Forasmuch as Jane, wife of Rob. Bell of Thirske, Sitha wife of John Richmond and Tho Langscarth of the same, have confessed the filchinge and stealing of corn in the feilds of Thirsk. Ordered that they shalbe presently whipped by the Constables of Thirske."

temptation arose when crops were scanty to steal food for them; people are frequently presented for stealing "a bottle of hay"—that is as much as they could carry in their arms.

It was so easy to take a haycock or a sheaf of corn out of another man's patch of ground, and very difficult to detect the robbery: consequently when people were convicted of such theft they were severely punished[1]. The only division between each man's arable land was a ridge or balk which was never ploughed[2]. As has been already noticed, the inhabitants of the villages were very lax in keeping the fences of their open fields in repair, so that cows, sheep and horses frequently went astray, and the pinfold[3] was in constant use. When the owner discovered his loss he set off to find his wandering stock, crying a description of them as he passed through every village and looking into every pinfold. If he were fortunate enough to find them impounded he sought the constable and regained his goods, but he must not "forcibly enter" the pinfold and take them away without the knowledge of that officer[4]. The straying of animals gave occasion also for theft. If a sheep found wandering on the highway was driven off and put among his flock by a dishonest person, it could not easily be discovered unless marked with the owner's name or sign. Hence sheep-stealing was a common offence and in some cases was even treated as petty larceny[5].

[1] *N.R.Q.S.R.* vol. v. p. 154. Thirsk, Ap. 1654. "A man for unjustly taking away two cocks of hay (2d. fined 5s.)." "A Nunnington labr. for stealing a bottle of hay (4d. puts himself guilty to a farthing, whipt)." "A woman for stealing one burthen of hay. To be whipped."

[2] *Ibid.* vol. v. p. 186. New Malton, July, 1655. "Two Yearme yeomn. for plowing without in trespass part of the common baulks in Yearme field."

[3] *Ibid.* vol. v. p. 54. Malton, July, 1650. "The inhabts of Farmanby for not repairing their common pyndfold."
"A Leeming Yeomn for not repairing his proportion of the common pinfold."

[4] *Ibid.* vol. vi. p. 25. Richmond, July, 1668. "A yeomn and two women of Marriske, for forcible entry on a common pinfold and taking out five cows."

[5] *Ibid.* vol. i. p. 206. Helmsley, Jan. 8, 1610. "John Metcalf of Newton

Horses or oxen sent to winter on the moors or large commons at some distance from any habitation were more often stolen by the professional thief. This, however, was felony, the penalty for which was hanging[1], or branding in the thumb of the left hand[2].

The open fields were not an unmixed blessing. They gave occasion for pilfering, such as the stealing of turf[3], or flax, the milking of other people's cows, etc., and they did not tend to encourage good farming. It was difficult to safeguard stock from cattle plague, since one diseased animal could infect the rest of the herd. For this reason many people were in favour of enclosures, which made possible better agricultural methods, and greatly increased the value of the land[4].

But the evil of enclosures lay in the fact that much of the common land was taken away from the labourers, and small freeholders, making it difficult for them to carry on their holdings. Mention is made of certain towns where enclosure had taken place in the North Riding quite early in the seventeenth century being "pittifully depopulated[5]."

on Ouse, labr. for stealing three ewes at Newton value 10d. belonging to some person unknown."

[1] *N.R.Q.S.R.* vol. v. p. 143. Thirsk, Oct. 1653. "Man to be hanged for horse stealing." Thirsk, Ap. 1654. "A labr for stealing 2 oxen (puts himself guilty, hanged)."

[2] *Ibid.* vol. v. p. 258. Helmsley, Jan. 1657. "A Maunby labr. for stealing a black heifer (20s. guilty to 9s. burnt in the left hand)."

Ibid. vol. III. p. 203. Richmond, July, 1624. "Lab. for stealing a stott 10s. another for stealing a black cow 40s. (Both plead guilty and are branded.)"

[3] *Ibid.* vol. v. p. 213. Thirsk, Ap. 1656. "An Easingwold woman for stealing a burden of turves. (1d. puts herself not guilty.)"

Ibid. vol. VI. p. 14. Helmsley, Jan. 11, 1658–9. "A woman for stealing 3 lbs of Paternoster flacks." (In considerable districts of Cleveland flax was largely grown.)

[4] Cp. Rural Economy in Yorkshire, *S.S.P.* vol. XXXIII. p. 129. "The landes in the pasture weare (att my fathers first comminge) letten to our owne tenants and others, for 2s. a lande; afterwards for 2s. 6d. a land, and lastly for 3s. a lande; but nowe, beinge inclosed, they will lette for thrice as much."

[5] *N.R.Q.S.R.* vol. I. pp. 78–9. Thirsk, July, 1607. "Moreover that the townes undernamed are inclosed and pittifully depopulated viz: Maunby by Will Midleton about xvi yeares since; Cristhwaite by the late Erle of Northumberland about xxxta yeares since; North Kilvington by Mr Mennell; the rest by whom ignoramus; Salton als. Sawton in Rydall by the late Lord Eure about xxiiii yeares sithence."

Various grades of rank were recognised in the social life of the period. Among the jury, who must be freeholders, at least one or two names head the list with the designation "Gentleman," the rest are "yeomen." No man of the rank of esquire appears in the list and no esquire expected to be returned as a juryman.

In 1619 the Bench ordered that

John Gower of Stainsby shall be fined £10 for not appearinge at this Sessions and being warned by the Baliffe gave these contemptuous speaches followinge; that he scorned to come, and he marvelled that Sir Tho. Belassis would returned him to serve amongst such a sorte of flatcapps, he being an Esquier (as by the oathe of Will. Greenside was affirmed in Courte) conditionally that if he appeare and do service att the next Sessions, the fine shalbe remitted[1].

Evidently John Gower had sent a man to swear to his rank expecting to be excused on that score, and that he was an esquire is clear from the Sessions Roll of January 9, 1616, where he is thus designated[2]. He never served as a juryman, but at Stokesley Special Sessions a month later he got his fine of £10 reduced to 10s., which he paid[3]. The freeholders were grassmen (who owned houses with commonable rights but no arable land) and yeomen. In the North Riding the latter class was numerous[4]. The yeomen were very turbulent and much of the disorder during the Interregnum was caused by them; they were frequently in trouble for riotous entry and unlawful assembly. In many cases their holdings were too small to render anything beyond a bare livelihood and the work on them was hardly sufficient to absorb the whole of a man's time and energy. Therefore yeomen tried to augment their income by trading[5]; in this, however, they were thwarted by Government.

---

[1] N.R.Q.S.R. vol. II. p. 206. Helmsley, July 8, 1619.
[2] Ibid. vol. II. p. 111.
[3] Ibid. vol. II. p. 214.
[4] Tuke estimated in 1794 that one-third of the North Riding belonged to the yeomanry, yet by that time many small freeholders had been ousted by enclosure; therefore the proportion was greater in the seventeenth century.
[5] N.R.Q.S.R. vol. IV. p. 231. Bedale, July, 1642. "47 persons almost

The Tudor and Stuart legislators had no conception of the doctrine of *laissez-faire*, therefore they regulated trade and labour in careful detail. The North Riding being so entirely an agricultural district, its trade chiefly consisted in the buying and selling of live stock, butter and other products of the land. Minute regulations were made by Government respecting these; stock had to be kept five weeks after it was bought, whether a man had sufficient food for it or not. The laws against forestalling and engrossing[1] were regularly enforced by the Justices. No one could buy goods except in the open market and on the appointed day[2], nor was the middleman allowed[3] unless he held a licence granted by the Court of Quarter Sessions[4].

After the Restoration an act[5] was passed for reforming abuses in butter, since farmers had been accustomed to weigh with stones, iron wedges, etc., and to add much salt to the butter to increase its weight "to the wrong and abuse of His Majesty in the victualling of his Navy and to the great dishonour of the English nation in the parts beyond the seas[6]."

Therefore every farmer was ordered to sell his butter in

---

exclusively described as yeomen for exercising the trade of a badger and buyer of corn without license. 9 others for using the trade of a buyer of butter and cheese; a man for using the trade of a drover of cattle."

[1] 5 and 6 Ed. VI, cap. xiv.

[2] *N.R.Q.S.R.* vol. I. p. 121. Helmsley, July, 1608. "John Foxe of Hovingham for bringing corne to Thirske, a markett-towne on the weekedaie before the markett, and not on the markett daie."

."Roger Lecke of Thirske for that he receyveth corne in the weeke tyme (out of the markett daie) into his chambers."

"John Frank of New Malton and Alice his wife, for forstalling the markett of divers paniers of fishe, buying the same of the fishermen of Runswick or Whitbye...before it came into markett."

[3] "Geo. Hesslupe, millner, of Russwarp, for buying of xii bushells of wheat of Rich. Jackson of Bargate, and reselling the same to him making VIIIs gaine of it."

"Rob Tyson of Seamer for buyinge foure quarters of barley about Candlemas last of a stranger who was carrying the same to the King's markett and also Will Langtofte of the same, for buying two qrs of barley when he was goeing to Skarbroughe Markett."

[4] 5 Eliz. cap. xii.

[5] 14 Car. II, cap. xxvi.

[6] 14 Car. II, cap. xxvi.

firkins and kinderkins of a standard weight and size[1], and to have his name stamped on the outside. The penalty for default was 2s., half of which was to go to the poor, half "to him who will sue."

Evidently the act was needed, for after its enactment there are numerous presentments of yeomen and farmers for selling butter under weight, and for neglecting to brand their initials on the casks. Firkiners also were summoned for making firkins "above the weight of 8 lbs which could not contain 56 lbs of butter[2]." At Whitby there was even an attempt to make a corner in the butter trade. In 1678 "five gentlemen and three women" were presented "for conspiring to lower the price of butter on a market day at Whitby and promising each other not to give more than 12s. a firkin[3]."

In rural districts like the North and East of Yorkshire, where there was no great trade centre, the circulation of money was slow and the custom survived of making payment in kind[4]. Temptation also arose to make counterfeit money; a man from the remote parish of Aysgarth in Wensleydale having the following charge made against him in 1659[5]:

Miles Hardcastle of Edgley in the parish of Askarth, yeomn, not having God before his eyes, but led by the instigation of the divell, as a traytor to his Highnes Decr. 11 1658, two pieces of money of false and impared mettall like unto the coin of the Commonwealth of England, falsely, feloniously and traitorously did counterfeet, make, and coin, contrary to the statute etc.

This and the clipping of coin were serious offences and persons suspected of the latter were committed to trial at the Assizes[6].

---

[1] Kinderkin = 132 lbs i.e. Butter 112 lbs cask 20 lbs.
　Firkin　 = 64 ,,　　　,,　 56 ,,　 ,,　 8 ,,
　Pott　　 = 20 ,,　　　,,　 14 ,, pot　 6 ,,
[2] N.R.Q.S.R. vol. VII. p. 12. Stokesley, July, 1678.
[3] Ibid. vol. VII. p. 15. Thirsk, Oct. 1678.
[4] Rural Economy in Yorkshire, S.S.P. vol. XXXIII. p. 155. 1622–3. "William Hutson hath payd by a quarter of veal 8d. of his rent. 1621. Bought of William Whitehead a cowe, to pay for her a qr of barley for bread."
[5] N.R.Q.S.R. vol. VI. p. 17. Richmond, Jan. 1659.
[6] Ibid. vol. V. p. 260. Helmsley, Jan. 1657. "A Thirske man to

Dealing in money was still looked upon unfavourably, the taking of excessive usury being an indictable offence[1].

The careful and detailed legislation of the time which demanded numerous briefs, testimonials and warrants, and the frequent litigation requiring oaths, produced in its train a certain amount of perjury and forgery[2].

Stealing, however, was by far the most common crime, in spite of the fact that its punishment was extremely severe. Indeed the heavy penalty for theft defeated its object, since in order to mitigate the severity of the law the Bench included quite considerable thefts in the category of petty larceny[3] (*i.e.* thefts of the value of 12*d.*), the punishment for which was whipping.

During the Interregnum the penalty for stealing was much less severe but was balanced by the strictness with which the ordinances of Parliament were enforced, and the heavy penalties imposed for political offences or for difference of opinion in religion.

In spite of the fact that for justice and police the country depended largely on unpaid amateurs, each department of work seems to have been adequately performed, and offenders seldom escaped punishment.

The constable was bound by his oath to present all offences within his cognizance; for many offences also one-

be sent back to the Castle of York there to remain to the next Assizes which shall first happen untill he shall be from thence delivered by a due course of Law, for the offence mentioned in the Mittimus upon which he was formerly committeed to the gaole, being for suspition of the felonious clipping of the currant coyne or money of the nation."

[1] *N.R.Q S.R.* vol. I. p. 46. Richmond, July, 1606. "Chr Paycock of New-by-super-Wiske for being a great usurer in haec verba viz: hath receyved of Tho Catterick of Brompton besides Allerton excessive usurie contrary to the statute, that is to say for the loane of iiii £ for one yeare xiiis. iiii*d.* and for the loane of the same for a yeare next after, other xiiis. iiii*d.* in malum exemplum etc."

[2] *Ibid.* vol. VI. p. 127. Richmond, July, 1668. "The three men who were indicted for forging of a warrant and for receiving £3. 2. by the same to repay the same to the constable of Long Coulton and the prosecutor to have his charges deducted out of the same."

[3] *Ibid.* vol. V. p. 208. Richmond, Jan. 1655. "A Hornby woman for stealing a green colored safegard (2*s.* 6*d.* putts herself guilty to 10*d.* whipt." *safegard* = riding-skirt.

half or a third of the fine was given "to him who will sue
for it," *i.e.* the person furnishing the information of misdeeds[1]. This led to the institution of the professional relator
or informer, a man who made it his business to find out
offences, in order to claim a share of the fine. His presentments usually concerned infringements of the statutes affecting trade, such as beaming and beetling cloth, buying
and selling stock without keeping it the requisite time, etc.[2]
The penalties for such offences were heavy, therefore the
occupation though odious was lucrative[3]. Consequently only
those people who received the sanction of the Justices in
Quarter Sessions and obtained a licence from His Majesty's
attorney were allowed to undertake it[4]. The case of Henry
Buttrye shows that rigorous penalties were imposed on un-
official informers and those who abused their power. Henry
Buttrye was charged with not considering nor fearing

the statute of 18 Eliz. for extorting 3s. from Leonard Heddon of
Welbury 9s. 6d. from Tho. Hunter xs. from Rich. Mathew of Hutton
Rudby husbn. under colour of certain informations laid by him
against them. Therefore he was condemned to stand on the pillorie
of Northallerton two severall days, with a paper on his head with
inscription testifying his cousinage etc., and that he used the office
of Informer without the authority or license from His Majties Attorney in the North, and to pay a fyne of xls. for each offence in
all £4[5].

---

[1] *N.R.Q.S.R.* vol. IV. p. 249. Easingwold, Jan. 1645. "Three of the
parties informed against as using the art of a baker etc. appear and submit
themselves, and are fined 10s. each, half to the informer, half to the King."
[2] *Ibid.* vol. III. p. 325. Helmsley, Jan. 1632. "An information by
Phil. Kendall (who claims half the penalty of £168) against Raph Hasell
of Huton on the Hill, gentn for buying 30 oxen and 12 whies, value 40s.
each and not keeping the same for five weeks, but resold them."
[3] *Ibid.* vol. III. p. 316. Richmond, July, 1631. "Long Mem. of information by Philip Kendall against Raph Hasell of Huton on Derwent gentn
for engrossing etc. ten quarters of rye (£40) twenty quarters of oats (£15)
and ten quarters of barley (20 marks) the value in all amounting to
£68. 6s. 8d. of which the said informer claims half under the statute cited
(5 Edw. VI)."
[4] *Ibid.* vol. VII. p. 47. Bedale, Jan. 1681. "Ordered that Fr Kitching
of Thornebrough yeomn be admitted as common informer for Richmondshire and Allertonshire, and continue the said imployment during the
pleasure of the Court."
[5] *Ibid.* vol. I. pp. 40–44. Helmsley, Jan. 1606.

Nevertheless the office lent itself to extortion[1] and it cannot be doubted that many people were frightened into paying the informer the sum of money he demanded.

There were few prisons, the chief penalties being the ducking stool, the stocks, the pillory, the public whipping or branding on the shoulder or the hand, and finally the gallows.

Certain offences, such as undutiful conduct, insolent words, cozening tricks[2], etc., had special punishment meted out to them, such as public penance in church and in the market place in full market time[3]. A Newbiggin man who is indicted for "cooseninge one John Hamond of £10 is to pay back one half to the said Hamond at Martinmas next and the other half at Lady-day after, and to be shaved close on one halfe of his head and the one halfe of his beard, and to be bound one whole year to the good behaviour." The publicity of all punishments produced coarseness in the manners of the period. The rigidity of the law, the lack of freedom of thought, word and action was not conducive to self-control and resulted either in narrowness of outlook or impotent revolt. Hence there were frequent assaults by both men and women. Evelyn in his *Character of England* speaks of the discourtesy to strangers, the familiarity of the innkeepers, the inartificial

---

[1] *N.R.Q.S.R.* vol. VII. p. 27. Thirsk, Oct. 1679. "Whereas it hath been made appear unto this Court that Jas. Phillips of Great Broughton, under the color of an informer, hath committed several misdemeanours and received sums of money of several persons unlawfully: Ordered that the said Jas. Phillips be put down from being an informer, and that hereafter no informations be drawn in his name."

Ibid. vol. I. p. 160. Malton, Oct. 1609. "Rich: Cotes of Thornton Beanes Lbr. an informer, for extorting colore officii sui, a fee of 19s. 10d. at Thirske from one James Scott of the same; and also for the like in the matter of 19s. 6d. taken from James Browne of Thornton in le Moore etc."

[2] *Ibid.* vol. III. pp. 238–9. Richmond, July, 1625. "Forasmuch as Tristram Hogg of Newbiggin is indicted for using cooseninge tricks etc."

[3] *Ibid.* vol. II. p. 237. Thirsk, April, 1620. "That Jane Philip, convicted of felonie and petit larcenie, for wch she beene whipped here at Thirske, and besides is to be taken to Stokesley and there sett in the stockes etc. yet the Courte is pleased that if she shall make humble acknowledgment at the Markett-crosse in Stokesley that she hath wronged Mrs Constable, her late Mrs, by laying an unjust imputation upon her for those matters conteyned in the indictment whereof she herself was founde guiltie, and desire forgiveness of her said Mrs, for her said offence, then the further sentence to be remitted."

congestion of the houses, the irregularities of public worship, the drinking and card-playing[1] of his time.

The insanitary conditions of the villages were not conducive to public health, and, as we have seen, the Riding in one place or another was frequently visited by the plague[2].

In 1604 the local authorities were authorised to levy a tax for the relief of people suffering from this scourge, not only on town or village but on the country round within a radius of five miles[3]. If, however, the infection continued for a long time, a larger sum was levied by the Justices on the whole Riding[4]. When the sickness broke out the richest people in the village provided the necessary funds and were afterwards re-imbursed from the rate[5].

In 1605 and 1610 the plague is mentioned in the Thirsk

---

[1] Evelyn, *Diary*, vol. II. p. 156.

[2] *N.R.Q.S.R.* vol. I. p. 3. Thirsk, April, 1605. " John Gill... for severally refusing to pay the cess imposed on them for the relief of the folk suffering under the visitation of pestilence contrary to Christianity &c. (Side Note: the Overseers did justifie in Court that this assessment was payd, and therefore the Court at Thirsk holden ye 8 of November 1605, thought good to dyscharge them.)"

In 1610 the visitation is again mentioned and in 1626 strict watch has to be kept at Sowerby near Thirsk on account of the pestilence.

[3] *Ibid.* vol. IV. p. 99. Malton, July, 1638. "Thornton in Pickering Leth infected with Plague. Whereas £25 was ordered to be assessed for the relief of the inhabitants of Thornton in Pickering lith now infected with the plague within 5 miles thereof and the infection still continues £100 to be levied throughout the Northe Riding for the relief of the inhabitants of the said town and Rog. Wervell and John Caley Esqrs (two J.P.s) are requested to see the same carefully applied."

[4] *Ibid.* vol. III. p. 214. Thirsk, Sept. 1624. "The towne of Scarborough (sore grieved with sicknes and infection of the plague) being not able to releive and maintaine themselves, their sicke and poore people, and forced to seeke releife of the countrie adjoyninge &c. Ordered that anie two of the next justices shall take order for the ratinge, collectinge and levyinge of £10 weeklie for releife of the said towne throughout the Wapes. of Whitby Strand, Pickering-Lieth, and Ridall &c. as in their wisdomes and discretions shall be thought most fitt etc., for so long as necessity shall require—the said rates to be levied according to the usual rates and proportions &c."

[5] *Ibid.* vol. III. p. 279. Richmond, Oct. 1626. "That all monies levied for the relief of the poor people of Leminge infected with the plague which continued there since Aug. 3, 1625 until Feb. 24 last and are now in arrear to be at once paid to Raph Smith and John Raper to be paid to such persons as did lend and laie for the money in the time of the visitation and to such as are behind for watch and to bring any balance over there may be to the next Sessions."

neighbourhood. In 1624 the town of Scarborough was so sore grieved with sickness and infection of the plague that the Justices order £10 weekly to be voted from the wapentakes of Whitby Strand, Pickering Lythe and Ridall for as long as shall be necessary, and they also make an order for relief for people at Leeming stricken with plague. In 1638 Thornton in Pickering Lythe is so infected with the plague that £100 is to be levied throughout the Riding for its relief[1].

The nearest Justice of the Peace took what measures he thought fit to prevent the spread of the infection; he appointed people to take care of those who were ill, and to guard the houses which were clear[2].

Day watch was strictly kept to prevent wandering people who might bring infection entering the parish, for the plague was by far the most dreaded illness in the seventeenth century. Monetary help was also given to sick people from the county fund for lame soldiers and hospitals, either to pay for doctors or to assist them in travelling to health resorts. The chief illnesses besides plague were cancer, the falling sickness and the king's evil. The cure for lunacy was still considered to be the treatment meted out to Malvolio: one Arth. Clarke appeared to the Court to be "a distressed and distracted person and not capable what he doth or saith"; his fellow-townsfolk were ordered "to take him into their safe-keeping...and to keep him darke, and otherwise releive him[3]." It is to be hoped that the relief did not partake of

[1] See note 4, p. 196.
[2] *N.R.Q.S.R.* vol. III. p. 261. Northallerton, Ap. 1626. "Sowerby near Thirsk visited by the plague and Raph Bell of that town, a rich man, refusing to be ordered by those that are appointed to take care and charge of the infected, and to contribute to their reliefe, and for guarding the houses which are cleare, as by the advise and consent of Rog. Gregory Esq. J.P. and residing near, as thought fitt." "Ordered by this Courte that the said Bell and his mother shall either remove out of the towne, to a house he hath built for that purpose or els that a sufficient watch be sett about the house he now dwelleth in, during his aboade therein, att his owne charge: and if he refuse to pay their wages Mr Lockwood and the other inhabts to disburse the same, and Mr Gregory shall take him bound to appear att the next Sessns after such time as the said toune of Sowerby shalbe sett at libertie: And in the meantime &c."
[3] *Ibid.* vol. III. p. 355. Malton, July, 1633.

the twofold nature of Rosalind's remedy for madness, "a dark house and a whip."

The system of local government through the medium of the parish tended to make permanent the local feeling which in the Middle Ages had given the feudal lord a strong position in the state. But conditions were changing; while the boundaries of the parish formed the horizon of almost all its inhabitants; beyond, out of sight and ken, appealing to the imagination by its very vagueness, lay the King's Majesty.

For all public authority was derived from the King, every order proclaimed at the market cross or in the church was made in his name. The constable kept His Majesty's Peace[1]. The King's liege people were not to be disturbed by the disorderly conduct[2] of individuals. All the parishioners were summoned in church to give their labour for the repair of the King's highway, or to assemble when the muster was held for His Majesty's service in war[3].

The freeholders went to Quarter Sessions to do service for His Majesty; finally His Majesty's Justices of the Peace held powerful sway over each parish as over the whole Riding.

---

[1] *N.R.Q.S.R.* vol. I. p. 9. Richmond, Oct. 8, 1607. "Tho. Best of Wath, a wavering person, for three assaults on the Constable of Melmerby, willing to kepe good order and His Maties peace: fined xxs."

[2] *Ibid.* vol. I. p. 213. Thirsk, July, 1661. "John Swyer of Thirske for a drunkard, and for disturbing the Kinges people with great disorder in his drunkenness."

[3] *Ibid.* vol. I. p. 104. Malton, Jan. 1608. "John Binckes son of Widow Binckes of Stonnykeld for flying and hyding himself from his Maties. service at the last musters...(Per Rob. Colling et Rob. Shawe, Cap. Const.)."

APPENDIX G

COMPENSATION FOR LOSS BY FIRE

Briefs.

Collected upon Breifes, 1675 Jany 20; Upon the breife for the fires in Redbourne within the liberties of St Albon's in the County of Hartford, being delivered to Mr Martin Minister whoe is to procure the acquittance for the same, 16s. 8½d. 1676 June 6th: Upon the breife for the fire in the towne of Northampton within and throughout the parish as by a schedule thereunto annexed doth and will appeare per ye Major, 2£. 6s. 7d. June 25th: Upon speciall orders for one Don Harasa, an outlandish and Caldean priest taken by the Turkes, and paid him, 1£. 0s. 0d. July 30th: Upon the breefe for the rebuilding of the parish church of Oswestree in the County of Salop and to Mr Martin paid, 13s. 11d. Aug. 27th: Upon the breefe for Niwent church in the County of Gloster. 13s. 2d.

> Vestry Book of the Parish of St Nicholas, Durham, 1665–1703, *S.S.P.* vol. LXXXIV. pp. 236–237.

1680–1. For riding about the parish with a breif, 2s. for carrying the breife money to Durham, 1s.

> Vestry Book of the Parish of Houghton-le-Spring, vol. XI, 1671–1704, *S.S.P.* vol. XLVIII. p. 340.

Upon reading the petition of Jas Wild of Greeta Bridge, setting forth that he is a milner and milne wreet by trade, and lived in good and creedable manner, contributed to the relief of the poor, to his utmost proportion, till about the year 1660, he having taken a water corn milne, with another partner, was by a sudden accident of fire wholly burnt down and consumed, to the poor petitioner's damage, of £60 and upwards, and further setting forth that since, to witt, the 21st of April instant about two of the clock in the morning, by the like accident of fire, consumed and burnt down a kilne, stable, woodhouse, and backehouse, with two horses standing in the stable, some corn, and all his work geare, and much considerable house-stuff, as bedding, tables and timbers, then standing and being in the same, to the poor petitioner's losse of £80 and upwards, so that he is now in a sad and necessitous condition, having little or nothing whereby to maintain himself, his wife and six little children, but is in much debt and like to be cast into prison, whereupon this Court, taking the petitioner's sad and miserable condition into consideration, doth think fit and so Order that the poor petitioner shall have free liberty and leave to aske and receive the gratuities and charitable benevolence of all well-disposed people in and throughout the whole North Riding, and doth earnestly recommend the petitioner, earnestly entreating and desiring all parsons, ministers, lecturers, vicars, and curates, for the better stirring up of charateable devotions deliberately to declare and publish the tenure hereof unto the people upon the Lord's Day next after the same shall be tendered unto them, and likewise the Churchwardens of every parish where such collections is to be made are ordered to collect and gather the almes and charateable benevolence of all and every such well-disposed people who shall be present at the publishing hereof, the sum and sums of money so collected and gathered forthwith to be paid unto the petitioner, or to such person or persons who he shall depute to be the bearer hereof, or to receive the same, and this Order to continue in force for the space of eight months now next ensuing the date hereof.

N.R.Q.S.R. vol. VI. p. 69. Richmond, July, 1663.

CHAPTER X

THE JUSTICE OF THE PEACE

SHOWING

THE RELATION BETWEEN THE PARISH AND THE COUNTY

The justices of the peace be those in whom...the prince putteth his special trust[1].

THE secret of efficient English local government lies in the close relation between the parish and the county.

The connecting link is the Justice of the Peace, who, as a parishioner, is a member of the village community, takes part in its life, shares its privileges, is subject to the control of its authorities, in the same degree as the poorest day labourer, and as a county magistrate is empowered with high judicial functions extending not only over his own parish, but also over the entire county.

Through his position as a local man of considerable wealth and influence the country Justice at any time would be an important factor in his neighbourhood; and when to this is added the judicial, administrative and even governmental power assigned to him by statute after statute, it is clear that in attempting to describe the parish economy, account must be taken of its most prominent member.

Every parish rested as it were under the shadow of some Justice, looked to him for pecuniary assistance in time of distress and depended on him to help it out of its difficulties, to be literally a friend at court when it got into trouble and was summoned for negligence in performing its civic obligations.

[1] *The Commonwealth of England*, by Sir T. Smith, Ed. 1589, Bk. II. ch. xxi.

While the influence of the Justices looms large in the parish, in Quarter Sessions they had such wide and varied functions in the area of local government that, when the central power for a time broke down, order was steadfastly maintained in the shires. Perhaps the work of the local magistrates, and the excessive duties of the parish officials supply one answer to the question why England attained a peaceful revolution in 1688.

The ordinary Englishman had so much to do in the affairs of his own village or town, that he had no desire for a larger sphere of activity, no thought for what lay outside his own little circle, within which for the most part stability and sound rule prevailed.

In order to understand how it came about that the Justices of the Peace exercised such full and varied powers in the seventeenth century it is necessary to consider briefly the origin of their authority.

In Edward III's reign the edict went forth that in every county good men and lawful should be commissioned to keep the peace[1].

By a series of statutes[2] these local magistrates were empowered to put down riots, to issue warrants for the arrest of offenders against the peace, and to hear and determine at the King's suit according to the law and customs of the realm, all manner of felonies and trespass done in their county[3].

For this purpose they were to hold meetings or sessions four times a year and any failure in this respect rendered them liable to punishment at the discretion of the King's Council[4].

The Justices were required also to administer Acts of

[1] 1327. 1 Ed. III, st. 2, cap. xvi. Conservators of the peace were appointed in 1285 under the Statute of Winchester.
[2] 1330. 4 Ed. III, cap. ii.
   1344. 18 Ed. III, st. 2, cap. ii.
   1360. 34 Ed. III, st. 2, cap. i.
[3] Maitland, *Constitutional History*, p. 206.
[4] 12 Rich. II, cap. x.

Parliament. Especially is this the case with regard to the Statutes of Labourers, which gave them authority to compel men to work for the legal wage and even delegated to them the governmental function of determining the rate of wages.

Moreover their Commission empowered any two or more Justices of the Peace (one being of the quorum):

1. To enquire (by a jury) of all offences mentioned within the Commission.

2. To take or view all indictments or presentments of the jury.

3. To grant out process against the offenders whereby to cause them to come and answer.

4. To hear and try all such offences.

5. To determine thereof by giving judgment and inflicting punishment upon the offenders according to the laws and statutes[1].

Any man holding lands or tenements to the value of £20 a year was liable to be made a Justice of the county in which his lands lay, or in the case of a borough, any member of the municipal corporation was qualified for the office[2]. At first only a few men, six or eight in each county, were chosen[3]; but their number steadily increased during the sixteenth and seventeenth centuries[4].

---

[1] Dalton, *The Country Justice,* chap. iv. "And whereas by the Commission of the Peace presently after and to this day the Justices of the Peace had and still have the Statute of Winchester given them in charge to execute the same, which Statute of Winchester (13 E. I) was long before there were any Justices of the Peace by this it may appear that the King by his Commission may commit the execution of the Statutes and Laws to whom he shall please. And so also a Justice of the Peace by virtue of the Commission may execute any Statute, whereunto he shall be enabled by the said Commission although there shall be no such express power given him so to do by the words or letter of the same statute."

[2] 18 Hen. VI, cap. xi. 13 Rich. II, cap. vii. 2 Hen. V, cap. i. st. 2.

[3] Maitland, *Constitutional History,* p. 209.

[4] Visitation of Yorkshire, Ed. by J. Foster, pp. 406–7 (*Harleian Soc. Publ.*). At the Visitation held in Yorkshire in 1584–5 by Norroy King-at-Arms four knights and nineteen esquires were in the Commission of the Peace for the North Riding. In 1635 the number had risen to thirty-nine.

Yet the number of Justices attending any Court of Quarter Sessions in that year was generally ten or eleven, very occasionally twelve or thirteen.

In spite of many petitions that these magistrates might be chosen by the freeholders of the shire, the King would never give way, and the Justices of the Peace have always been appointed by commission of the King, and hold their office at his good pleasure[1].

Thus the central government secures its control over the local authority, and the office is a compromise. The Justice, a local man, generally of considerable influence in the shire where he has jurisdiction, is appointed and supervised by the Crown[2] and serves "durante bene placito regis."

Every Justice before he entered upon his duties was required to take the oath concerning his office and the oath of the King's Supremacy[3].

These oaths bound the Justices to be loyal to King and government, to do equal right to rich and poor, to be impartial in giving judgment, to hold their sessions at the appointed times, to pay all fines, etc., unto the Exchequer, to take no bribe and to make the King's officers execute their warrants.

The work of the Justices may be considered from two standpoints, (1) collectively in the Court of Quarter Sessions, (2) individually each in his vicinity.

The Quarter Sessions were held at certain fixed times: after Easter, after the Translation of St Thomas, after the Feast of St Michael, and after the Epiphany[4].

They generally lasted three days; in the spring the Court opened at eight o'clock in the morning[5], in summer at

In 1662 no less than twenty Justices attend the Court, therefore the whole number in the Riding must have been considerably larger than in 1635.

See *N.R.Q.S.R.* vol. IV. p. 32. The full list of J.P.s for the North Riding in this year is given in Appendix K.

[1] Maitland, *Constitutional History*, p. 207.

[2] The Justices of the North Riding received orders from the Privy Council and (until 1641) from the Court of Star Chamber while the Council in the North ensured that these orders were carried out.

See also Redlich and Hirst, *Local Government in England*, ch. ii. p. 13.

[3] See Appendix N for oath concerning his office, 1 Eliz. cap. i. sec. ix. for Oath of Supremacy.

[4] Lambard, pp. 579–80; 2 Hen. V, cap. iv.

[5] *N.R.Q.S.R.* vol. v. p. 180. "The next sessions to be at Northallerton April 24th next by eight of the clock in the morning."

seven[1]. They could be held in any of the towns in the county at the discretion of the Justices; in the North Riding they were usually held at Helmsley and Thirsk, with adjournment in January and July to Richmond; sometimes they were called at Malton and very occasionally at Northallerton, Stokesley, Bedale. Wensley, Middleham, Guisborough, Topcliffe, and other smaller towns[2].

The Justices in the North Riding still received in the seventeenth century their allowance of 4s. a day for attending the Court[3]; at the Helmsley Quarter Sessions held on the 10th and 11th of July, 1610, the Bench was exceedingly annoyed at the sheriff's deputy because he refused "to disburse his Majestie's allowance to the justices now present for their wages; we do therefore," the entry continues, "in respect of his contempt in this behalf with one consent set upon Mr Sheriff's head, for a fine to be presently (i.e. immediately) estreeted the somme of £10, and this to be entered emongest the Orders of this session[4]." It would be interesting to hear the deputy sheriff's side of the case; it may be that some work remained for the Justices to finish and they were not willing to sit a third day at Helmsley. The statute which allows them their wages enacts "that they should keep their sessions every quarter of the year at the least and by three days if need be[3]," and it is worthy of note that out of the twelve Justices who sat at Helmsley, only one appeared among the eight who sat at Northallerton at the adjourned Sessions, and of the six attendances it was possible for them to make during the year it was the first appearance of two Justices, while seven had only attended twice, one had been at three Sessions, and two had made four attendances. As the Act only allowed for the payment of eight Justices perhaps the deputy sheriff had reason on his side. However

[1] N.R.Q.S.R. vol. v. p. 61. New Malton, July, 1654.
[2] Chiefly at the smaller towns by adjournment, during the last quarter of the seventeenth century. Ibid. vol. VII.
[3] 12 Rich. II, cap. x. and 14 Rich. II, cap. xi.
[4] N.R.Q.S.R. vol. I. p. 195.

this may be, it would seem that the sheriff had to pay the fine, and at the next Sessions in October he had also appointed a new deputy.

As an instance however of the time given by some Justices to their magisterial duties it may be noticed that in the spring of 1616 Sir Henry Frankland attended the Thirsk Quarter Sessions on April 10th, a meeting of certain Justices to compound for purveyance in York Minster on the 16th, the Special Sessions at Sutton on the 22nd, at Wath on the 28th, and at Guisborough on May 2nd.

Special or Petty Sessions, which may have taken their origin from the enactments in the Statute of Labourers and Apprentices, were held twice a year in each wapentake in the North Riding, at Hutton Bushell for the Liberty of Whitby Strand[1], at Sutton for the Forest of Gaultres[2], at Wath for the wapentake of Hang East[3], at Richmond for the Liberties of Gilling East and Gilling West[4], at Guisborough for the Liberty of Langbargh[5], at Cuckwold[6] for the wapentake of Birdforth, and at Northallerton[7] for the Liberty of Allertonshire. They were attended by those Justices who lived in the neighbourhood, ranging in number from two to five, and by the sheriff's deputy. The Justices tried in Petty Sessions, with the help of a jury from the wapentake, all offences, except felony, which came within the competence of the Quarter Sessions. Such were infringement of the statutes relating to trade (forestalling and engrossing), the brewing and selling of ale, the assize of bread, labourers and apprentices, rogues and vagabonds; also such offences as petty larceny, assault, the playing of unlawful games, and the neglect of civic duties[8].

---

[1] *N.R.Q.S.R.* vol. II. p. 120. 4 and 5 April, 1616. 8.5 Eliz. cap. iv. sec. xxxi.
[2] *Ibid.* p. 127. 22 April, 1616.   [3] *Ibid.* p. 128. 28 April, 1616.
[4] *Ibid.* p. 129. 29 April, 1616.   [5] *Ibid.* p. 130. 2 May, 1616.
[6] *Ibid.* p. 133. 8 May, 1616.   [7] *Ibid.* p. 134. 1 May, 1616.
[8] *Ibid.* vol. III. p. 288. "Special Sessions (for the Liberties of Lanbargh Gisborough and Whitby Strand) at Gisborough 21 Feb 162⅔ before Sir Daved Foules Bart. and Nich Corners Esq. Tho Clarke gent. Deputy for

Before considering the work of the Justices in detail it will be necessary to take some note of those public officers over whom they were expected by their commission to exercise a general supervision, and who were more or less their coadjutators.

The most eminent of these was the high sheriff of the county, who, as the representative of the sovereign, held the highest rank in the shire; he was appointed by the King for one year only, and during that year could not be an active Justice of the Peace. He had gradually lost his ancient powers and functions, and, in the seventeenth century, his chief work consisted in returning lists of freeholders[1] to serve on juries and in carrying out the sentences passed on offenders by the criminal courts. With this latter duty was connected the charge of all prisoners committed to him and the maintenance of the county gaol. The sheriff could only hold office for a year, too short a time to allow him to gain much insight into the nature of his duties; therefore his work was always performed by deputies who were permanent officials. The Justices exercised a careful supervision over the sheriffs, fining them if they appointed unsuitable deputies who neglected their work[2] or whose position in the county was not adequate to the dignity of the office[3], and holding them

High Sheriff and a Jury consisting of 3 Gent. and 10 yeomen. Three women for stealing chickens (4d.) a husb^m for sheep-stealing; 126 alehouse keepers for selling their best ale above 4d. a gallon; a widow for harboringe of tinkers; a Skelton lab^r for an assault on a man in the presence of the Court. Submits etc. is fined £5 and to sit in the stocks for four hours with a paper on his head setting forth his offence."

[1] *N.R.Q.S.R.* vol. II. p. 32. New Malton, Sept. 1613. In 1613 "the Sheriffe of the Countie of Yorke for his Bailiffes Generall Default in not returning sufficient Jurors for his Maties service is fyned 40s."
See also *ibid.* vol. IV. p. 31. Thirsk, April 8, 1635.
The Bench ordered "That the Sherife of the County of Yorke shall send into this Court the booke of the whole N.R. conteyning the names of all the freeholders within the same to the next Quarter Sessions."

[2] At Helmsley in Jan. 1619, the High Sheriff (Sir Robert Swift) "was fined £10 for allowing a prisoner in his custody to escape." At Richmond in Aug. 1657 the Sheriff "to be fined £20 for allowing two men committed to his custody to escape, unless they are apprehended and brought before a Justice of the Peace within twenty days."

[3] In July, 1614, Sir George Savile, the High Sheriff, made a certain bailiff, William Robinson, his deputy Sheriff and for so doing was fined

responsible for all misdeeds on the part of their employees[1].

This supervision seems to have been effective; in April, 1620, a fine of £20 was imposed on the sheriff because the bailiff of Bulmer wapentake did not attend the Sessions[2]; in the following October, however, the Bench ordered "that the fine of £20 imposed on the High Sheriff...for the negligence of his Bailiff of Bulmer be remitted as the Courte has been satisfied by his (the Bailiff's) better service since." Evidently the fine was of the nature of a warning and caused the sheriff to put pressure on his negligent bailiff.

The North Riding contains the liberties of Allertonshire, Richmondshire, Whitby Strand, Pickering Lythe, and others. In these lands the King's writ did not run, yet the Court of Quarter Sessions held jurisdiction over their bailiffs, who were great lords as powerful as the sheriff.

The Justices exercised an even greater authority over the high constables (the chief officers of the wapentakes or hundreds). Originally elected in the Sheriff's Turn of the Hundred Court, on its decline they were appointed and sworn in the Court of Quarter Sessions. Thus they were directly under the power of the Justices and were useful intermediaries between them and the officials of the parish.

From time to time the Court of Quarter Sessions issued charges[3] to the high constables respecting their own duties and the orders from the Bench which they were to deliver to the constables and churchwardens.

£10. William Robinson "being adjudged insufficient for that service and not able to make any sufficient return modo et forma."
    In the Sessions held at Malton in the following October, Sir G. Savile had obtained "Will. Henlake, gentleman," to do his work.
    In April, 1656, the Sheriff was fined 20s. for appointing a bailiff "not having sufficient land in the county."
    [1] N.R.Q.S.R. Helmsley, Jan. 1651. "Sir Ed. Rodes Knight, High Sheriff, Tho. Reed and Rich. Lealand, Gaolers for exacting 4d. for receiving a prisoner."
    Ibid. Helmsley, July, 1667. "The gaoler of the Castle of York for extortion under colour of his office."
    [2] Ibid. vol. II. p. 235. Thirsk, April, 1620.
    [3] See Appendix H.

For example in 1676 "Copies of the Articles underneath written" were ordered to be sent

by the respective Chief Constables within this Riding unto the several petty Constables within their divisions, and the Ministers of the several parishes within the Riding are desired to publish them in the parish Church after divine service and sermon in the morning, once every month.

1. That due watch and ward be kept by persons fit of able body by house-row, or at the charge of the Constablery, for the apprehending of all wandering and suspicious persons and for the punishment of them according to law.

2. That a privy search be made every month (or oftener) for the discovery of such persons and to prevent the harbouring of idle people and settleing of strangers.

3. That the Parish Officers do meet monthly according to the Statute, to consider of their poor, to provide stock, and get them to work, and give them convenient allowance according to their several necessities.

4. That such poor as having weekly relief or other maintenance, shall wander or beg out of their parishes (or townships) shall lose such maintenance and relief.

5. That for the better provision of the poor, the several statutes for levying the 12*d.* per Sunday, and the penalties for swearing tipling and drinking, driving cattle to markets carrying loads and burthens, and using unlawful pastimes on the Lord's Day, be speedily and duly executed, and the Officers failing to make their presentment to the next J.P. to be forthwith proceeded against.

6. That the Constableries through which any rogues or sturdy beggars, shall pass unapprehended or unpunished, shall pay after the rate of 2*s.* per head to such persons as shall seize and secure those wanderers.

7. That all tinkers, pedlars, and petty Chapmen, Bedlam common players of enterludes, gypsies, fiddlers, and pipers, wandering abroad be apprehended by the Constables and watchmen where they shall so pass, and be carried before some J.P. to be dealt with all according to law.

And while the magistrates collectively in Quarter Sessions enumerated the chief duties of the parish officers, individually they enforced these duties, each in his own neighbourhood; this was not the least important work done by them. For each group of parishes in his vicinity the Justice was

the chief authority, exercising control over constables, churchwardens and overseers[1] alike; remedying abuses[2], settling
disputes[3], binding apprentices, giving orders for the relief
of the poor and impotent[4], granting licences to beg, determining the differences regarding the rates to be levied by
adjacent townships, or by the several townships in one
parish[5], inspecting the work of the surveyor and of parishes
as regards the repair of the highways and bridges[6], in short
keeping an eye on all the parishes under his jurisdiction and

[1] N.R.Q.S.R. vol. v. p. 114. Ordered, "the overseers for the Poor of
Osmotherley having neglected to yield obedience to a warrant from Col.
Lassells whereby they were to pay 6d. weekly for the relief of a poor man
and his wife, they are to be carried before the next J.P. to become bound
etc."
   Ibid. vol. I. p. 72. Thirsk, April, 1607.
[2] Ibid. vol. VI. p. 242. Richmond, July, 1675. "Whereas Margaret
Binkes of Hipswell widow hath complained unto this Court that Robert
Ripley of East Whetton and his son and a stranger, which they said was
a Constable, did lately by force enter into her house and took away certain
goods for 2s. which she (as they pretended) was in arrear for hearth money,
and offered then to pay, though in her own wrong, and they refused to take
except she would pay 4s. more for charges and therefore did carry away and
as yet do detain, the said goods: and whereas the poor woman not being
able to prosecute law against the said persons hath petitioned for relief
here: this Court doth therefore refer it to Sir William Dalton J.P. to take
a hearing of the matter and Order relief to the petitioner according to his
discretion."
   [3] Ibid. vol. v. p. 110. "On hearing the differences bet. Sir Henry Vaghan
and F. R. Wright of Whitwell, gent: and for preventing the breach of the
peace hereafter Ordered that Sir Rich Darly and Henry Hall Esq. shall
hear the case and mediate an end if they can."
   [3] Ibid. vol. v. p. 120. "Col. Lassells (on the Bench) to call a man and
a woman before him and to mediate an end to the difference betwixt them
if he can."
   [4] Ibid. vol. v. p. 178. "A J.P. to inquire of the condition of a
woman of Helmsley alleadged to be a poor impotent innocent and to give
Order for her present relief and certify &c."
   [5] Ibid. vol. v. p. 120. "The inhabitants of Northallerton and the
inhabitants of Lazenby to pay their proportionable parts one to the other
in all Constable's assessments touching highways and if any difference
arise amongst them Col. Lassells to determine it."
   [6] Ibid. vol. v. p. 114. "Col. Lassells certifies that both Lazenby and
Hutton Bonville have both scowered the River Wistle sufficiently within
their townships."
   Ibid. vol. v. p. 119. "Whereas £10 was estreated against the
inhabitants of Pottoe for not sufficiently cleansing a water sewer or still
called Traineham Sike, and alsoe £13. 6s. 8d. upon the inhabitants of
Traineham for the like offence £10 for not making a sufficient horsebridge
over the said sike: forasmuch as it appears by the certificate of Fr. Lassels
Esq. J.P. that the said sike or stell is sufficiently scoured and a convenient
bridge laid by the inhabitants the C.C. for Langbargh to repay the said

performing executive work delegated to him by the Court of Quarter Sessions[1].

When presentments were made about which the evidence appeared unsatisfactory or insufficient the Court appointed a Justice who lived in the locality to enquire into the matter and report on it at the next Sessions[2]; or again the Bench delivered over to the nearest Justice the power of dealing with a refractory constable or a recalcitrant township[3]. It was the presence of "the next J.P." which was valuable for the interests of justice. Living in the neighbourhood the country magistrate knew or had means of finding out what was the true state of a case sent up to the Sessions. Considerable power was given to a single Justice by many of the statutes. He could order flesh killed in Lent to be confiscated and given to the poor[4]; condemn people found trespassing to be whipped, and send vagabonds to gaol[5]; set

inhabitants, the money collected by him for the offence aforesaid, excepting such charges as the law allows for levying the sum."

At the same sessions a J.P. is "to see the law put in execution against a Surveyor for detaining money which he ought to have paid to the mason who repaired Smeaton Bridge."

[1] "John Heslerton Treasr for the Hospitalls for this yeare now past tendering his accompt and the Court being busied, so as not to have time to examine the same, Rob. Brigges and Tho. Davile, Esquires, to receive it and deliver the same to the Clerke of the Peace."

[2] *N.R.Q.S.R.* vol. IV. p. 227. At Thirsk Quarter Sessions in April, 1642. "Two persons presented for non-payment of sums owing to the High Constable of Bulmer to be summoned by some Justice near adjoining, who shall examine the trueth and settle a peace or certifie this Courte at the next Sessions in whose defaulte."

[3] *Ibid.* vol. v. p. 33. "Kirby Moorside, July, 1649. Upon a petition preferred by the Ministers of Thornton in Pickering Lythe, Kirbymoorside, Edston, Lastingham and Helmesley, and other Ministers in the N.R., of the great profanation of the Lord's Day in and thorow the said Rideing, and the Ordinance of Parliament, for the suppressing of vice and punishing of offenders, neglected by the Constables and Churchwardens, who are to see the same put in execution, to the great Dishonour of God and Discouragement of painfull and laborious Ministers, the Constables are required from time to time to take speciall care the said Ordinance of Parliament for better observance of the Lord's Day, and penall statutes in that case provided, be put in due execution, by carrying the offenders before the next J.P. to receive condign punishment, and the Ministers, where such offences are committed, from time to time to inform the next J.P. if neglect be in the Constables and Churchwardens in pursuance of their office, that they may receive punishment, according to the nature of their offence and high contempt of authority."

[4] 5 Eliz. cap. iii.   [5] 14 Eliz. cap. v.

a price at which certain articles were to be sold in the markets; determine offences in tilemaking[1]; and commit to prison any persons using seditious words, unless they gave sureties to appear at the next Quarter Sessions or gaol delivery[2]. He had also considerable powers with regard to recusants[3]. He could receive their submission, administer the oath of allegiance to them, and at any time demand of a person suspected of recusancy that he should take the oath. On his warrant the churchwardens levied the fine of 12*d.* for absence from church, and if the offender refused to pay and had not sufficient distress, the Justice could commit him to prison[4].

Any two Justices of the Peace received by statute even greater administrative and judicial powers[5].

They could license or discharge alehouse keepers, appoint overseers of woollen cloth by the year[6], and punish clothiers for making deceivable cloth[7]. They were empowered to fine head officers in boroughs and market towns for not viewing weights and measures and burning the defective ones, and they fined all buyers and sellers using unlawful weights and measures[8]. They were expected to see that poor soldiers obtained work, and were allowed to tax the hundred for their relief; they might also assess proportionally parishes within the hundred towards a contribution for anyone who had been robbed. They administered the greater part of the statutes, relating to the poor, to rogues and vagabonds, and to labourers and apprentices.

The Court of Quarter Sessions was a court of record, and the office of keeper of the Records—Custos Rotulorum—was held by the Lord Lieutenant of the Shire.

"In the County of Gloucester, justice of peace and coram," says Slender of Robert Shallow, Esq., "ay, and ratolorum too; and a

---

[1] 17 Ed. IV, cap. iv. sec. vi.   [2] 23 Eliz. cap. ii. sec. vi.
[3] 3 and 4 Jac. I, cap. iv. sec. xviii. 7 and 8 Jac. I, cap. vi. sec. iii.
[4] 3 and 4 Jac. I, cap. xvii.
[5] Dalton, *The Country Justice*, chap. vi. p. 20.
[6] 4 Ed. IV, cap. i.   [7] 21 Jac. I, cap. xviii.
[8] 11 Hen. VI, cap. viii.

gentleman born, Master parson; who writes himself armigero, in any bill, warrant, quittance, or obligation, armigero[1]."

Those country gentlemen who had had some legal training were named "of the quorum," and in many of the laws which were given to any two or three Justices of the Peace to administer, it was provided that one of them should be "of the quorum"; in time it became usual to make all Justices members of the quorum, so that the distinction lost its importance[2]. The seventeenth century was a litigious age, and it was the custom for elder sons to spend some terms at the Inns of Court reading law.

Fuller's "true Gentleman" goes to the University, then "At the inns of court, he applies himself to learn the laws of the kingdom," because "law will help him to keep his own, and bestead [*i.e.* benefit] his neighbours'[3]."

A Justice's position in his own shire was one of great power and dignity and was eagerly sought after. Fuller would not have his true gentleman invite the office, but having become so worthy that the Commission of the Peace finds him out "he compounds many petty differences betwixt his neighbours which are easier ended in his own porch than in Westminster Hall...yet he connives not at the smothering of punishable faults."

> "Your dead father," says Tapwell talking to Wellborn,
> "My quondam master, was a man of worship,
> Old Sir John Wellborn, Justice of Peace and quorum,
> And stood fair to be custos rotulorum;
> Bore the whole sway of the shire, kept a great house,
> Relieved the poor and so forth[4]."

From King James I's proclamation it is clear that country gentlemen were expected to keep a great house and relieve the poor. In 1603 and again in 1622 they were commanded to return to their houses in the country so that they might relieve the poor by their ordinary hospitality, take action

---

[1] *Merry Wives of Windsor*, Act I. Sc. I.
[2] Maitland, *Justice and Police.*
[3] Fuller, *The Holy State*, p. 138, Ed. 1841.
[4] Massinger, *A new way to pay old debts*, Act I. Sc. I.

for the prevention of the plague, and keep order in their districts[1].

Moreover, the Justices in the North Riding appear to have taken the responsibilities of their position seriously.

In 1621 and 1622 the harvests had been very bad and the Privy Council issued orders for the reduction in the number of alehouses, since barley, used for malting, "is in time of scarcity the bread corne of the poore[2]."

Mr Wm. Aldborough, of Ellingthorp, being unable to attend the January Sessions in 1623 wrote to Sir Timothy Hutton declaring his readiness to obey His Majesty's orders and call a Special Sessions "for the spede preventing and re-midinge of the dearth of corne[3]."

In the Quarter Sessions the Justices made arrangements among themselves conducing to the better administration of the statutes[4], tried civil and criminal cases presented by a Grand Jury, fixed the rate of wages, or price of labour[5], and made general arrangements concerning public health and prevention of disease among animals. Any matter directly affecting the welfare of the individual, such as relief of the poor, pensions for lame soldiers, compensation for fire, came within their competence; they authorised the various assessments and arbitrated in many disputes arising out of rating,

[1] Leonard, *Early History of English Poor Relief*, p. 146, quoting Little Proclamation Book, James I, Nos. 22 and 23; Large Proclamation Book, James I, Nos. 108 and 109, 20 Nov. 1622.

[2] *Ibid.* p. 145, quoting Dom. S.P. Jac. I, vol. cxxxiii. No. 52.

[3] See Appendix I.

[4] Records printed from 1605 onwards.

In 1619 the Justices each take charge of separate districts in order to carry out more effectively the laws against Recusants. *N.R.Q.S.R.* vol. ii. p. 202.

In 1632 each Justice is ordered to inform himself of the condition of the bridges in his neighbourhood. *Ibid.* vol. ii. p. 342. Thirsk, Oct. 1632.

In 1635 the Justices agreed to divide themselves into groups, each group to be responsible for performing the "Country Services" in one particular Wapentake or Liberty, and to hold an annual sessions "to enquire into abuses committed by petty Constables, Churchwardens, Overseers and ale Conners." *Ibid.* vol. iv. pp. 32–34. See Appendix K.

[5] See Appendix E for wage assessments; also *N.R.Q.S.R.* vol. vii. p. 128. Thirsk, April, 1692. The J.P.s order that all carriers shall charge no more than 2*d.* a lb.

enclosure, and right of way, decided on whom rested the liability to repair a road or a bridge: and in all these difficult and uncertain duties they showed an evident desire to get at the real facts of the case, before declaring judgment.

The records of the Court of Quarter Sessions held during the seventeenth century justify the opinion that on the whole the Justices did their work in a fair minded and capable manner. Instances of oppression are few, and there are frequent indications of sympathy for people in distress and consideration for the well-being of the community. In spite of political changes the judicial and administrative work still went on, and it is difficult to conceive that any other system of local government could have performed its functions so lawfully or so well. In those distracted years which followed the outbreak of the Civil War, when one party was striving against another at Westminster, no efficient control was maintained by the central authority over the country districts after the abolition of the Star Chamber.

Yet the Court of Quarter Sessions were held with little intermission[1], and all the machinery for local government

---

[1] The Oct. Sessions in 1642 and the January Sessions in 1643 were not held. Oct. 1643 and April, 1645, no minutes and orders are recorded.

N.R.Q.S.R. vol. IV. pp. 233–4. On the 18th March, 1643, Henry Belasyse, Robert Strickland and Charles Tancred, three of the Justices, sign an order in which they authorise the Clerk of the Peace to issue writs to summon the next general Quarter Sessions of the Peace to be held at Thirsk on Ap. 13th. "Forasmuch," they say, "as the said North Riding hath been soe troubled with several armyes of soldiers ever since Michaelmas last, soe that noe Sessions of the Peace cold be held ever since untill this tyme that the armyes are drawen from these partes." However, the armies still remained, consequently the Easter Sessions were not held, for a further order, signed by Henry Belasyse and Charles Tankard, at Coxwold on the 20th July, again declares that no Sessions could be held on account of the armies "until now that they are withdrawn from these parts," and orders the next general Quarter Sessions shall be held at Thirsk on October 3rd, 1643, which accordingly was done.

Between Oct., 1643, and April, 1645, no minutes and orders are recorded; after this, with the exception that there were (intentionally) no Easter Sessions in 1648, the Justices met continuously until the end of 1659. There are no records of Epiphany, Easter or Summer Sessions in the year 1660. Then they are held in their regulai course until another period of indecision occurs in 1688.

was kept going; roads and bridges were not allowed to get out of repair, lame soldiers received their pensions, the poor were relieved, losses by fire were compensated, disorderly alehouses were rigorously suppressed and a steadfast determination to maintain order was shown in a time of general misrule.

Even when no Sessions were held the Justices met together to transact business and there was a Standing Committee, which seems, however, to have occupied itself mainly with the assessment of rates. Any orders made by the Justices at these informal meetings were brought to Quarter Sessions later to be confirmed[1].

The Justices, living among the people, knew and sympathised with the burdens imposed by the billeting of soldiers and the heavy taxation, and endeavoured to lighten them. In 1642 the Court ordered that

forasmuch as the countrie hath been very sore oppressed and put to greate charge by reason of soldiers billeted in most parts of the North Riding, soe that diverse poor men and others have been forcete by meanie of the saide souldiers to keep an alehouse and to brew ale, and to sell as well withoũt license as with license...all such persons as nowe remaineth in prosses or are only presented for the same within these two years last past shall be discharged[2].

In 1646 when the Scottish army was in Yorkshire, and the North Riding had to pay an assessment of £7000, the burden of carrying provisions and draughts (*i.e.* pair of horses) to Leeming fell heavily on the western part of the wapentake

[1] *N.R.Q.S.R.* vol. IV. p. 243. Thirsk, July, 1645. "Whereas an Order was made att Gisborough 30 April 1645 by Geo Trotter, Fr Lascells, and George Ewre, Esquires Justices of Peace within the Riding, that £10 should be weekly collected in the wapentake of Langbargh for relief of the poor and infected people in Yarme soe long as the sickness shall there continew, and that the same be weekly paid to the H Cs on every Saturday, and if any shall refuse to satisfye the proportion assessed upon them, the Constables are then commanded to distreyne the refuser's goods, and to prise and sell them, sending the overplus to the owners according to the expressions of an Order made at the last Quarter Sessions. Ordered that the same Order made by the said Justices shal be observed and performed, and is now confirmed by this Court."

[2] *Ibid.* vol. IV. p. 215. Thirsk, Oct. 1641.

of Langbargh, costing it about £300; therefore the Justices
ordered that the east part should share the expense and the
proportion "shall be equally charged on every several Constablery[1]."

In 1647 Geo. Marwood, Esq., J.P., is requested to convey
to Major-General Skippon the humble desires of the inhabitants of Cleveland, and "to be a sutor unto him on the
behalfe of this Court that hee will be pleased to afford them
his assistance and mediation as hee shall conceive most con-
duceing to the reliefe of the poor exhausted country[2]."

Although justice and good government were maintained
there are indications of the disorder caused by the Civil War.

A miller and two labourers were presented for forcible entry
into a man's house, for assaulting his wife and saying to her
"unless you give 40s. I will not leave your husband worth
one groat, but will bring a troope of soldiers and drive all his
goods (i.e. cattle) away[3]."

Petitions were brought to Court regarding the billeting of
soldiers[4] and many people were presented for refusing to pay
assessments.

In 1643 the high constables complained that the parish officers
in Richmondshire "do refuse to pay to them such moneys as
are charged upon their several towns and parishes, for bridges,
Purveyor's money, House of Correction, Muster Master's fee,
Prisoners in Yorke Castle, Hospitals and Lame Soldiers[5],"

---

[1] N.R.Q.S.R. vol. IV. p. 249. Easingwold, Jan. 1646.
[2] Ibid. vol. IV. p. 264. Helmsley, Jan. 1647.
[3] Ibid. vol. IV. p. 235. Thirsk, Oct. 3, 1643.
[4] Ibid. vol. IV. p. 253. Thirsk, April, 1646. "Whereas by the petition of Peter Clarke of Oldstead it appears that hee hathe been chardged
with billitting of souldiers, both horse and foote, which was in the service
of the King and Parliament, farr above his proportion; and sometimes
quartered souldiers when his neighbours had not any, the Constable and
inhab[ts], then promiseinge att the same time for his soe doeinge and easinge
them of the burthen, they would be bearers with him, and that an assesse
should be cast thorough the towne for satisfyeinge of the said chardge,
but as yet they have utterly refused to performe the same, it is therefore
Ordered that such an ass[t] be forthwith made etc., and the refusers are
required to repair before the next J.P., whoe is desired to examine the
premisses and doe justice therein."
[5] Ibid. vol. IV. p. 236. Thirsk, Oct. 3, 1643.

and two additional constables were appointed to help those in the wapentake of Birdforth[1].

During the period of the Civil War, while cases of assault, forcible entry and unlawful assembly were more numerous, fines and punishments increased also in severity. Occasionally alongside with the admittedly useful work done by the Justices of the Peace, there are instances of oppression, of arbitrary fines, of orders which encroach far on the liberty of a freeman. In 1652 a yeoman of Husthwaite is presented "for speaking scandalous words against John Worsley, Esq., J.P., that is to say 'he is a fool,'" he submitted to the mercy of the Court and was fined £1. 6s. 8d. He had also brought an accusation against Colonel Lassells in that he said "Col. Lascelles is a partiall man," for this he was fined 40s. on his submission; there was still a third indictment against the said yeoman, he had refused "to set the watch in Husthwaite according to custom." But for this fault he was fined 12d. The contrast in the fines is surprising; for two sentences the outspoken yeoman paid £3. 6s. 8d., for evading a weary night's work he escaped with a penalty of a shilling[2]. Verily a man during the Commonwealth had need to follow the advice in *The Wanderer*, "Brave is the hero who holdeth his troth: nor shall he too hastily ever, give voice to the woe in his breast, before he can work out its cure."

In the seventeenth century the free and independent spirit characteristic of the people in Yorkshire was not allowed much scope. Nevertheless though some sentences pronounced by the Justices might be harsh and aggravated by political bias, the entries show that the law was put in force against Cavaliers and Roundheads alike, and that there

[1] *N.R.Q.S.R.* vol. iv. p. 237. Thirsk, Oct. 3, 1643. "Forasmuch as the H.Cs of Birdforth are sore troubled with many collections of moneys and executions of several warrantes, which these troublesome times dailey produce, soe that they of themselves are not able to performe the service, but desire that they may have 2 Chiefe Constables more to assist them, it is therefore Ordered (dureinge these troublesome times onely) that 2 C.Cs. more be named &c and that Rob Wilson of Thirske gent[n] and Ch[r] Baine of Kilburne gent[n] doe forthwith repaire to a Justice &c."

[2] *Ibid.* vol. v. p. 116. Thirsk, Oct. 1652.

was need of vigorous measures. Even Parliamentarians of the rank of gentlemen are found taking advantage of their position and extorting money from ignorant people when taking their subscription to the engagement[1].

In the Court of Quarter Sessions the various oaths of loyalty to the government of the day were taken: these were in early Stuart times the oath of supremacy, during the Interregnum the oath to the Commonwealth[2], and at the Restoration the oath of allegiance and supremacy.

No government during the seventeenth century was able to gain much feeling of loyalty from the English people, therefore at no time were "false and seditious words" allowed against authority. In 1616 a Flaweth labourer was presented "for uttering opprobrious, presumtuous, and disgraceful words viz 'I care not for the Constable or the King[3],'" and in 1633 Ch^r. Thompson, a blacksmith, was summoned "for uttering scandalous and defamatory words against the King as follows, 'the Devil go with the King and all the proude packe of them, what care I[4].'"

The severity of sentences for any kind of political offence during the Interregnum is especially noticeable. The Justices left the difficult task of deciding what was treason to the government judges, but they bound men to appear at the Assizes with very heavy recognizances[5]. Anyone who spoke "contemptuously" against authority[6], anyone who drank a health to King Charles during the Commonwealth ran the risk of a fine. Men paid a heavy price for open loyalty to the Stuarts; in 1652 John Watson of Easingwold is discharged from keeping an alehouse "for that he confessed that he hath bin an officer in the service of the late Kinge against the people of England," and so late as July 1658 a

---

[1] See Appendix L.
[2] For the Oath to the Commonwealth see Appendix M.
[3] *N.R.Q.S.R.* vol. I. p. 90. Helmsley, 1616.
[4] *Ibid.* vol. III. p. 356. Richmond, 1633.
[5] *Ibid.* vol. v. p. 104. "Philip Howseman of Ferlington in £60. Geo Watson of Cowton gent^n in £100. Ja^s Wilkinson of Cowton in £100."
[6] *Ibid.* vol. v. p. 110. Malton, July, 1652.

New Malton innkeeper was committed to gaol on a charge of high treason "for promoting Charles Stewart's interest, eldest son of the late King by drinking of a health[1]."

In spite of, or it may be owing to, the repressive measures of the Justices, there was a general feeling of unrest. Royalist hopes revived after the great Protector's death, but discipline was maintained; one "Robert Myles of Marriske, gent[n]" was summoned in Jan. 1659,

for that he intending and imagining to more Sedition, discord, dissention, and rebellion within the Kingdom of England, maliciously did speak and utter these seditious and scandalous words "that Oliver Lord Protector was burning in Hell fyre for taking so many honest gentlemen's lives away[2]."

Then the Restoration of the King saw the return to power of the royalist Justices; all men who appreciated the Protector must keep their thoughts to themselves, and there were some persons in the Riding who failed to do so. A yeoman of Keld in the parish of Grinton uttered the following

seditious and defamatory words to another yeoman "thou had best be quiet for those that thou buildest upon I hope they will not last long,...I lived as well when there was no King and I hope to do so again when there will be no King[3]."

Another yeoman declares that "Cromwell and Ireton was as good as the King[4]," and a third uttered

opprobrious words against Simon Douglas of Fremington, "Thou and thy father are rogues and traitors and all is traitors that do fight for the King[5]."

Heavy fines and punishments were inflicted in Quarter Sessions for refusal to take the oath of allegiance and supremacy: one Anne Lambe was fined 5s. in 1662, and twenty-two Roman Catholics were committed to gaol in 1679. Among the

---

[1] *N.R.Q.S.R.* vol. VI. p. 7. New Malton, July 13, 1658.
[2] *Ibid.* vol. VI. p. 1. Richmond, Jan. 1659.
[3] *Ibid.* Thirsk, Oct. 1661.
[4] *Ibid.* Richmond, July, 1662.
[5] *Ibid.* Richmond, July, 1663.

latter were some names of note in the Riding, Sir John Lawson of Brough, Edward Saltmarsh of Newby Wiske, James Thornton of Bedale. Charles II did nothing to gain popularity in the North, and there was much criticism of his methods of government. Moreover, though the sentences imposed for seditious words seem to err on the side of severity, there is evidence that the Roman Catholics were well organised. Away up in the dales of the North Riding there were many who still hoped for the return of the old faith, and by some means or other obtained a shrewd insight into the character of the King and his policy. A Scawton woman was fined 40s. and committed to gaol until she paid the money for seditious words as follows:

The King of France is our King: I pray God he may get the victory this battle, and then I hope in God he will be in ere it be long, and the Protestant Ministers must be put forth of the Churches and ours put in, and except all the Protestants will turne they must all be killed.

To which another woman responded "Many will lie on the ground before that come about," and the aforesaid woman continued, "The King is nothing to us, the Queen is; the King is a Protestant in outward show and a Catholicke in his heart[1]."

The priests who acted as chaplains and schoolmasters for the Romanist families carried news from house to house. Religion took the place of loyalty. Thus the fear of rebellion probably lay at the root of many of the arbitrary decisions of the Bench. The Justices of the Peace, knowing well the sense of the country, had ever before their eyes a fear of the return of Roman Catholicism; therefore men found travelling on Sunday (their only day of leisure) had to give a satisfactory reason for so doing[2]. Recusants had to explain their

---

[1] *N.R.Q.S.R.* vol. VII. p. 12. Stoxley, July, 1678.

[2] *Ibid.* vol. V. p. 224. Northallerton, July, 1656. "Tho Lassells Esq having brought before us Tho Thorpe and Rich Purslaw for being convict of travelling on the Lord's Day and he not approving of their excuse they having confessed the said fact, the Court concurrs with him therein and thinkes it fitt that Mr. Lassells doe issue his warrant to leavy 10s. of

presence in any town at the bidding of a Justice[1]; hasty words were atoned for by fine or imprisonment. And it cannot be denied that their fears had some foundation. As fortune turned her wheel the grandson of the man (Simon Scroop of Danby) who had humbly to petition Parliament that he might contract for his estate "$\frac{2}{3}$ of it being in sequestration for recusancy only[2]," and who needs must ask permission of the Bench to carry a gun, is himself (Simon Scroop, the younger) in 1688 found among the number of Justices.

It was in his administrative work that the Justice came into the closest connection with the parish. The constable or the churchwarden had to obtain a warrant from him before any offender could be presented at the Quarter Sessions; thus the conduct of each parishioner came directly under the Justice's surveillance. It is probable that at times warrants were too easily granted. An Askrigg labourer uttered "false scandalous words" against Thomas Metcalf, Esq., J.P., in that he said "if a dog or cat went to Mr Metcalf for a warrant they might have it granted[3]." Unquestionably it was difficult, after the abolition of the Star Chamber and the Council in the North, to obtain redress for any capricious or tyrannical act on the part of a Justice. The charges brought in a petition of fourteen Askrigg men and two Bainbridge men against the same Justice Metcalf in 1678, seem to qualify him for the company of Shallow and Greedy. He was accused of taking bribes, embezzling money, protecting offenders, and misusing warrants; but without knowing more of the facts of the case it is impossible to judge his conduct. The petition may have been merely malicious; at any rate it failed and was used instead to present the sixteen men "for combining to scandalize and villify Thos. Metcalf, Esq., J.P.[4]" But on the

each of them and for want of sufficient distress the said parties to sitt 6 hours in the stocks."

[1] See Depositions from York Castle, *S.S.P.* vol. IV. p. 44. No. xxxvi. John Robinson and another.

[2] Composition Papers, No. 523, Yorks Archaeological Soc. vol. III.

[3] *N.R.Q.S.R.* vol. VI. Thirsk, Oct. 1676.

[4] *Ibid.* vol. VII. p. 5. Richmond, Jan. 1678.

whole it does not seem that the freedom from all government restraint affected adversely the work of the Justices, and Sir Roger de Coverley in his parish at the end of the century probably bears a closer resemblance than Robert Shallow, Esq., at its beginning, to the country Justice of the North Riding.

In conclusion it may be of value to quote the orders given at a Sessions of the Peace, because they serve to illustrate what has been already noticed regarding the power of the Justices, their numerous activities, their knowledge of and relations with, not only public officials, but also private individuals, living in the country parish.

Richmond.

Qr Sessions, at, by adjournment 13 July 1613. Before Coniers Darcy, Arth Dakens, Henry Jenkins, Knts., Tho. Davile, Rob Pepper, Adam Midleham, and Will Tankard Esquires, Tho. Clerk gentn, Deputy pr Sir Chr. Hildyard. (A grand jury of (1st panel) 3 Gentlemen and 14 yeomen.
2nd panel 2 Gentlemen and 13 yeomen.

Orders made etc.

Whereas all Recusantes within these divisions of Richmondshire and Allertonshire ought to have prescribed and delivered to the Head Constables to draw all the said presentments in forme of Law:

And forasmuch as such presentments for Recusance are altogether imperfect for want of informations and directions of the said forme in that behalf; Therefore time is given by this Courte untill the next Sessions to perfect and bring in the same. And in meantime every Constable to take copies of the said forme and instructions from the Head Constables of everie division, paying 6d. for everie copie, or otherwise, if they will copy yt, to pay nothing for the same.

That whereas Fr Wright of Covenbury, gentn, refuses to pay the assessments "imposed upon him for the King, bridges and otherwise" a warrant be directed to Tho. Waggett, Dep. Bailiffe of Gilling East, to attach him, etc.

That the Overseers of Massam do relieve a poor man upon his petition, providing a suitable house for him and his family with 12d. weekly towards their maintenance, and until such home be found for him 18d. weekly, and if they refuse to do so then a warrant etc. To issue a warrant and attach a man and his wife to be taken bound with two subsidie men, himself in £40 and each of the latter in £20 to appear etc (Direct. this warr. to all Bailiffs and Constables).

A warrant to attach the Constable of Ilkton for not duly executing a warr^t of Sir Arth Dakins etc, and a similar warrant to attach other two persons etc.

That Tho. Jackson, Head Constable of Hang East, and Roger Whitey, Deputy-bailiff of Hang West, be for adequate reasons discharged of the fines formerly imposed upon them.

That a partly blind man complaining that he does not get his allowance of 4d. a week paid regularly, there being an arrear of 5s. due, the Overseers of his parish (Hunton) shall at once pay "the arrearages" and for the future at every months end 16d. etc.

Whereas there was severall Orders conceived and made at Helmesley Sessions, the eight of this moneth, touching some arrearages due to the Purveior for the provisions of his Ma^{tres} wax; As also touching some augmentation of the allowance to the Prisoners in Yorke Castle; This Courte thinkes fitt that the same Orders shall be likewise confirmed in this Division, and that the monie be hereafter levied accordingly.

That a carpenter of Massam having his arme broken and so become disabled, &c have £3 presently paid him by the Thres^r to the Hospitalls as a benevolence towards his maintenance.

Whereas Peter Patteson of Pattrick Brompton, a poore man, hath a daughter infected with a disease called the Kinges Evill, and intendes to travell with her to the Kinges Matie for cure thereof, and being destitute of meanes for such a long journey, hath craved of this Courte some releife in that behalfe; Therefore the (Courte) thinkes fitt and so order(s) that he shall have presently paid unto him 20s. by the Thresurer.

A poor man, burdened with a son six years old, both lame and dumb, petitions aid, and the Court orders that he shall have 6d. a week paid him by the Churchwardens and Overseers of his parish (Croft).

Ordered that £3 left out of the £30 levied for the "building and erecting" of Tanfield bridge, to be "paid by the Thres^r for the Hospitalls to Ralph Hutchenson, Collector for the same bridge; Provided always that such other summes as are now allowed by this Courte to other Charitable uses be first paid, and then this to be next."

That a Warrant &c to apprehend eleven different men of Healey Ilkton and Ellengstring and bring them and to appear at the next Sessions, and in the meantime keep the peace etc and especially towards one Cuthb. Browne.

That Ralph Milner of Richmond for his abuse in Court be fined 2s. 6d.

The offender in the third case of rescue be fined 10s. and a second for a fraye made &c be fined 20s.

Whereas the decay of Ulsey bridge is now by the Jury found dangerous, the necessary repairs being estimated at £40. Ordered that the sum be estreated and levied &c. That a warrant &c to apprehend a man and take him bound etc that he shall neither brew to sell nor tipple ale or bere for thre yeares next ensewing; as also to be of good behaviour during that time.

That the father of a bastard child shall pay to the mother, for a yeare and a halfe (if he do so long live) 6d. a week &c. (Fr Hunter gent[n] Head Constable of Halikeld being present in Courte, hath undertaken to se this Order performed.)

Whereas John Metcalfe gent[n] Lame Soldier, bringing letters recommendatory from the Lordes of the Privie Counsell, as also from Sir Will. Wade, and craving some present releife and benevolence to support him in his travaile to the Baith, and so unto the Low Countries, promiseing never to crave further allowance &c Ordered that he have £4 presently paid him by Will. Rymer Thres[r] for Lame Soldiers.

Next Sessions at Richmond 5 Oct[r] next. Roll signed by Arth Dakins, Knt., Adam Midleham and Will Tanckard, Esquires.

APPENDIX H

Charge to the High Constables[1].

All and every the High Constables within the N.R. shall keepe precizely the orders presented unto them in calling the Church-wardens and Petty Constables at convenient tymes before them betwene every Quarter Sessions, and give them severall copies of the said orders or articles for 8*d*. copie, and to take their present-mentes to very the severall articles upon their Othes, if they be not formerly sworne. And if any difficulty happen in any of these pre-sentmentes to let it be sensured by the Justices at the next Sessions[2] *And if there be defalt of presentment in any of the offices abovesaid according to the said Articles in every respect then the same de-falters to be presented* by the High Constables at every Generall Quarter Sessions[3], and the Head Constables for every devition (division) to enter in a fair booke all such presentmentes as they shall so receyve of the Petty Constables from tyme to tyme, and shall attend some of the Justices of the devition with the saide booke of presentmentes and of defaltes of Petty Constables and Church-wardens and Overseers of the poore, one moneth before every Sessions, to thend that such Justices upon consideration thereof may give order to enjoyne such of the offendours to appeare at the then next Sessions as they shall thinke fitt to be ordered, as to justice shall appertaine. And it is ordered that every of the said officers and ministers shall carefully behave themselves therein for the good example of the Commonwelth and freeing the good sub-jectes from oppresion and reforming common disorders at their and every of their perills.

---

[1] *N.R.Q.S.R.* vol. I. p. 118. Thirsk, Ap. 5, 1608.
[2] The reading here is difficult and uncertain, partly because the writing is not so clear as usual.
[3] The writing from * to * is underlined.

APPENDIX I

REFERENCE TO THE ORDER OF THE PRIVY COUNCIL
IN 1622

Will Aldbrough (to Sir Timothy Hutton) Januarie 15, 1622–3

Ryght Worshippful,

Forasmuch as I am not able in bodye to come to your sessions at this instant, having formerly bene att the sessions at Hemsley; therfore I thought fitt to signifie unto you, thatt yf yt stand with your good likinge, that according to his Majestie's orders, there shall be a division of ourselves into sundry wapentakes for the spede preventing and remidinge of the dearth of corne and other victualls according to the said orders, I shall be redye for the spede execucion of the said service to joyne with those of our assosiats as you shall think fitting for the execucion of the said service within the wapentake of Hallikell and Hangeast, upon notice of the tyme and place which I thinke fitting afore your departure from sessions to be sett downe, and notice thereof to be given to the head constable now present at your sessions. The place I think fitting to be att Burneston; the tyme as shortly as you can; the charge to bee that the pettie constable and bring (*sic*) a note to all brewsters lycensed and lycensed malsters, and the malsters to be present, all badgers and ingrossers of corne, and whatt further derections you will sett downe. Thus, upon notice of your pleasures hearein, I will be redye to the best of my knowledge to do his Majesty service, both now and all other times.

Yours in all kindenes

Will Aldiburgh.

Ellingthorp, Januarii 15, 1622

William Rey of Kirbie Super Moram, I hold him not fitting to tiple, for that he doth harbour by a whole weak together contemptououse persons to the law; therefore I pray you lett him be disallowed by sessions.

The Hutton Correspondence, *S.S.P.* vol. XVII. p. 231. Letter C.L.I.

APPENDIX J

REFERENCE TO THE ORDER OF THE PRIVY COUNCIL IN THE QUARTER SESSIONS RECORDS

Whereas the Lords of the Privy Counsell, by letter, dated 19th Oct[r] last, for the suppressinge of all disordered and unfitt alehouses, and whereas the Justices here present have also taken into consideration that the abundance of maltsters (having their dependencie of those unnecessaree alehouses) do also as much prejudice the common wealth: Ordered that not onelie all those maltsters whose names are hereunder written, but also all others unlicensed shalbe discharged hereafter from maltinge of any barlie to sell otherwise than as the Statute doth provide; that all manner of persons within the N.R., that have been formerlie indicted for brewinge or sellinge of ale without license in the year 1619, shalbe absolutely discharged out of proces without payinge, either fine to the King or fee to the Clarke of the Peace.

The following note appears at the end of the same Sessions, "touching the above Order as to maltsters, the Court was not unanimous, several of the Justices left before the matter was settled, some doubt grewe in the penninge of the Order, and so was not perfected by the whole Bench, Wee, whose names are hereunder written, do Order that this cause shall rest till the next Sessions, or such other time as the most part of the Justices do meet, &c."

N.R.Q.S.R. vol. III. p. 158. Helmsley, Jan. 1622–3.

APPENDIX K

An agreement made by the Justices within the N.R. for devideing themselves into the severall Wapentacks and Libertyes within the said N.R. for the performance of Country Services, 8 April 1635.

1. That Sir Tho. Gower, Bart., John Gibson, Arthur Ingram, Will Sheffeild, Rich. Darley, Hugh Bethel, Will Strickland, Knts, and Bryan Stapleton, Esq. shall attend the same services within Bulmer Wapentage.

2. Henry Belassis, Esq., Sir Tho. Dawney, Will. Franckland and Geo. Metcalfe Esquires, in Birdforth.

3. Sir Will. Pennyman, Bart., Sir Tho. Laiton, James Morley, Nich. Conyers and Ja[s] Pennyman, Esq[res], in Langbargh.

4. The R^t Honble Tho. Viscount Fairfax of Emeley, Sir John Gibson, Sir Arthur Ingram, Sir Will Strickland, Tho. Heblethwaite and Will. Caley, Esq^{res}, in Ridall.

5. Sir John Hotham, Bart., Sir Tho. Posth. Hoby, Sir Rob Napier, Sir Hugh Cholmeley, Rich. Egerton, Roger Wyvell and Will Caley, Esq^{res}, in Pickering-lith, and Whitby Strand.

6. Sir Tho. Layton, Will Mallorie, Chr Wandesford, Math. Hutton, Tho. Harrison, Tho. Best, John Dodsworth, John Wastell, and Geo. Metcalfe in Richmondshire and Allertonshire.

And it is meant by all the said Justices that each of them may joyne with the rest which was assigned, to performe the said services in any of the said divisions as occasion shall require[1].

APPENDIX L

The following entry gives an illustration of the facility with which it was possible for corrupt officials to impose on ignorant people under the guise of authority and it indicates the value of the local magistrate.

forasmuch as Leon Conyers, Clerke, of Lastingham, Tho. Dove, gent^n of Newton, Rob. Harding, gent^n, of Pickering, and Rob. Hunter, gent^n, of Thorneton, being intrusted for the use and comoditie of the inhab^{ts} of same parishes, to take subscriptions to the Engagement in theis words:—(I doe declare and promise that I will be true and faithfull, to the Commonwealth of England as it is now established, without a king or house of Lords) appointed by Act of Parliament, that the said gent^n did, in the month of May 1650 at Kirby Misperton and other places, (54^b) for their own covetous ends, and to procure money to themselves, and to oppress the said inhabitants, publiquely and falsely devulge, to the great scandall of this Commonwealth, that there was a necessitie of all persons having subscribed, should have certificate from them, testifying such subscription and in case such persons had not such certificate to produce, that they could not travaile above five myles from home, or go to the markett, but any persons might take them prisoners, and take away their horses, cloathes or other goods from them, and the persons soe taken prisoners, and having their goods soe taken away could obtain no remedy in that behalf, and that by which false and indirect dealings they persuaded the inhab^{ts} that there was a

[1] *N.R.Q.S.R.* vol. IV. p. 32. Thirsk, April 8, 1635.

necessity of having their certificate, and yett notwithstanding would not give or signe any such certificate under 6d. each, all which is contrary to law to the scandal of the Commonwealth, and contrary to the publique peace and deceipt of the people, and that they were found guilty by the Grand Jury and were not willing further to prosecute the business, but did submit to the censure of the Court, and for that it doeth appear unto us that the parties were not equally guilty but that Mr Conyers and Mr Hunter were most to blayme, and Mr Conyers did act most in the said misdemeanors, the Court doeth Order that Mr Conyers be and is fined to the Commonwealth, £6. 13. 4. and Mr Rob. Hunter, £3. 6. 8, and the others £1 each (55) and that all the parties do enter recog^{ce}, to repay unto the country all the moneys exacted upon them before the next Sessions and that they appear at the next Sessions to certify such repayment, and to stand committed till this Order be performed;

N.R.Q.S.R. vol. v. p. 96. Malton, Jan. 1651.

APPENDIX M

THE OATH OF ABJURATION

(262[1]) The Oath of Abjuration. I, A.B., doe abjure and renounce the Pope's supremacie and authoritie over the Catholique Church in generall, and over myself in particuler, and I doe believe that there is not any transubstantiation in the Sacrament of the Lord's Supper or in the ellements of bread and wyne after consecration thereof by any person whatsoever, and I doe alsoe beleive that there is not any Purgatory, and that the consecrated Hoast, crucifixes or images out not to be worshipped, neither that any worshipp is due unto any of them, and I doe alsoe believe that salvation cannott be merretted by workes, and all doctrines in affirmation of the said points I doe abjure and renowce without any equivocation, mentall reservation, or secrett evasion whatsoever, taking the words by me spoken according to the common and usual meaning of them.

Soe help me God.

[1] *N.R.Q.S.R.* vol. v. p. 180. Richmond, Jan. 1655.

APPENDIX N

THE OATH SWORN BY A JUSTICE OF THE PEACE

Sir William Dalton, writing in the seventeenth century on The Country Justice, gives the form of oath as taken at that time:

Ye shall swear that as Justices of the Peace in the County of (Yorkshire) in all articles in the King's Commission to you directed you shall do equal right to the poor and to the rich, after your cunning wit and power and after the Laws and Customs of the Realm and Statutes thereof made: And ye shall not be of counsell of any quarrel hanging before you. And that ye hold your Sessions after the form of Statutes thereof made. And the issues, fines and amercements that shall happen to be made, and all forfeitures which shall fall before you, ye shall cause to be entered without any concealment (or imbezzling) and truly send them to the King's Exchequer; ye shall not let for gift or other cause but well and truly you shall do your office of Justice of the Peace in that behalf. And that you take nothing for your office of Justice of the Peace to be done but of the King and fees accustomed and costs limited by Statute. And ye shall not direct nor cause to be directed any warrant (by you to be made) to the parties, but ye shall direct them to the Bailiffs of the said County or other the King's officers (or Ministers) or other indifferent persons, to do execution thereof. So help you God and by the contents of this book[1].

[1] Dalton, *The Country Justice*, ch. iv, p. 13, Ed. 1635.

PREFACE TO BIBLIOGRAPHY

I SHOULD like to express gratitude to the diarists and writers who give us glimpses of the life of their day: Shakespeare, Fuller, John Evelyn, Butler, Ralph Thoresby, Sir John Reresby, and the later authorities on the customs, folklore and antiquities of various parts of Yorkshire. Here are also to be remembered the amateur and professional specialists on Local Government: Coke, Lambarde, Blackstone and Dalton; E. W. of Gray's Inn, Paul and Ritson who wrote manuals to instruct the constable, Ralph Dunning that most alert and intelligent overseer, Adam Moore and Matthew Hale who specialised on Poor Relief, and Henry Best of Elmswell in the East Riding, whose carefully detailed farming book spreads out before us the agricultural life of the time.

There are some excellent histories on the Stuart period by modern authors, but for old customs still surviving in the seventeenth century Pollock and Maitland's *History of English Law* is invaluable, for it gives a picture of medieval life which forms the necessary background for the understanding of seventeenth century ideas.

All students of the history of Local Government are greatly indebted to the late Canon J. C. Atkinson, who not only calendered the records of the North Riding Court of Quarter Sessions but prefixed to each volume an introduction full of interesting observations and illuminating ideas. These records were published privately, and are, unfortunately, scarce and difficult to procure. I am indebted for the loan of those I used to the Rev. A. T. Coore of Scruton Hall, who kindly lent me his copies for an indefinite time.

It is the privilege of few people to be pioneers: most of us benefit by the work of others: I should like to express my obligations to all whose work contributed to the making of this small book and in particular to the following: Archdeacon Cunningham, Mr and Mrs Sidney Webb, Professor Sir William Ashley, Miss Leonard, Professor Hearnshaw and the great English historian Dr Maitland.

ELEANOR TROTTER.

BIBLIOGRAPHY

CONTEMPORARY SOURCES

Army Lists of the Roundheads and Cavaliers, xvii Cent. Ed. E. Peacock, 1863.

Burton, R. The Anatomy of Melancholy, 1621.

Coke, Sir E. Institutes of the Laws of England. Ed. 1648.

Dalton, M. The Country Justice, 1618; 5th ed. 1635.
Domestic State Papers.
Dunning, R. Plain and easy method of showing how the office of Overseer of the Poor may be managed, 1686.

Evelyn, John. Diary, 1818; ed. A. Dobson (3 vols.), 1906.
E.W. of Gray's Inn. The Exact Constable, 1660.

Fuller, Thomas. The Holy State and The Profane State, 1642.

Glover, R. The Visitation of Yorkshire, 1584–5. Ed. J. Foster, 1875.

Hale, Sir M. A Discourse touching Provision for the Poor, 1683.

Lambarde, M. Eirenarcha, 1581.
—— The Duties of Constables, Borsholders, Tythingmen, and such other lowe and lay Ministers of the Peace, 1602.

Mather, William. Of repairing and mending the Highways, 1696.
Moore, Adam. Bread for the Poor and the advancement of the English nation promised by enclosure of the wastes and commons, 1653.

Quarter Sessions Records, Vols. i.–vii. Ed. by the Rev. J. C. Atkinson, published by the North Riding Record Society.

Register Book of Ingleby Greenhow, The. Ed. 1889.
Royalist Composition Papers. Yorks Archaeological Society Record Series, Vol. iii. (xvii Century), 1893–6.

Select Statutes and other Constitutional Documents. Ed. by G. W. Prothero. 3rd ed. 1906.
Smith, Sir Thomas. De Republica Anglorum, 1583. Ed. F. W. Maitland and L. Alston, 1906.
Standish, A. The Commons' Complaint, 1611.
Statutes of the Realm.

Stuart Tracts, 1603–1693. Ed. C. H. Firth, 1903.

Surtees Society Publications:
Best's Farming Book, Vol. XXXIII. 1641.
Depositions from York Castle, Vol. XL. 1640–90.
Durham Parish Books, Vol. LXXXIV. 1580–1700.
Ecclesiastical Proceedings of Bishop Barnes, The. Vol. XXII. 1575–87.
Hutton Correspondence, The. Vol. XVII. 1565–1628.

Thoresby, Ralph, Diary of. Ed. J. Hunter, 1677–1724.

LATER SOURCES AND AUTHORITIES

Ashley, W. J. An Introduction to English Economic History and Theory, 1901.

Beard, C. A. The Office of Justice of the Peace in England in its origin and development, 1904.

Blackeborough, R. Wit, Character, Folklore and Customs in the North Riding of Yorks, 1898.

Blackstone, Sir W. Commentaries, 1765–9.

Cambridge Modern History, III. xvii. (1905), IV. viii.–xii. xv. xvii.–xix. (1906), V. v. ix.–xi. (1908).

Cannan, E. The History of Local Rates in England, 1896.

Cartwright, J. J. Chapters in Yorkshire History, 1872.

Constable's Assistant, The. 1818.

Cunningham, W. The Growth of English Industry and Commerce in Modern Times, Vol. II. 1907.

Francis, Const. Decisions of the Court of King's Bench upon laws relating to the Poor, 1793.

Gardiner, S. R. A History of England from the Accession of James I to the outbreak of the Civil War, 1603–1642.

Garnier, R. M. History of the English Landed Interest, 1908.

Godfrey, E. Home Life under the Stuarts, 1903.
—— Social Life under the Stuarts, 1904.

Hallam, H. Constitutional History of England, 1827.

Hasbach, W. A History of the English Agricultural Labourer (translated by R. Kenyon), 1908.

Hearnshaw, F. J. C. Leet Jurisdiction in England, especially as illustrated by Records of the Court Leet of Southampton (Southampton Record Society), 1908.

Ingledew, C. J. D. History and Antiquities of Northallerton, 1858

Lawton, G. Collectio Rerum Ecclesiasticarum. 2 vols. 1840.

Leach, A. F. English Schools at the Reformation, 1896.

Leonard, E. M. The Early History of English Poor Relief, 1900.

Lodge, R. Longman's Political History, Vol. VIII. 1910.

Macaulay, Lord. History of England, 1849–61.

Mackay, T. Public Relief of the Poor, 1901.

Maitland, F. W. The Constitutional History of England, 1908.

—— Justice and Police, 1885.

Mayhall, J. The Annals of Yorkshire, 1860.

Montague, F. C. Longman's Political History, Vol. VII. 1907.

Odgers, W. B. Local Government, 1907.

Paul, J. The Compleat Constable, 1785.

Pollard, A. F. Factors in Modern History, 1907.

Pollock, Sir F. The Land Laws, 1883.

Pollock, Sir F. and Maitland, F. W. History of English Law, 1895

Redlich, J. and Hirst, F. W. Local Government in England, 1903.

Reresby, Memoirs of the Hon. Sir John, 1734. Ed. J. J. Cartwright, 1875. Ed. A. Ivatt, 1904.

Ritson, J. The Office of Constable, 1791.

Rogers, J. E. T. Industrial and Commercial History of England, 1892.

—— A History of Agriculture and Prices, Vol. V. 1887.

Simpson, W. B. The Office of Constable (*E.H.R.* 1895).

Slater, G. The English Peasantry and the enclosure of Common Fields, 1907.

Smith, J. Toulmin. The Parish, 1857.

Traill, H. D. and Mann, J. S. Social England, 1901.

Trevelyan, G. M. England under the Stuarts, 1904.

Unwin, G. Industrial Organisation in the XVI and XVII Centuries. 1904.

Ware, S. L. The Elizabethan Parish in its Ecclesiastical and Financial Aspects, 1908.

Webb, S. and B. English Local Government, 1906–13.
  I. The Parish and the County, 1906.
  V. The King's Highway, 1912.

Whitaker, T. D. History of Richmondshire, 1823.

Yorkshire Archaeological and Topographical Journal, 1870 ff.

Yorkshire Notes and Queries, 1885–90.

Yorkshire, Victoria County History of, Vol. II.

INDEX

OF PLACES MENTIONED IN TEXT AND FOOTNOTES

DVCATVS
EBORACENSIS
PARS BOREALIS
THE NORTHRIDING
OF YORKSHIRE

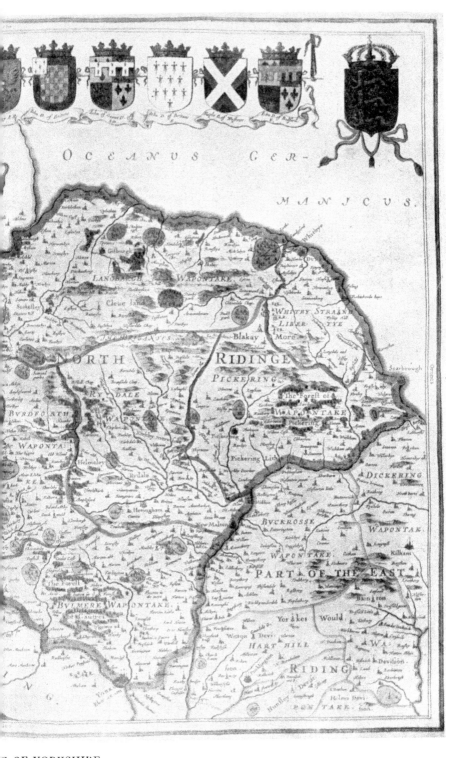

G OF YORKSHIRE

map, 1662)

For EU product safety concerns, contact us at Calle de José Abascal, 56–1°,
28003 Madrid, Spain or eugpsr@cambridge.org.

www.ingramcontent.com/pod-product-compliance
Ingram Content Group UK Ltd.
Pitfield, Milton Keynes, MK11 3LW, UK
UKHW010341140625
459647UK00010B/742